Journalist

KU-141-240

Also by David Randall and published by Pluto Press

The Great Reporters (2005)

David Randall

The Universal Journalist

Fourth Edition

PlutoPress
www.plutobooks.com

First published 1996
Second edition published 2000
Third edition published 2007
Fourth edition published 2011 by Pluto Press
345 Archway Road, London N6 5AA

www.plutobooks.com

Distributed in the United States of America exclusively by
Palgrave Macmillan, a division of St. Martin's Press LLC,
175 Fifth Avenue, New York, NY 10010

British Library Cataloguing in Publication Data
A catalogue record for this book is available from the British Library

ISBN-13   978 0 7453 3077 8 Hardback
ISBN-13   978 0 7453 3076 1 Paperback

Library of Congress Cataloging in Publication Data applied for

This book is printed on paper suitable for recycling and made from fully
managed and sustained forest sources. Logging, pulping and manufacturing
processes are expected to conform to the environmental standards of the
country of origin.

10   9   8   7   6   5   4   3   2   1

Designed and produced for Pluto Press by Chase Publishing Services Ltd
Typeset from disk by Stanford DTP Services, Northampton, England
Simultaneously printed digitally by CPI Antony Rowe Ltd, Chippenham UK
and Edwards Bros, United States of America

Contents

Acknowledgements

At the risk of sounding like an Oscars-night bore, there is a long trail of people whose advice and spirit inhabit this book. It begins, at the first newspaper I worked on, with the late Geoff Collard (from whom I learnt that journalism without a sense of honour is not worth the name) and news editor Cathryn Sansom, whose hectoring lessons in professionalism seemed a curse at the time but have proved a rich blessing ever since. At the *Observer*, Peter Corrigan (by careful supervision) and writers like Peter Dobereiner, Hugh McIlvanney and the late Lawrence Marks (by example) showed me what sharp, clear writing really is. At the same paper, Paul Routledge and John Merritt gave me permanent lessons in how the best reporters think and breathe. On lecture tours in Russia, John Shirley taught me so much about 'how to take command of the material'. And at the *Independent* and *Independent on Sunday*, where I continue my fourth decade in journalism, I learnt yet again that you never stop learning. In particular, Simon Ritter's running commentary on each day's content improved my ability to spot written nonsense, working with Michael Williams was akin to attending a private master class in handling daily news, and Keith Howitt has been a constant reminder that quality journalism begins and ends with attention to detail. Barely a day goes by without me testing in my head some potential intro, headline or news judgement against the standards these people set.

Finally, thanks to Giovanni De Mauro, editor of Internazionale in Italy, for letting me reproduce parts of my columns on journalism from that magazine. And a salute, too, to my son Simon who spotted at the proof stage several errors I had missed.

Preface

This book contains all the best advice I have learnt or collected in three decades as a journalist. Some of it came direct and uninvited from wise old heads, some from observing classy reporters at work, some from picking their brains, some from books, some from websites and a lot from making mistakes and learning the hard way what was the best, most inventive way to do the job. But whatever the origins of the lessons contained here, they have helped to save my skin on numerous occasions and have earned me some wonderful jobs on others.

The book is called *The Universal Journalist* in answer to those who think that each type of publication produces its own distinct form of journalism, inevitably regarded by its practitioners as superior to other kinds. It doesn't. If you write and read enough stories, in the end you realise that there really are only two types of journalism: good and bad. The bad is practised by those who rush faster to judgement than they do to find out, indulge themselves rather than the reader, write between the lines rather than on them, write and think in the dead terms of the formula, stereotype and cliché, regard accuracy as a bonus and exaggeration as a tool and prefer vagueness to precision, comment to information and cynicism to ideals. The good is intelligent, entertaining, reliably informative, properly set in context, honest in intent and effect, expressed in fresh language and serves no cause but the discernible truth. Whatever the audience. Whatever the culture. Whatever the language. Whatever the circumstances. Such journalism could be printed in any publication, because it is, in every sense of the word, universal. This book sets out to tell you how to achieve it.

The second rationale for the title is that these days, in a world where both the available media and the amount of information bombarding us is multiplying all the time, anyone hoping to be a good journalist needs to acquire a range of new skills. A facility with words is no longer enough, You also have to be a sharp and sceptical questioner, be comfortable with statistics, understand how online media works, be able to use the Internet for research, know how to handle increasingly sophisticated sources and their spin doctors, and be able to produce journalism that is more informative, fresh and reliable than that of the proliferating competition. If that sounds like a tall order, that's because it is. This book aims to describe these new techniques which, when added to the more traditional ones, make a universally skilled journalist.

To the memory of
JOHN MERRITT,
the best reporter I ever met.

1

What Makes a Good Reporter?

The only qualities for real success in journalism are ratlike cunning, a plausible manner and a little literary ability.

Nicholas Tomalin

The heroes of journalism are reporters. What they do is find things out. They go in first, amid the chaos of now, battering at closed doors, sometimes taking risks, and capture the beginnings of the truth. And if they do not do that, who will? Editors? Commentators? There is only one alternative to reporters: accepting the authorised version, the one the businesses, bureaucrats and politicians choose to give us. After all, without reporters, what would commentators know?

Reporters are, like almost all heroes, flawed. As a group, they have a more soiled reputation than most; for enough of them routinely exaggerate, simplify and contort the truth to have made parts of the trade a by-word for calculated dishonesty. Not for nothing do screenwriters and dramatists, in search of a booable villain, regularly opt for a tabloid reporter. It saves time. They don't have to spend pages establishing a lack of morals, the mere announcement of the character's line of work is enough for audiences to grasp that this person is going to wheedle and deceive. Then there are the lazy – those who opt for spoonfeeding and the facile, rather than the hard, painstaking, often exposed job of getting it as right as they can. There is, to be sure, a lot of calculated malice and shoddy workmanship in the history of journalism.

But there is a lot that is heroic, and far, far more of it than most media critiques and journalism schools would have the beginner believe. There is John Tyas's exposure for *The Times* of British atrocities against demonstrators in Manchester in 1819; William Howard Russell's accounts of the bungling of the British army in the Crimea; William Leng's exposure in the *Sheffield Telegraph* of corruption and violence in that city (he was threatened so often that he kept a loaded revolver on his desk and had a police escort home every night); Emily Crawford, who incessantly risked her life to report the 1871 Paris Commune for the *Daily News* and then scooped the world at the subsequent Versailles Conference; Nellie Bly, who feigned mental illness to get inside an asylum and wrote a series for the *New York World* that described the terrors and cruelties she found and which led to improved conditions; W.T. Stead's exposure in the *Pall Mall Gazette* of child prostitution; and Ida Tarbell's articles in *McClure's* that documented the corruption and intimidation of the Standard Oil Company 1902–1904 and prepared the way for the dissolution of the firm.

Then there is Emilie Marshall, who broke several all-male preserves in becoming the first woman reporter in the House of Commons press gallery and the first woman staff reporter on both the *Daily Mail* and *Daily Express*; John Reed's reporting of the Russian Revolution; the unmasking of the violently racist Ku Klux Klan by Roland Thomas of the *New York World*; the exposure by freelance George Seldes of the links between lung cancer and smoking – a decade before the mainstream press reported it. Ilya Ehrenburg's reporting for *Red Star* first revealed the Nazi extermination camps; John Hersey and Wilfred Burchett's reporting from Hiroshima disproved the official lie that there was no such thing as radiation sickness; and there was the courageous opposition of the *Observer* and *Manchester Guardian* to the Suez invasion of 1956; Alice Dunnigan facing down – and defeating – racial prejudice to report Washington in the 1950s; the relentless pursuit of high-level security breaches by the whole British press in the early 1960s; the uncovering by Seymour Hersch, then a young freelance, of the full horrors of the My Lai massacre in 1968; the *Sunday Times*' campaign for the limbless victims of the drug thalidomide; Carl Bernstein and Bob Woodward's Watergate investigation in the *Washington Post* that proved a US President a corrupt liar; Randy Shilts's reporting on the emergence of Aids for the *San Francisco Chronicle* that forced health authorities to wake up to the crisis; and Robert Fisk's refusal to swallow the Nato line (or, for that matter, anyone's line) in reporting the Kosovo conflict in the *Independent* in 1999 and the conflicts in the Middle East that still continue in 2007.

There are also those whose names are read fleetingly, but rarely remembered; the ones whose efforts to inform their communities are met, not with an obstructive official or evasive answer, but with intimidation or worse. Every year, thousands of reporters are arrested or threatened, hundreds imprisoned, and scores killed. In its most extreme form, this is what Peruvian journalist Sonia Goldenburg has called 'censorship by death'. In 1994 no fewer than 103 journalists died for getting too close to the truth. That toll fell by the turn of the century and then rose again in 2005, with 63 journalists and five assistants killed, 807 arrested and 1,308 attacked or threatened. Each one of them is a definitive answer to those, both inside and outside the business, who think that journalism is a branch of marketing that organises and exaggerates trivia. After all, no authority would bother obstructing, jailing or murdering people for that.

Finally, there are the tens of thousands of other, often local, journalists whose lot is nothing more glamorous or heroic than discovering the most complete version of what happened in their areas and reporting it. They don't expect gold or glory, and there is no particular reason why they should get it. But they are, nevertheless, an antidote, socially and professionally, to those who have traded in their credibility for a high salary or easy life.

And all these good reporters share something. They may keep it well hidden under the journalists' obligatory, hard-bitten mask, but the immortals, the persecuted and the unsung all share a belief in what the job is about. This is, above all things, to question; and, by so doing, then to:

- Discover and publish information that replaces rumour and speculation.
- Resist or evade government controls.
- Inform, and so empower, voters.
- Subvert those whose authority relies on a lack of public information.
- Scrutinise the action and inaction of governments, elected representatives and public services.
- Scrutinise businesses, their treatment of workers and customers, and the quality of their products.
- Comfort the afflicted and afflict the comfortable, providing a voice for those who cannot normally be heard in public.
- Hold up a mirror to society, reflecting its virtues and vices and also debunking its cherished myths.
- Ensure that justice is done, is seen to be done and investigations carried out where this is not so.
- Promote the free exchange of ideas, especially by providing a platform for those with philosophies alternative to the prevailing ones.

If you can read that list without the hairs on the back of your neck beginning to stand up, then maybe journalism is not for you.

Attitudes

To meet the aims listed above on a regular basis is a tough assignment. The idea, common among those outside journalism, that what a reporter needs more than anything is the ability to write well is not even the half of it. Literary ability is only part of the job, and often not the largest part. Neither is good reporting a matter of acquiring a little bag of tricks and tools, out of which the appropriate one is selected according to circumstance. What is needed to succeed as a reporter are the right attitudes and character.

The most important equipment reporters have is that which is carried around between their ears. Some of these attitudes are instinctive, others are learnt quickly, but most are built up through years of experience – by researching and writing, re-researching and re-writing hundreds and hundreds of stories.

Reporting is one of those trades that you learn by making mistakes. In my first week in journalism, for instance, I was working on a small weekly paper in southern England and, by a combination of luck and my determination to make an impact, got on to a good story about river pollution. I went off, did the research and then rushed back to the office dreaming of the accolades that would be coming my way when I turned in the story. 'What the hell is this?' shouted the news editor when he read it, 'Where are all the names?' I had been so thrilled with the story that I had forgotten to ask the names of the people I had interviewed. There were lots of good quotes but all of them were from 'worried resident', 'water engineer', 'safety inspector', etc. I spent the next 24 hours rushing around, getting names, re-interviewing people and repairing most of the damage. And the story led the paper that week. I have since been so grateful for my stupidity, for I learnt two invaluable lessons in my very first week. One was that quotes are not much good without names attached to them. The other, even more important, was that reporting was a very difficult job. Clearly being enthusiastic and having a good degree was not enough; you also needed the right attitudes. The following are the key ones:

Keen news sense

You need this – and for three reasons. First, in the positive sense of knowing what makes a good story and the ability to find the essential news point in a mass of dross. Second, in the negative sense of not wasting time by pursuing stories that will never amount to much. Often you have to ask yourself: 'What is the best this story can be? What is the strongest news point it will have if I get all the information I need?' And sometimes the answer is that it will not be much of a tale. So drop it. The third reason is that if you don't have a news sense, or have it but don't use it, you will miss things and make a fool of yourself. Take the case of Duncombe Jewell, a reporter for the *Daily Mail* in its early days. He was sent to cover the launch of HMS *Albion* at the Thames Ironworks in London and in due course returned to the office with a piece of purple prose that was, in his own words, 'the nearest thing to a Turner sunset that you could get in manuscript'. As he handed it in, news reached the paper that 30 people had drowned at the launching. His news editor was beside himself with anger. 'Well,' said Jewell, 'I did see some people bobbing about in the water as I came away but...'

Passion for precision

As a news editor, this is the one attribute I valued more than any other in reporters. Could I rely on their work and trust their accuracy? As a reporter you also speedily appreciate that your reputation for accuracy and not exaggerating, either in print or beforehand, is a valuable commodity. Lose it, and it will be very difficult to regain.

Precision means three things. First, the obvious one of recording and writing accurately what people tell you. Second, taking care that however accurate each little part of your story, the whole thing is true to the spirit and atmosphere of the situation or events – which means adding background and context. Third, not falling into the dangerous and widespread habit of saying, 'Well if that happened and the other happened, then this other thing must be true.' You should not wish but report your stories into print. If there are any gaps in a sequence of events that you are reporting, find out precisely what is missing: don't think that if A happened, then something else and then C, then the missing part must be B. It may not be.

Determination to find out

There is no surer sign of a bad reporter than the one who keeps wimpishly going back to the news desk to say: 'I can't find out.' A determination not to be defeated by a few unanswered telephone calls or stonewalling sources is a hallmark of the decent reporter. What makes them a good one is the determination to go that little bit further (or longer) to get the story. In 1996, for instance, a man suspected of being the notorious Unabomber (whose campaign of letter bombs to universities and on planes killed three and wounded 29) was arrested in remote Lincoln, Montana. A stringer for *People* magazine called Cathy Free made a name for herself by asking a school secretary to fax her the Lincoln phone directory (fortunately only four pages long) and then rang everyone in it to collect information on the suspect. If it means, as George Esper of the Associated Press once discovered, that you have to call the father of a suicide victim seven days in a row before he will agree to talk, then that is what you have to do. Extraordinary reporters will go a lot further than that. In 1917, Floyd Gibbons of the *Chicago Tribune* booked himself onto a ship likely to be sunk by the Germans so he could report its torpedoing. It was and he did. And then there was Evelyn Shuler of the *Philadelphia Ledger*, who knew she would beat the opposition on a murder case if she could witness the exhumation of a victim's body. So she stayed up for three days and nights keeping watch in a cemetery, and, early on the fourth morning, got her story.

Never make assumptions

This applies to all assumptions – either of logic, identity, fact or motives. The great problem with assumptions is that most of them turn out to be correct; that is what makes them so dangerous and tempting. Play safe, report only what you know, not what you think you know. That way you will avoid being inaccurate, dishonest and misleading – or sacked.

There was a famous occasion when a freelance photographer gave a British mass-market newspaper a picture of Prince Charles putting his arms around a lady who was not his wife at a time when he was known to be unhappily married. The paper published the picture under a headline that suggested a romantic relationship, because the editors assumed that was what was taking place. They were wrong. Unknown to them, the picture was taken at the funeral of the woman's child, who had died of leukaemia at the age of four. The Prince was doing what any of us might have done in a similar situation – he was comforting the distressed mother.

Never be afraid to look stupid

However rudimentary you may imagine your ignorance to be, if you don't know, ask; if you don't understand, request an explanation. Don't worry if anyone laughs at you. The really stupid reporters are the ones who pretend to know, who sit there nodding throughout an interview they only partly understand and who then try to write the story – and find that they can't. The place to show your ignorance is when questioning people, not on paper in your subsequent story.

Be suspicious of all sources

An essential general attitude for reporters, indeed all journalists, is to be suspicious of all sources. Why is this person telling me this? What is their motive? And are they really in a position to know what they claim to know? This complex issue is dealt with in Chapter 6.

Being resourceful

Using your wits and charm to overcome obstacles is part of the fun of reporting. Sometimes that means pushing your luck in asking for a phone number of an important potential source, or, maybe, blagging your way into where you are not really allowed. Many is the reporter who has done something similar to Margueritte Higgins, who, in order to get a story on a 1940s society wedding, borrowed a hotel housekeeper's uniform and so slipped unnoticed into the back of the reception. In 1989, *Daily Mail* reporter Ann Leslie was so disgusted at how far from the main action the press had been placed at Emperor Hirohito's funeral that she wore a luxuriant fur coat and marched imperiously past the security checks and found herself sitting by President George H. Bush. And then there was the technique of Floyd Gibbons, when he needed to impress Polish border guards that he was someone important. He found a military-looking uniform, and hung on his chest a line of gaudy medals (a couple of which were actually awarded at dog shows). The guards saluted him through. On another occasion, during the Great War, he was about to write a story about the arrival of US general John J. Pershing, when he was told British censors would not permit reporters to say where Pershing landed. So Gibbons cabled his office: 'Pershing landed at British port today and was greeted by Lord Mayor of Liverpool'. Smart.

Leave your prejudices at home

You cannot be expected to shed all your cherished beliefs, but you should never allow them consciously to affect your work. Reporters should accurately relate what happened, not strain everything through the sieve of their own prejudices, cultured and intelligent though they imagine these to be.

This invocation applies to newly minted prejudices as well as old ones. Don't let the opinions you form early on in the research prematurely colour your judgement of the story. A great sin of some reporters, particularly those often asked to write colour and atmosphere pieces, is that they will write the intro in their heads on the way to an interview. Their intro may be smart, it may be a beautiful piece of writing, but the chances are that it will say more about them than their subject.

Realise you are part of a process

Reporters are subject to what editors want. By all means argue with them, shout at them and try to sweet-talk them, but, in the end, you have to accept their decision – or go and work elsewhere. That is professionalism. So, too, is the acceptance of the discipline of the schedule of your paper. A lot of reporters think it is somehow a mark of a literary talent in full flower to be late and over length. It is not. It is the sign of an unreliable amateur. So too is the reporter who, when out on a story, fails to call into the office regularly. You can often, however, use the paper's needs to your advantage, getting prominence for your stories by calculating when in your paper's production cycle they are most in need of early stories or ones illustrated by pictures, graphics, sidebars, etc. – and delivering them.

Empathy with readers

Unless people read your story, you might as well be muttering it to yourself in a darkened room. They will read it if you consider them – when you write, but especially when you research. What will readers want to know? What do they need explained? And what will bring this story home to them? Find anecdotes, show how the events will impact on readers' lives, or impact on other lives; use examples that will be relevant to their own experience; above all, where possible, tell the story in terms of real people.

The will to win

Sooner or later the new reporter experiences the dawning realisation that the rest of the world is not run for the convenience of newspapers. Stories happen at bad times and in awkward places, telephones are not always available or working; and, if you are out of the city or country, you can be running out of money, time, food, drink and energy. You need a strong desire to beat whatever circumstances are strewn in your path, get to the story and then file as fast as possible. To be like Ed Cody of the *Washington Post*. Mort Rosenblum's excellent book *Who Stole the News?* tells the story of how Cody was in Paris one night in December 1988 when word reached him that a Pan Am jumbo jet had crashed on Lockerbie, a little town in Scotland. It was 8.20 p.m. and the last flight to Britain that evening had already left. Cody found a charter operator, persuaded his foreign editor in the United States to authorise the cost and, a few hours later, the reporter was in Glasgow. Lockerbie was 60 miles south and by that time had been sealed off by police roadblocks. Miraculously, Cody found a cab driver who was from the town and, with his local knowledge and contacts, Cody made it to the scene. The driver even had a friend who owned a pub, which he opened up so that the reporter could call Washington to file his story.

The crash, in which all 259 passengers and 11 people on the ground died, was one of the biggest stories of the 1980s. Cody's excellent job on it was possible because he had the will to win. He may also have had a paper prepared to pay $6,000 for a charter aircraft, but, on most occasions, a reporter's desire to get to the story will not cost as much and it will always bring rewards.

Sense of urgency

Newspapers want their reporters to file the earliest and fullest account of a story that they can get. A little healthy, or even unhealthy, competition to be first is part of the reality – and fun – of the job. And it serves readers well, just so long as not too many corners are cut.

Beating the rival agency, for instance, was uppermost in the minds of the Associated Press (AP) and United Press International (UPI) photographers who were assigned to take pictures of the Dalai Lama as he fled Tibet in 1959. Both chartered planes and organised relays of motorcyclists so that they could get their pictures from the Chinese borders to the nearest transmitter in India. When the Dalai Lama emerged from his aircraft, the photographers leapt forward, took their pictures and ran to their already-revving planes. After a break-neck race in the air and on the ground, UPI won.

The AP man was devastated. He went back to his hotel room and sat there, full of recrimination about what might have been and the shame of being beaten. Then he received a cable from his office: 'Opposition's Dalai Lama has long shaggy hair. Yours bald. How please?' The AP man cabled back: 'Because my Dalai right Dalai.' In his desperation to be first, the UPI man had photographed the interpreter.

Taking pleasure in beating the opposition

Using your wits and charm to overcome obstacles is part of the fun of the job, as is beating the opposition to be first with the story. But acceptable rivalry has its limits, and they were surely reached – and considerably exceeded – by the former *New York Post* reporter Steve Dunleavy when he was a young man on a paper in opposition to his father's one. Both were assigned the same story, and Steve was so keen to be first to the scene that he immobilised his father's car by slashing its tyres. (The shocking thing here is not the sabotage, but the crudity of the method. In Britain, a matchstick thrust into a tyre valve was the rather more dainty technique.)

But discovering that your rivals were already up and running in their vehicle called for other measures. On the kinds of newspapers I have worked for, the sight of rivals in your wing mirror would provoke no more than a sigh of regret, but to intensely competitive tabloid reporters it was a cue to guerrilla action. Wensley Clarkson of the London *Sunday Mirror* once persuaded a sex-change couple to tell their complicated story to him and him alone. Rivals swarmed outside. So he threw a blanket over the transsexual pair's heads (to stop other papers taking their photograph), bundled them into his car, and sped off towards a hotel where he could interview them at his uninterrupted leisure. His competitors naturally set off in pursuit. What to do? Well, Clarkson waited for the next set of traffic lights showing red, got out of his car, ran back to that of his pursuers, and tapped on the driver's window. It opened. 'Give me a break, guys,' he said. 'No,' they replied, whereupon Clarkson reached inside, grabbed the car keys, and threw them down a nearby drain. End of problem.

Being professional

This is the opposite of taking the attitude 'that will do', and it means learning to be as efficient, thorough, and fast as your talents will allow. And if you want a yardstick of professionalism, I can do no better than cite the performance of Meyer Berger of the *New York Times* on 7 September 1949. That morning, reports began to filter in of a gunman randomly shooting people in Camden, New Jersey. Berger was despatched, and by the time he reached the scene, a young army veteran called Howard B. Unruh had shot dead 12 neighbours and passers-by. For the next six hours, Berger retraced Unruh's steps as he went about his killing in the blocks around his East Camden home. Berger interviewed 50 witnesses, including prosecutors who carried out the initial interview with the arrested killer, then went back to the New York office, sat down, and wrote in just two and a half hours a 4,000 word account for the first edition, not one word of which was changed by any editor. It began:

> Howard B. Unruh, 28 years old, a mild, soft-spoken veteran of many armored artillery battles in Italy, France, Austria, Belgium, and Germany, killed twelve persons with a war souvenir Luger pistol in his home block in East Camden this morning. He wounded four others.
>
> Unruh, a slender, hollow-cheeked six-footer paradoxically devoted to scripture reading and to constant practice with firearms, had no previous history of mental illness but specialists indicated tonight that there was no doubt that he was a psychiatric case, and that he had secretly nursed a persecution complex for two years or more.

Berger's story contained not a single quote stating the obvious, not even half a sentence of police jargonese, and the words 'shocking', 'tragic', or 'I' do not appear once. And all written on a typewriter at a rate of nearly 2,000 words an hour. The story brought Berger a deserved Pulitzer. He gave the prize money to the killer's traumatised widowed mother.

Individuality

All around the world governments are getting ever more sophisticated in their management of news, tightly controlling what information they distribute and who gets it. In some places access to these channels even involves reporters joining a kind of informal 'club', with rules about what constitutes 'responsible' behaviour and the threat of exclusion from the official information for those who stray. This is unhealthy, as is the habit of reporters sometimes to co-operate with each other, sharing quotes and phone numbers. But good reporters should always be prepared to strike out on their own when necessary, to go where no one else is going, and – when it does not work out – take the flak. They are ready to spurn pre-digested meals from the official spoon because they know there is something far tastier to be found if only they go foraging for themselves.

Character

Almost any intelligent human being can, with sufficient application, learn how to be a competent reporter. But to rise above that, to be good or great, you must have real talent and flair for either research, or writing, or both. And you should have the right kind of character; for if there is one thing that separates outstanding reporters from the ordinary, it is this.

Most of what I know about the personality of a true reporter I owe to one man. He was ten years my junior and I only knew him for a few brief years before he died from leukaemia at the age of 32, but he was as near to perfection as a reporter as I ever expect to meet. He was the chief reporter of the London *Observer* and his name was John Merritt. This slim, sharp-faced young man had every virtue, and most of the vices, needed in a great reporter. The first thing that struck me about John, even before I realised he was a great reporter, was that people liked him. He was open-looking and he could be funny, but the reason people warmed to him was because he was interested in them and showed it with his *outgoing nature*. This did not mean that he toured the world with a fixed grin on his face, oozing phoney friendship, greeting people like a game show host. But the ability to strike up relationships with perfect strangers was of recurring assistance to him. With rough and ready types (like fellow journalists) he could drink, smoke and swear, and with bishops he could drink tea and talk theology. Whatever he thought of people, he could be easy with them and make them feel at ease with him.

This pleasantness masked, until he wanted it uncovered, the characteristic which is typical of all classy reporters – *determination*. John had a resolve both to find stories of the right standard and to fight through all the obstacles, delays and evasiveness that he found between him and the finished article. His determination was especially visible when a particular piece of information was proving difficult to find. Then he was prepared to sit at his desk for hours on end, making phone call after phone call, trying all kinds of unlikely places until he had got what he needed.

It helped a great deal that this determination was allied to considerable amounts of that other great reporting quality – *cheek*. He had the audacity to ring that top official at home, ask for a copy of that report or that favour from a perfect stranger. You never heard from him the poor reporter's whine of 'Oh, it's no good asking for that, they would never speak to me'. He was careful about the timing of his approach, but never shied away from making the call. 'The worst they can say is bugger off,' he would say as he picked up the phone to try one last call – and often that call produced the goods. John was never afraid to ask.

Neither was he afraid of much else, least of all threats, hard work, big name officials or governments. This was not due to arrogance (although he had plenty of that at times), but the *passion and sense of injustice* that he brought with him to work. John was not a saint (anybody who disagreed with him in the office was soon aware of his sharp tongue), but he cared deeply about the victims of society and governments. He saw it as a major part of his job to give a voice to those who did not have one.

For him, impartiality did not mean indifference; it did not mean being inoculated against caring about wrongs in society. He believed that anger and a sense of injustice should constantly inspire journalists, informing their judgements about the subjects to be tackled and powering their enquiries to their end. John could write light stories, but he was distinguished for the stories he wrote about the victims of torture throughout the world, the homeless and their exploitation by greedy landlords, and the appalling conditions in which the mentally handicapped were kept in places like Greece. But he was always professional – he never forgot the difference between a story and a sermon.

He also had, to an extent that was overwhelming at times, *enthusiasm*. It is easy for a reporter to be excited by a big story, but the test of their quality is whether they have the appetite to make the best of the unpromising-looking story. John had this enthusiasm, always prepared to come in early and stay late when necessary. And not just in the office. Reporters who fly into meetings or press conferences or any other assignment at the last minute and then leave at the earliest opportunity may think this is how the grown-ups behave, but it isn't. Good reporters often get stories by being at meetings early or hanging around late and talking to officials.

Then there was his incessant *curiosity*. He asked questions. Constantly. John Merritt was interested in anything and everything. He wanted to find out why things are like they are, what they are, why they work, or don't work. Wherever he went, he never stopped asking questions. He could probably have found a story in the middle of an empty field.

A great reporter

If one was to select one piece of reporting that in its quality and impact represents the best of journalism, one could do a lot worse than go back a century and a quarter to a Central Europe riven by nationalist claims and systematic violence. In what follows, any resemblance to contemporary events in that part of the world is almost certainly not a coincidence. The story started with allegations of atrocities, the simultaneous lying of several governments, censorship and a dying empire. It drew in Turkey, Russia, Britain and a nascent Bulgaria, continued with heroism and a war, and concluded with nothing less than the creation of several new nations in the re-drawing of the map of Europe. And what drew all these disparate strands together was a former St. Petersburg correspondent, an Irish-American called Januarius Aloysius MacGahan.

Even by the adventurous standards of his day, MacGahan was a thrill-seeker of the first order. In an age when men in an international hurry used the horse and the steamship, MacGahan in five hasty years reported from the Paris Commune (where he was imprisoned), the court of St. Petersburg, Central Asia, Cuba, the Arctic, the Caucasus and the Pyrenees. Famously distinguished for his impartiality and sharp eye, MacGahan was also never one to shirk a challenge. In 1875 he sailed through the Arctic's ice-choked waters in a wooden boat and two years earlier he defied a Russian embargo on reporters to make a remarkable ride over the Central Asian steppes. His goal was to catch up with a Russian military expedition on its way to Turkestan. Cossacks bent on his destruction pursued him for nearly 1,000 miles but after 29 days, accompanied by two attendants, sometimes forced to wade knee-deep in sand and several times lost, he reached the camp. His towering reputation for reliability and bravery reached new peaks.

By the summer of 1876, this 32-year-old reporter was in London with his Russian-born wife, Barbara, and a young son. He was planning a third book and some rest. But his relaxation was short-lived. The *Daily News*, a prominent liberal London paper, contacted him. They had an urgent assignment.

The *News* was in some trouble. A day or so before, on 23 June, they had published a story from their man in Constantinople, Sir Edwin Pears, based on rumours of terrible atrocities in southern Bulgaria by Turkish forces against the Christian population. The British Foreign Office was furious. So too was the pro-Turkish Prime Minister, Benjamin Disraeli. Describing the reports as 'coffee-house babble', he flatly denied them and openly charged the paper with misreporting and with, that old standard whine of the politicians, 'irresponsibility'. The Turks, who had imposed a total censorship on events, denied the whole thing.

It was now up to the *News* to prove their charges, or humiliatingly to climb down. So they sent for MacGahan and commissioned him to go to Bulgaria and try to discover the truth. By early July he was on his way; by the middle of the month he was there, investigating and interviewing hundreds of survivors. What he found was beyond even his hardened imaginings: the frenzied and wholesale butchery of some 12,000 Bulgarian men, women and children.

In the first of his dispatches, published by the *News* on 28 July, MacGahan wrote: 'I think I came in a fair and impartial frame of mind ... I fear I am no longer impartial, and I am certainly no longer cool ...'. His most telling account was from the village of Batak. Despite his own remarks about impartiality, it is a model of how the controlled reporting of facts, rather than emotions, is the most effective form of journalism:

As we approached the middle of the town, bones, skeletons, and skulls became more numerous. There was not a house beneath the ruins of which we did not perceive human remains, and the street besides was strewn with them... The church was not a very large one, and it was surrounded by a low stone wall, enclosing a small churchyard about fifty yards wide by seventy-five long. At first we perceive nothing in particular, ... but upon inspection we discover that what appeared to be a mass of stones and rubbish was in reality an immense heap of human bodies covered over with a thin layer of stones.

... We were told there were three thousand people lying here in this little churchyard alone ... There were little curly heads there in that festering mass, crushed down by heavy stones; little feet not as long as your finger on which the flesh was dried hard by the ardent heat before it had time to decompose; little baby hands stretched out as if for help; babes that had died wondering at the bright gleam of sabres and the red hands of the fierce-eyed men who wielded them; children who had died shrinking with fright and terror; young girls who had died weeping and sobbing and begging for mercy; mothers who died trying to shield their little ones with their own weak bodies, all lying there together, festering in one horrid mass.

They were silent enough now. There are no tears nor cries, no weeping, no shrieks of terror, nor prayers for mercy. The harvests are rotting in the fields, and the reapers are rotting here in the churchyard.

MacGahan's reports (which were reprinted across the world and later published as a booklet in many languages) instantly detonated a chain reaction of enormous proportions. Amid the worldwide indignation that followed, the British government was forced to concede the truth, pressure for military intervention built up and, in the spring of 1877, Russia launched a war against Turkey.

Eighty correspondents arrived to cover the Russian side but such were the rigours of the campaign that by its end less than a year later, only four of the original reporters were still in the field. MacGahan, of course, was among them. He had gone off to war with one foot in plaster, after injuring it in a fall. He ignored this and two further accidents which seriously crippled him, and carried on reporting, watching the fighting from a gun carriage. Six months and two treaties later, the nations of Bulgaria, Serbia, Montenegro and Romania had come into being, Russia was enlarged and the British had Cyprus.

MacGahan, however, was not alive to report it. A few weeks after the end of the war he went to Constantinople to nurse his friend, Francis Greene, through typhoid fever. Greene survived, but MacGahan caught it himself and on 9 June 1877 he died, aged 34. The Bulgarians, who had already christened him 'The Liberator', buried him in Pera, masses were said for his soul in St. Petersburg and he was mourned in London, Paris and America. In Sofia a statue was erected to him and for years afterwards his death was commemorated with an annual requiem at Tirnova.

Five years later his body was brought by an American warship to New York, where it lay in state in City Hall, and thence was taken to its final resting place in New Lexington, Ohio. His wife, who had been the Russian correspondent of the *New York Herald*, crossed the ocean with her husband's body and became the American correspondent for the Moscow paper, *Russkaya Viedmosti*. Later that year an official inquiry confirmed, in the cool calm of hindsight, everything that MacGahan had written from the chaotic killing fields of Bulgaria. Universal journalism is nothing new.

Whenever you find hundreds and thousands of sane people trying to get out of a place and a little bunch of madmen trying to get in, you know the latter are reporters.

H.R. Knickerbocker

2

The Limitations of Journalism

Newspapers are owned by individuals and corporations, but freedom of the press belongs to the people.

Anon

Every daily newspaper ought to print a disclaimer in each issue. It would read something like this:

> This paper, and the hundreds of thousands of words it contains, has been produced in about 15 hours by a group of fallible human beings, working out of cramped offices while trying to find out what happened in the world from people who are sometimes reluctant to tell us and, at other times, positively obstructive.

There are limits to the process of journalism. Shortage of time and the frequent unavailability of information are two which are endemic. So too are the errors that journalists make when working under pressure. There are also limitations on good journalism which are created by journalists themselves and by those who control or own newspapers. One of this trade's great myths is that coverage of events is shaped by a paper's style and news values. Would that it was all as simple as that. Instead, the quality and nature of a paper's journalism is also shaped by the owners' priorities, the prevailing journalistic culture and what readers' values are perceived to be. And there is often conflict between these factors.

Owners' priorities

Owners may pay lip service to concepts of truth, light and the virtuous way, but they are generally in the business to make money or propaganda or both. The way those who control newspapers' purse strings use them for propaganda is so well attested that it does not need re-stating with all its gory details here. Promotion of their own views, exclusion of opposing ones, slanting coverage to fit a point of view or commercial interests and pursuing personal vendettas are major themes of press history.

One example will suffice: William Randolph Hearst, the American newspaper magnate who behaved all his life as if he and honesty had never been properly introduced. He it was who, when a film called *Citizen Kane* was made patently based on his life, offered money to the studio to have the master and all prints destroyed before distribution. When that failed he had his gossip columnist, Louella Parsons, ring studio executives and distributors and threaten them with the exposure of personal details. She told them: 'Mr Hearst says that if you boys want private lives, he'll give you private lives.'

Like many non-corporate newspaper owners, Hearst paid his journalists very well; not through philanthropy but because it meant he had staffs who, through fear of the sack or a wish for the high-life to continue, compliantly shaped the news to fit their proprietors' prejudices. Once bedded in, they rarely needed specific instructions but would echo their master's voice unbidden. The pattern is a familiar one. In 1919, for example, Hearst papers reported the outbreak of communist revolution in Turin. The story was illustrated by a picture of workers armed with swords, guns, and bayonets, standing in front of a wall at the Fiat factory on which was daubed 'Viva Lenin'. It later turned out that the man who took the pictures, Ariel Vargas, had paid someone to paint the slogan on the factory walls, toured antique shops buying up every old weapon he could find, handed them to the 'revolutionaries', and told them not to laugh while he took their picture. Why? Well, his New York office had heard rumours of an uprising and evidence of it, true or otherwise, was what he felt he had to give them.

Nothing, however, better illustrates Hearst's attitude towards journalism, and that of many other proprietors down the years, than one exchange of cables from 1898. Hearst was very anxious, for personal political reasons and circulation purposes, that there should be a Spanish–American war over Cuba. His main paper, the *New York Journal*, ran slanted, jingoistic stories with lurid, distorted headlines ('Feeding Prisoners To The Sharks' and 'The Worst Insult to the United States In Its History', etc.). He also sent his staff on all kinds of escapades to find evidence of Spanish 'atrocities'. The honest ones filed nothing (and found their careers suffering), others used their imaginations. One of the former was an artist called Frederic Remington. Finding all quiet and no bloodshed, he cabled Hearst: 'There will be no war. I wish to return.' Legend has it Hearst replied: 'Please remain. You furnish pictures. I will furnish war.' Whether he sent such a cable is now widely doubted, but by running a series of distorted and invented stories, he duly did help supply the resultant conflict.

(Eccentricity was also often a hallmark of the single proprietor. Colonel Robert McCormick, owner of the *Chicago Tribune*, once ordered his Paris correspondent William Shirer to the French countryside to try to locate a pair of binoculars he had left in a barn nine years before. The champion lulu, however, was James Gordon Bennett Jnr. Not only did he insist his *International Herald Tribune* print the same weather report for 24 years, but also once marched into its offices and dismissed all the men standing on the right hand side of the room, sacked a music critic for the length of his hair and celebrated New Year's Day 1877 at the home of his fiancée's parents by urinating in the fireplace and then fighting a duel with her brother.)

His father was rather nicer for journalists to know. He commissioned Henry Morton Stanley to search for missionary David Livingstone, then lost in Central Africa. Before he left, Stanley told Bennett he was worried about the cost of the assignment. Bennett said: 'Well, I will tell you what you will do. Draw a thousand pounds now; and when you have gone through that draw another thousand, and when that is spent, draw another thousand, and when you have finished that draw another thousand, and so on. But find Livingstone!'

Nowadays owners are far more likely to be a corporation and their propaganda requirements are likely to be confined to supporting a known political party, stroking politicians able to favour them (or kicking those who can't) and urging stories that aid and abet their business interests. As a general rule, corporate owners are less active propagandists than individual proprietors and some show very little interest in editorials until it frightens the advertisers. What they are supremely focused on is maximising profit margins and urgently so if their debt is being financed by outsiders. This has meant, in the last two decades of the twentieth century, a concentration on lowering costs and, especially in monopoly situations, a fierce reduction of editorial staff. The experience of the regional weekly I once edited, which has seen its newsroom cut from 21 reporters to fewer than 10, is common.

The result, in terms of coverage and of scrutinising officialdom, has been devastating. In the case of covering local authorities, for instance, the former practice of assigning a reporter to track each department (education, leisure, environmental health, social services, etc.), has now been widely abandoned. Add the proliferation of public relations departments at local councils, health authorities, etc., and you have the recipe for coverage that is haphazard at best and spoonfed at worst. These staff cuts, and the expectation of more stories per reporter than was once the case (often formalised into half-baked schemes to measure reporters' 'output'), has meant that many reporters who now pass their days glued to a telephone behind a desk would not recognise the experiences of their predecessors, only a generation ago, who routinely tramped the streets meeting contacts (and readers) in search of stories. If that sounds like nostalgia, look around your newsroom, imagine its staff doubled and think how your coverage (and your own working life) would be changed.

Owners' priorities have probably imposed more limitations on how journalism is practised than any other factor in the last 20 years.

The journalistic culture

This culture sets what editors and their executives regard as a good story or dismiss as 'boring' and determines the subjects they think of as 'sexy' and those that are not. It also creates the moral atmosphere of a paper and is thus far more responsible for the ethics that are in daily use on a paper than any theoretical commandments.

In this culture, one of the most admired skills is 'a nose for a story'. This can either be a genuine ability to see meaning and interest in what others might overlook, or, in its degenerate form, the artful technique of presenting the mundane as the unusual. This journalistic conjuring trick is normally performed by excluding context, as when, in the early 1980s, the editor of the *New York Daily Post* filled the front page on a slow news day by asking reporters to collect details of every little crime committed in the city and then wrote them together in one breathless story under the headline 'Mayhem On Our Streets'.

A feature of such dishonest ingenuity is that a broadly accurate series of parts add up to a totally inaccurate whole. And it is not just admired on the tabloid papers where it originated. It has a wide influence on what is thought to be smart, slick behaviour everywhere. Sleight of hand with the facts and judiciously selecting information that is then presented out of its true setting is often copied, albeit in a milder form, throughout journalism. Part of this is unavoidable because any reality, which by its very nature is messy and complicated, has to be simplified, or at least have language and coherence imposed upon it, when it is related in words. A lot of journalism, however, wilfully omits context and unduly magnifies this effect for the sake of rendering reality in a more dramatic way. After a while the process is barely a conscious one.

The culture of mass-market papers also prizes the writing of facile narratives. What is involved here is certainly some talent, but also, far more, a stretching of facts and the meaning of words to give an arresting construct. Its most common form is where the story is given a false intro by deducing from some of the elements some spuriously dramatic (but probably far-fetched) possibility. The giveaway is often the words 'could', 'may' or 'claims'. As with the conjuring tricks referred to above, the sneakiness is in the way in which some sort of plausible defence of each component can be mounted. The finished article, however, still amounts to a lie. Neither is the writing and editing process on more serious, 'quality' papers free of this corruption. There it originates with the desk editors who talk of 'running the story through their machines' to 'beef it up'. Often stories do benefit from such attentions, but frequently this amounts to, and is openly acknowledged as, putting a synthetic gloss on a story, stretching the implications of each fact to the utmost and thus producing a misleading overall picture.

And what is done in the editing process today is liable to be done at the reporting stage tomorrow. Reporters competing to get their stories published anticipate executive values and are prepared (or feel obliged) to adopt practices which are at odds with their private values. This professional schizophrenia is at its most chronic where the prevailing culture is known to favour stories that are composed of vivid blacks or whites and not the messy greys and ambiguous mid-tones of reality.

To an extent all journalism favours such stories. A story where A cheats B with provably false documents and then uses the ill-gotten gains to live it up in the Caribbean, is obviously more immediately interesting to all of us than one where A and B are in dispute over a deal, both are claiming to be cheated and the trip to warmer climes turns out to be a business visit to service off-shore accounts. In any language, for any paper, the first version of that story would be preferred to the second. It is more unusual and it patently has greater news value. The problem is that such preferences get understandably formalised into the journalistic culture. Reporters and editors, knowing that simplistic stories of black and white are the most attractive to editors, can then look for these to the exclusion of more subtle, and certainly more realistic, tales. Worse is the way that this view of what constitutes a 'good, hard story' can affect the research and writing and rob a story of balance. There is an unconscious tendency to stop asking questions at the nice and simple, clear-cut stage. 'Don't check it out too closely' is the cynical, sniggering advice of too many news editors.

It is not a very large step from this to regarding news as something to be packaged to conform to a pre-conceived recipe, or formula. On mass-market papers in particular, editors are determined to have stories of certain types – light, frothy ones or breathless, dramatic ones. Executives hear of a story in the early stages, decide the kind of headline or treatment they want and then they (or the reporter) organise the facts or the treatment of them to force the story into the formula. It is journalism by headline. It presents to readers a world where the extraordinary always happens, there are only certainties and simplicities, rights and wrongs, and only stereotypes exist.

British papers are far worse offenders in this than American ones. For various reasons, the most powerful of which is the influence of the national mass market press, there is a pervasive 'journalistic' style of writing, of deploying 'journalese'. Entire newspapers are filled with tired old puns, hackneyed ideas (no story about cats are complete without a reference to 'nine lives'), clichés, and a jaunty and routine hyping (political disagreements, for instance, being described as a 'furious row'). For reasons that are beyond sense or explanation, many journalism trainers and not a few news editors actively encourage such unoriginal and limited language as evidence of 'professionalism'. There is something almost totalitarian about the widespread insistence on this journalese. In America, lacking a tabloid press that has any influence on what is thought to be good journalism, there is far less conforming to a 'journalistic style'. News and feature writers are allowed far more latitude, and the result is better writing. And the US press takes the study of writing far more seriously than all but isolated pockets of its British counterpart. Some US papers bring in writing coaches. Suggest this to a British paper, and you'd probably be sent to the company doctor for medication.

These are the limitations of the journalistic process seen at their most extreme. Many papers do not go this far, but those that do, and those journalists on other papers who have absorbed some of this culture, have one standard answer to objections: the readers. No group of people are more often invoked to defend the otherwise indefensible. No group of people have their appetites more regularly or wilfully taken for granted, nor their vocabularies and intelligence more patronisingly underestimated. 'Time to go and write my 200 words for people who move their lips when they read', as one British tabloid correspondent always used to say.

Readers' values

Readers are the ones in whose names stories and subjects are selected, treatments applied, intros written and re-written, and presentation and design carried out. Yet, of all the conflicting elements in journalism – those who supply potential information (sources), those who process it (reporters, editors, owners or controllers) and those who consume it (readers) – the latter are the only ones who are not actually present during its creation. Their tastes have to be anticipated.

Newspapers in established, sophisticated markets do this in a variety of ways. They and their journalists build up over the years, through responses they have had to stories, readers' letters, telephone calls, complaints and so forth, an anecdotal 'knowledge' of what their readers want. Or rather what they believe their readers want. This internal folklore may or may not be successful and it may or may not be accurate. Unless it is put to the test with some serious research, no one will ever know.

Often it is not. It is instead combined with the prejudices of journalists, executives and owners to produce a highly personalised idea of what readers want, or what they think they ought to want. Times without number one hears in editorial conferences the phrase, 'What the reader wants is ...'. Too often this is based on the speaker's own preferences and tastes, or those of friends; or, even worse, those he or she wants to impress.

A danger here is that journalists often inhabit circles and have lifestyles, habits and tastes that are far removed from those of their readers. They might, if they are a 'serious' journalist, mix constantly with figures in authority and officials and so absorb some of their values. In many developed countries the payment of relatively fancy salaries on many papers has meant that journalists breathe a different air, eat different meat and live a life far removed from that experienced by their readers. It takes more imagination than most such journalists have to appreciate that the restaurants they dine at, the clothes they buy and the holidays they take are not pleasures enjoyed by their readers. And if they do use their imagination, they run the risk of conjuring up a patronising pastiche of their readers' tastes.

Research, if scientifically done, is part of the answer. Some papers rightly use research companies to find out as much as they can about readers: ages, male/female ratio, incomes, occupations, education, interests, concerns, tastes, how they spend their leisure time, spending patterns, etc. They then know, for instance, how many of their readers aged 35–50 take holidays in France, or how many aged 25–35 own a mobile phone. The only problem is that this information is collected for the benefit of the advertising department and is only rarely passed to journalists.

The research normally initiated by the editorial department is into reader attitudes, both to the paper and to the issues and subjects they might cover. This can either be simple surveys via a form printed in the paper, 'readers' panels', or by research companies whose structured questioning finds out what people do read (or, rather, what they claim to read). Surveys are, however, strung about with trip-wires for the unwary. They should ask very specific questions on detailed points of the paper's coverage. It is no good asking people if they want more news – of course they do, but what kind? And what would they like less of to make room for it? Then there is the problem of respondents telling researchers what they think they want to hear, or, even worse, stating preferences that they would like to be thought of as having, rather than their real ones.

Just after 1945, the British *News Of The World* was the largest-selling paper in the world. Each Sunday some 7,000,000 copies were sold to people who lapped up its diet of murders and sex cases. A few 'respectable' features were mixed in. Then the editor had a hunch that morals and tastes were changing and so commissioned a survey. Men were hired to visit readers' homes and quiz them about what they liked and did not like in the paper. Since this work was done during the day, it was mainly women who answered the door. None, understandably, was prepared to say to their male inquisitors: 'Yes, I like the rape cases and the indecency and my husband is very fond of stories about priests and small boys.' Instead, respondents assured the researchers that they only took the paper for the respectable features. The editor read the results and immediately dropped all mention of sex from the paper. After just two weeks, circulation had fallen by 500,000. By the third week, the paper had a new editor, the content returned to its seedy normality and sales eventually reached 8,500,000.

Readers do have a disorientating tendency to say they like one thing while preferring another and publicly disdain some forms of journalism while consuming them avidly in private. That is why some researchers use two-way mirrors to observe a focus group reading a paper or uninhibitedly discussing its contents. There are even visor-like devices which fit on to people's heads, monitor their eye movement and so give a precise record of what they read, merely glance at, or ignore. If the technology or money is not available for those black arts, there is an alternative which, for journalists, is probably more effective than any research. That is to spend as much time as possible with readers and observing them. How many journalists have ever stood and watched people as they select a paper at the newsstands? Or studied them in bars or on trains and seen how they read papers? This is all part of the unquenchable curiosity that journalists should have about readers. It should make them want to talk to them at every opportunity, meet them and get to know as much as they can about them.

Advertisers are the other element in the paper's audience and for smaller circulation papers they are economically more important than readers. This commercial power is what makes many think that advertisers are continuously exercising this muscle to intimidate papers into tailoring their coverage to suit them. The surprise is that the instances of this, and there are many, are not even more frequent. Of course large advertisers have sometimes withdrawn advertising in protest of a paper's coverage (or lack of it), many have threatened to do so and even more have tried a chummy phone call to an editor or publisher to get their way. And some have succeeded.

The dangers of this are greatest when papers, normally provincial ones, are inordinately dependent on one advertiser or group of advertisers. But far more common than this overt pressure is the influence of potential advertisers on feature coverage. Editors are often under enormous pressure from the commercial side of the paper to run features on certain subjects because it is known, or anticipated, that this will generate advertising. This can result in some subjects getting more attention than they otherwise would. A lot of this is relatively harmless in itself, but then proves to be the precursor of more demanding attentions.

These limitations on the journalistic process – the ones endemic to information gathering and those imposed by owners' priorities, editorial culture and readers' tastes – mean that perhaps the disclaimer suggested for most papers at the opening of this chapter should be a little longer:

This paper, and the hundreds of thousands of words it contains, has been produced in about 15 hours by a group of fallible human beings, working out of cramped offices while trying to find out about what happened in the world from people who are sometimes reluctant to tell us and, at other times, positively obstructive.

Its content has been determined by a series of subjective judgements made by reporters and executives, tempered by what they know to be the editor's, owner's and readers' prejudices. Some stories appear here without essential context as this would make them less dramatic or coherent and some of the language employed has been deliberately chosen for its emotional impact, rather than its accuracy. Some features are printed solely to attract certain advertisers.

These limitations have all the inevitability of recurring bad dreams. In the end, journalists have only one answer to them: to develop universal standards and skills and act upon them. They are our only protection. If journalists do that, they can beat the limitations. It can be done; for every day, somewhere on this planet, it is being done. Reporters are exposing corruption, uncovering negligence, revealing dangers, unmasking criminals and reporting hard facts that someone wanted kept secret. Papers are publishing information and, to paraphrase *The Times'* editor of a century ago, making it the common property of the people. Even bad newspapers do more good than harm – and you can't say that about governments.

I cannot give you the formula for success, but I can give you the formula for failure – which is: try to please everybody.

Herbert Bayard Swope, US editor

3

What Is News?

Newspapers are unable, seemingly, to discriminate between a bicycle accident and the collapse of civilisation.

George Bernard Shaw

A newspaper's role is to find out fresh information on matters of public interest and to relay it as quickly and as accurately as possible to readers in an honest and balanced way. That's it. It may do lots of other things, like telling them what it thinks about the latest movies, how to plant potatoes, what kind of day Taureans might have or why the government should resign. But without fresh information it will be merely a commentary on things already known. Interesting, perhaps, stimulating even; but comment is not news. Information is.

The oft-quoted dictum on this issue was written by C.P. Scott, the editor of the then *Manchester Guardian*, in a signed editorial on 5 May 1921. He wrote that the newspaper's:

...primary office is the gathering of news. At the peril of its soul it must see that the supply is not tainted. Neither in what it gives, nor in what it does not give, nor in the mode of presentation, must the unclouded face of truth suffer wrong.

This is a tall, if not impossible, order. But then he added, and this is the bit that has since been trotted out a million times, 'Comment is free but facts are sacred'.

The real point of this statement is what it says about the comparative values of facts and comment. If you take a room full of journalists and ask them who has got an opinion on an important topical news event, every hand will go up. Ask who has some fresh, unpublished information on this event and almost every hand will go down. The fact is that almost everyone has a comment, be it interesting or not, and very few have new information. The one is a commonplace, the other is a thing of scarcity and hence value.

What is news?

There are almost as many definitions of news as there are stories. The most common hackneyed definition is one coined in 1882 by John B. Bogart, city editor of the *New York Sun*: it is not news if a dog bites a man, but it is news if a man bites a dog. This reminds us that news is the unusual. But there is more to news than that. It is also something fresh, something that people have not heard before and, crucially, is of interest to readers. That means not just matters which affect the public or have an impact on public life, but also what is *of* interest to the public. News of a divorce between two well-known actors is not a matter that is *in* the public's interest, but it is *of* interest to the public. The best illustration of this is still the old *New Yorker* cartoon of two men on a train. One holds a paper headlined 'Lots of Important Stuff You Have to Know' and the other has a paper headlined 'Rumors, Gossip and Wacky Stunts'. The joke is that the one with 'Lots of Important Stuff' can't keep his eyes off 'Rumors, Gossip and Wacky Stunts'.

News values

News then is the fresh, unpublished, unusual and generally interesting. The first three elements can nearly always be objectively established; it is the last part – what is generally interesting? – that causes all the arguments every day in newsrooms around the world.

There is not generally a problem at the two extremes. If 450 people are killed when a plane carrying the President crashes onto a city-centre department store, that is plainly very big news, guaranteed to make anyone who reads say 'Wow!', even if only to themselves. On the other hand, I have just bought a new car. Is that news? It is fresh, unpublished and it is certainly unusual. But it's not news because it is only of interest to my family, bank manager and car dealer.

It is all the stories in between these two extremes that journalists argue about, trying to decide if a story is strong or 'sexy', worth 200 words or 700, a news brief or a splash lead on page one. To the novice it is, along with intros, one of the great mysteries of their working lives, made all the more impenetrable by the ease with which experienced hands pass swift and seemingly sure judgement on a story. Fortunately, there is some detailed and practical help available.

News value factors

Let's get one thing established at the outset: there is no escaping subjectivity in judging news stories. It pervades the whole process of journalism and no reporter or news editor, try as they might professionally to suppress their own prejudices, will ever be able to do so completely. This is most obvious when they judge the basic story subject. I think homelessness is interesting and important, you think it is inevitable and boring. Such subjectivity, although unavoidable, is an ever-present danger, especially when journalists (often news editors) try to pass off their personal prejudices as objectivity. Awareness of the tendency is, however, some protection against its worst excesses.

Subjectivity is not what a lot of young journalists see when they first step into a newsroom. Nor, sometimes to their amazement, do they often witness lengthy debates on a story's virtues. Instead they see a lot of news judgements being made swiftly and surely and seemingly based on nothing more scientific than gut feeling. The process is, however, a lot more measured than that. It just appears to be instinctive because a lot of the calculations that go into deciding a story's strength have been learnt to the point where they are made very rapidly – sometimes too rapidly.

The following is an attempt to identify what is – or should be – whirring around inside journalists' heads when they judge a news story. For want of a better phrase, we can call them news value factors. There are eight of them. Five are concerned with the story (subject, news fashion, development, source, knowledge and timing); one with audience (the readers); and another with the world that the audience and paper inhabit (context).

Subject

This is the broad category that the story falls under – crime, environment, health, diplomacy, economy, consumer, military, politics and so forth. All subjects are in theory equal, but some are more equal than others. Crime, for instance, has a higher value than fashion because it is patently of broader interest. Each of these categories then breaks down into sub-divisions, for example, crime breaks down into murder, fraud, abduction, racketeering, drugs, robbery, blackmail, rape, assault, etc. For the general audience, each of these has its own rough value which is normally based on its rarity in a given society or area. This is where 'context' (see below) comes in. For instance, abductions generally have more news value than assaults because they are rarer.

News fashion

There is also such a factor as news fashion – subjects which suddenly swim into the news consciousness and are, for a time, flavour of the month. This is seen at its most glaring in activities which have perhaps been around for a long time in a fairly unobtrusive way, but which suddenly acquire a phrase or word to describe them. Under the new catchy title they then get reported out of all proportion. 'New crimes', such as air rage, are a classic example. Robbing people in the street, bust-ups between motorists and using cars to break into premises have been around for as long as there have been streets and cars. But given the names 'mugging', 'road rage' and 'ram raiding' they acquire an extra frisson and have all been the news fashion for a period.

The history of this phenomena goes back a long way. In 1862, *The Times* whipped up a fair old panic over the sudden outbreak of what the paper called 'garotting' – attacks from behind. In some areas, when the stories were at their height, people refused to leave their homes. The panic, however, soon subsided. Since then, news fashions have included the Great Cyclist Terror of 1890s, when the *Daily Graphic* set middle-class hearts aflutter with reports of hordes of cyclists who 'rang their bells and expected people to get out of the way while pedalling as fast as eight to ten miles an hour.' In the 1950s every working class male youth was a Teddy Boy, in the 1960s every biker a rocker, in the 1970s every long-haired youth was a drug-crazed hippie, in the 1980s every large gathering of the young was an acid house party and in the 1990s every minor contretemps between motorists was 'road rage'. Easy to sneer now, but hard to resist when everyone is talking about the latest scare. Some stories coolly examining the data on the phenomena are usually the antidote.

There are other, more lasting, mood swings in the news business. Some are due to changing lifestyles and technology; others are not. Thirty years ago, investigations, stories about consumer rights, and examinations of poverty and deprivation were very prevalent. These days they have been replaced by stories about celebrity, the media, lifestyle, surveys, and new trends, many of which are almost entirely spurious. The reasons for the change are twofold: cost (celebrity and lifestyle stories are, since they often come via PRs, a lot cheaper to generate than investigations), and the need felt by many editors to make their papers 'more featurey' and 'more accessible'. Or even, as some of them put it, 'more women friendly' – the patronising assumption in many newspapers being that women are interested in stories about trends and relationships to the exclusion of hard news.

Development

This is the specific event within the subject and sub-division which is the point of the story. Its rarity is the main part of its value and this exists without any reference to the audience. It is the straightforward assessment of how uncommon this particular development is. As an example, take the long-running dispute between Britain and France over the latter's refusal to allow UK beef to be sold because of possible BSE contamination. A development which involved plans to hold talks would be a minor development (unless one side had previously declined to meet).

Talks on issues are, after all, held all the time. But a development which consisted of one side or the other walking out of the talks would be a lot rarer and thus a bigger development. A low rarity value is the chief cause, along with a lack of timeliness, for a story being disregarded or downgraded. The development has three other elements:

Source

The value of the development depends in part on the source from which it was obtained. An opposition politician might tell you that the president is about to resign, but if the president, or one of his close aides, tells you this then it is clearly a stronger story. It will be an even better story if you discover that he is about to resign, but also that he does not want the real reason known – and you know it and pass it on to your readers.

Knowledge

This is a question of how many people know about the development. The highest value attaches to stories which are the first report of a development unknown to all but the source(s), including perhaps their colleagues and private circle. The story's value is lowered if it is already in the public arena because it has already been reported by another newspaper. Stories that have already been broadcast on TV or radio may have their value lowered, but not to the same extent. You frequently hear people in national newspaper newsrooms say of a story: 'I thought we knew that', meaning that this angle may already have been reported. If a search of the cuttings turns up a prior example then out of the paper goes the story. The statement is, however, frequently an excuse for news executives to downplay a story they otherwise don't like. If you hear it spoken frequently without good reason, your prejudice alarm should ring.

Timing

News, unlike wine, does not improve with keeping. Elapsed time, however, is not the most important of factors in itself. If you learn of a major development three weeks after it has occurred, the crucial factor is not the delay, but how many people have learnt of this development in the meantime. If the story is still not public knowledge, the three-week interval will not significantly reduce the news value. It may, depending on the reason, even increase it. While shortness of time elapsing between the development happening and your report of it can add value, timing is more often a negative factor, subtracting value when there are delays which allow the story to become widely known.

Readers

This is the first of the factors that does not relate directly to the specifics of the story. The importance of the audience in judging news stories is why you should make every effort to learn as much as you can about readers. Unless you do, you cannot possibly judge their interests and tastes and so properly weigh the value of the subject and development. It would be like lecturing in a dark room to an unknown audience.

But you should use your knowledge of readers to inform your judgements in general and not to influence them incessantly in a detailed way. The day you see news reporting as a commodity to be marketed is the day you cease to be a journalist. There is a point where pandering too avidly to what you think are the readers' preferences also becomes filtering to remove stories which do not fit readers' known prejudices or omitting inconvenient parts of them such as context, explanations and qualification. This is important. It is part of the journalists' mission to debunk popular myths and to challenge comfortable assumptions. You cannot do that if you are too conscious of readers' reactions and too anxious to placate them. You will end up being about as reliable as some eager-to-please lover who speaks only the words he thinks want to be heard.

The English satirist Michael Frayn had this in mind when he wrote in *The Tin Men* of a computer being programmed to produce daily newspapers according to the results of mass surveys. People were asked what stories they liked best, how often they wanted them to recur and which details they enjoyed. Should there be an air-crash story every month or more frequently? Is it preferred, or not, that children's toys should be found among the wreckage? If a murder is reported, should the victim be a small girl, an old lady or an unmarried pregnant woman? And should the corpse be naked, or 'partially clothed'? There are a lot of mass-market journalists around the world who, equipped with their own assumptions about readers' appetites rather than any survey results, approach reporting in much the same way as Frayn's imaginary computer.

Other assumptions about readers come into play. In recent years, there has been a resurgence of the 'vox pop' (in which members of the public chip in comments – not all of which are high in originality – on a story) and case histories, in which someone tells of their experiences in a sidebar to the main story. More often than is healthy, an editor's main obsession with these is not the quality of the personal drama being told, but the age, gender and appearance of the subject. An attractive thirtysomething woman, even if her remarks are utterly banal, is nearly always preferred to the moving testimony of an older, less photogenic one. This may not be defendable or edifying, but it is a fact of life on most newspapers.

Readers' hypocrisy

When I give public lectures on journalism to older audiences, a man at the back will invariably stand up and, in the guise of asking a question, make a short speech deploring what he calls 'the media's obsession with sex and intrusions into private lives'. This will be greeted with a storm of applause. After it dies away, I will ask: who here reads the .... ? (naming the tabloid newspapers most famous for their scandal content). Not a hand will go up. This is odd, because in Britain the papers in question sell more than 25 million copies a week and yet I have never met a single person who admits in a public meeting to reading them.

Such hypocrisy is at the heart of so much criticism of the press. People will condemn in public the content which they will avidly read in private. If they genuinely objected to scandal and invasions of privacy, they wouldn't buy the papers which peddle these stories, and the papers would rapidly change. Survey after survey may report that what people want in their papers is less trivia and celebrity, and more serious analytical articles, but mass market behaviour says otherwise. This is not to justify the journalism of the lowest common denominator, but it does go some long way to explaining it.

Context

This is the situation in any given circulation area (society, town, city or region) that relates to the subject and development and helps you to judge rarity. This is why the news value of a story will vary depending on where it happens. It explains why a rural Danish weekly will rate the story of a shooting far higher than a New York tabloid would. In one place it is the exception, in the other it is an event that happens many times a day.

Sometimes this works in what appears to be reverse, when many instances of a particular development accumulate. For instance, it may not be thought to be news if a dog bites a man. But if a certain breed of dog repeatedly bites people – and badly – then it will become news. Every single event adds to the rarity of the accumulation of cases. This is a reminder of why context should always be reported, sometimes in substantial detail. Occasionally the context is generally known, but more often it has to be researched and so becomes inseparable from the development in the story. It should always then be reported.

Context is also important for defending journalism against the allegation that it is negative, sensationalist or only interested in bad things. For instance, if you live in a place where people entering hospital are routinely cured and cared for, then it will be news if someone is suddenly neglected and dies. To report that is often condemned as negativist. Apart from the fact that it is not the job of journalists to be either negative or positive, those who make that allegation should ask themselves what atrocious standards of medical care it would take to produce headlines like 'Man Enters Hospital and Lives'.

A sliding scale for stories

Once you are aware of these general factors, judging the strength of news values can really only be done on a story-by-story basis. So here are some:

- A new UN peace initiative in an African state torn by civil war.
- Government ban on the import of all foreign-made cars.
- Famous soap opera actress to divorce.
- Opposition politician calls press conference to condemn government finance policy.
- Another opposition politician calls press conference to announce he will probably stand for leader.
- Four young girls murdered in small area of your city within three days by sex maniac.
- Government announces major new initiative to clean up dirty restaurants.

So which story do you think is the best? What would you put on the top of the front page? Well, of course, it is an impossible exercise unless you know what paper we are talking about and who its readers are. So try it first with your capital city's biggest-selling paper in mind and then again with a leading paper for the businessman.

My choices would be the murdered girls for the popular and the ban on foreign car imports for the businessman's paper. To reach those decisions I tested the stories against a kind of scale of story strength I have used over the years. Never committed to paper until now, it has largely been automatic and unconscious, as these things often are. Here it is:

At the bottom end of the scale are stories about what people are saying

These are stories about conflicts of ideas or new ideas. These are 'say stories' – nothing has happened, someone has just said something. A classic giveaway of this kind of story is the word 'warns', 'urges' or 'calls' in the headline. A May 1994 issue of the *Moscow Times*, an otherwise excellent English-language paper, once had nine out of 13 news stories which were say stories. Were they really saying that in a huge country covering eight time zones only four newsworthy things actually happened over a weekend?

There are two common traps for the journalist here. First is the assumption that because a politician says something, we ought to record it. Not true. Every journalist should have the motto on his or her desk:

'They are only politicians'. Just because some middle-aged man in a grey suit has chosen to make a speech or a statement does not make it news. Most speeches and statements are expressions of the entirely expected. It is only when they say something surprising that it becomes news. A leading reformist, liberal politician condemning the slow pace of change in a society is nothing new. But if he announces his conversion to communism, then it is news.

The second trap is what has been called the pseudo-event: press conferences, interviews and the like. Press conferences are not, as some journalists seem to think, news in themselves. Nothing has actually happened. The world has not been changed one bit. All that has happened is that some politician or celebrity has wanted to make a statement, usually for their own motives, the prime one of which is publicity. The only thing that matters is the content of their message. Treat all such pseudo-events with scepticism.

Next are stories about what people say will happen

These are stories about threats or demands for action. Such exhortations are over-used by politicians, aided and abetted by lazy journalists who find attendance at press conferences so much more congenial than scuffling around looking for genuine stories. But at least such events sometimes have the virtue of having good, hard information about a situation imparted along with the hot air and waffle.

Then there are stories about what people say is or was happening

These are stories about research, about people passing on to you what they have found out. Something concrete will have occurred.

At the top end are stories about what has happened

These are about developments, events, accidents, disasters, court hearings and many other hard, real, provable occurrences.

An important concept for judging news value is the number of your readers who will be affected by a story

The more people affected by an event, the stronger the story about it will be. If the readers are affected directly, then so much the better.

The more permanent the effect of what it is that you are reporting, then the better and stronger the story

Something which affects people only for a day or so is clearly weaker than that which affects them permanently.

As with all such rules of thumb, there will always be occasional exceptions to this scale. News fashion can often be responsible for these. Stories which a week before would have hardly merited a small inside piece are suddenly transported to the front page because they have caught the present news wave. Other developments, an incident, acccident or disaster, means that suddenly the story's subject is news flavour of the week. It can also work in reverse and often explains why being first to publish on an issue does not bring the kudos that it ought. In news, timing is often everything.

Finally, reporters should always remember that the fact that they have found something out does not make it news. The 'story' they are trying to sell to their editor may have taken days and even weeks to research, they may have had to brave all kinds of difficulties and overcome all kinds of obstacles – but that does not make the story stronger. Only in very exceptional circumstances does the reader care how the reporter came by the story.

> *On this newspaper, the separation of news columns from the editorial and op-ed pages is solemn and complete. This separation is intended to serve the reader, who is entitled to the facts in the news columns and to opinions on the editorial and op-ed pages. But nothing in this separation of functions is intended to eliminate from the news columns honest, in-depth reporting or analysis or commentary when plainly labelled.*
>
> Ben Bradlee, then editor of the *Washington Post*

Beauty and news values

One day in 2007 I came across, on page 29 of my favourite daily paper, the story of someone who had committed suicide on the other side of the world. She was quite unknown in my country, and of no significance to us whatsoever. What, you may ask, was the story of this sad and common occurrence doing in a newspaper 11 time zones away? The answer was in the picture that accompanied the story. The person who had taken their own life was a young Australian television newsreader. She was young, female, and, crucially for the editor who ran the story, strikingly pretty. She would not have looked out of place as the love interest in a Hollywood movie, and this, I think, was the sole reason the story was printed. If the subject had been over 40, or anything less than beautiful, or male, then the story would simply not have been published 11,000 miles away.

Physical attractiveness and gender have always been a factor in deciding what stories get printed, but these days they are major factors in news values. I know several papers in London where human interest stories – unless they are utterly extraordinary – will not be published unless they involve people who are attractive or female, or both. Here, and on many other papers, the people whose experiences are used as case histories to illustrate a news story or feature must conform to certain social, age, gender, and attractiveness standards. If the story is at all sympathetic, the subject must not be ugly, untidy, poor, or even just unyouthful and male. One paper whose news editor I know published a very moving account from a man in his fifties to illustrate a story. After the first edition appeared, the editor rang the news desk to angrily demand that an account from a 'smart' woman in her twenties or thirties was found to replace 'this old bloke'. Never mind that his story was a moving one, and fitted the story perfectly.

This preoccupation with appearance infects the news values even of stories where beauty and celebrity are – or should be – irrelevant. Would the famous murder case in Perugia, Italy a few years ago have been given such prominence if the victim, British student Meredith Kercher, been seriously overweight, or the American student convicted of her killing, Amanda Knox, had a skin problem and a squint? No. Editors are very marketing and image-conscious these days, and patrol the pages of their papers making sure the people written about are the kind they think readers aspire to being (young, successful and attractive). Newspapers are also much more heavily illustrated now, and it is but a small step from putting in occasional pictures of attractive people and things where relevant, to demand that stories are written primarily about them, or references to them are routinely inserted, just so their pictures can be used. It is an obnoxious trend which we should all resist where we can. My advice: leave beauty fascism to the glossy magazines.

4

Where Do Good Stories Come From?

It is hard news that catches readers. Features hold them.
                                        Lord Northcliffe

Some of the best stories appear to come from nowhere – out-of-the-blue accidents, resignations, and catastrophes so startling that the essential facts alone are enough to make major headlines. Journalists can do nothing to influence whether such stories exist; all we can do is produce the best-researched and written versions of them. A lot of other good stories, however, depend on journalists for their very existence – stories which start life as lesser incidents but are transformed into the startling by the discovery of some hitherto hidden aspect; and true off-diary stories, unknown to the public until a journalist discovers and reports them.

There is nothing accidental about this process. Good stories like these do not come out of the blue; they come from successful journalists knowing where to look and doing certain things right – which is why they come up with far more of such stories than ordinary journalists. The apparent mystery of where good stories come from is not a riddle at all. It is a matter of having solid working practices, plus knowing where to look – and where not to.

The habits of successful reporters

The best reporters get the best stories because they have sharp news instincts and they know where to look, who to talk to and what to ask. The details of these are covered in the next three chapters on sources, research and questioning. But there are other, perhaps less obvious but just as vital, reporters' habits which consistently produce good stories.

Exploring all avenues

Determination is perhaps the biggest difference between the ordinary and the good reporter. It is when other reporters are saying: 'Oh it won't be worth calling them', or 'No point hanging round here anymore', that the best reporters get busy. A classic example, all the more relevant for its everyday nature, is the story found by Derek Lambert, then on a trial with the *Daily Mirror*. It seemed at first like a routine murder case: a Polish man had been found stabbed in the basement of a seedy lodging house in Manchester and Lambert was sent out to find out what he could. It did not look very promising. The neighbours knew (or were saying) nothing, the policeman guarding the murder scene would not speak and, when Lambert went to the police station, he was told they could not add to their earlier brief statement.

It is at this point that the ordinary reporter would have headed back to the office and reported there was nothing much in the story; and indeed that is what Lambert's rivals did. He, however, was not an ordinary reporter. He hung around, determined to get more, hoping to grab a few words with an off-duty policeman. After a while he saw detectives emerge and get into a car. Hoping they were working on the murder, he returned to the scene. There he saw two men in suits knocking on doors. He introduced himself to the detectives and got talking about the case. The dead man, they told him, was a police informer who had been run over by a car and then stabbed. Lambert had his story and soon he was dictating it to his office. It began: 'Police were last night investigating the mystery of the man who was murdered twice.' It made front page lead and secured a job on the *Mirror* for Lambert.

Getting out and about

Good stories do sometimes come to those who sit and wait in an office, but most people are a lot more forthcoming in person than they are down a phone line. And experiencing life at first, as opposed to second, hand tends to produce good stories, whether it is the official lurking around at the back of the press conference who tells you the real story behind the announcement, or something that you see for yourself. For example, William G. Shepherd, a United Press reporter, just happened to be walking through New York's Washington Square on 25 March 1911, when his eye was caught by a puff of smoke coming from a nearby building. The premises belonged to the Triangle Shirtwaist Company, and the fire there became a famous tragedy, not least because of Shepherd's account of the young women working on the upper floors who flung themselves off window ledges as the flames leapt nearer. 'I learned a new sound, a more horrible sound than description can picture,' Shepherd wrote, 'It was the thud of a speeding, living body on a stone sidewalk. Thud-dead, thud-dead, thud-dead, thud-dead. Sixty-two thud-deads ... There was plenty of chance to watch them as they came down. The height was eighty feet.'

Of course, Shepherd was lucky to stumble on such a major story, but then, as someone once said: 'I've met a lot of lucky reporters. I've never known a single lazy lucky reporter.' And luck can come in the strangest form. There was the bizarre case, a few years ago, of Norwegian reporter Lars Gustavsen, sent by his paper to cover a police car chase. On the way, he picked up a hitch-hiker, and chatted with him for about ten minutes before being flagged down at a check-point, whereupon the hitch-hiker was immediately arrested. He was the very man the police had been pursuing. Exit reporter with a great, if rather embarrassing, story.

Keeping your eyes open for potential stories

The best reporters soon learn to filter almost everything they experience outside of their private life (and sometimes in it) for potential stories, much in the way that whales sift sea water for krill. Routine examples pop up almost every day, but one young British reporter shows how an ever-alert news sense can pay off. Ruth Lumley was travelling by train in the southern county of West Sussex one day in 2005 when she noticed some graffiti scrawled on a toilet door. It read: 'Girls aged 8 to 13 wanted for sex' and gave a phone number. It might have been the work of some warped prankster, but, being a good reporter, Ms Lumley investigated. Posing as an 11 year old girl, she sent a text to the number on the wall, and back came a series of obscene messages. She contacted the police, who investigated, arrests were made, four men duly jailed for sex offences, and Ms Lumley had a fine story to write. Less sensationally, it was keeping his eyes constantly open that provided *New York Times* reporter Meyer Berger with such a rich crop of human interest stories for his weekly column: from the descendant of Borneo head hunters who ran a Manhattan barber shop and Miss Delphine Binger and her collection of 500,000 chicken, turkey and goose wishbones, to Sig Klein's Fat Men's Shop on Third Avenue (74-inch trousers a speciality) and New York's only praying mantis farm.

Hanging around

The best reporters do not, unless they cannot possibly help it, arrive late and breathless to cover an event. They tend to arrive early and, if they have time, hang around afterwards. By doing this they get a feel for the event and its characters, hear things, observe useful detail, speak to people and ask questions. Whatever the event – whether it is a court case, public inquiry, political meeting, campaign launch, release of a report – the best stories are often found not in the public part of the event, but in the time spent before and after chatting to those involved. After all, most non-journalists have no idea what makes a good news story. It is only when they are talking informally before or after a meeting, interview or whatever, that they may mention something which is a far better story than the one you originally came for. And you never know what might happen when you do hang around. Perhaps the best example of being in the right spot when a major story breaks is the Associated Press's Lawrence Gobright. He was working late in Washington on the night of 14 April 1865, when a friend who had been at the nearby Ford's Theatre burst in and told him President Lincoln had been shot. Gobright filed a brief bulletin and then ran to the theatre. He was on the scene so quickly the place was still in uproar, and he was able to get into the presidential box, examine the blood on the back of Lincoln's rocking chair, see the rip in the flag made by the assassin's spurs as he leapt from the box, and was even able to take charge of the weapon that the killer had dropped as he fled. Then there was the BBC's Alistair Cooke, on hand in the right part of the Ambassador Hotel, Los Angeles when Senator Robert Kennedy was gunned down.

Making your own luck

To be lucky, you have to put yourself in the position where good fortune can occur. This is partly a matter of persistence, partly an instinct for where the happening part of the story is and, especially on the big stories where there are many reporters on the same case, partly a matter of not following the mob. In 1981, the Pope was shot and journalists from all round the world were sent to Rome. Among them was John Edwards of the *Daily Mail*. Like quite a few others, he arrived in Rome at 11.30 p.m., but instead of going straight to his hotel like the herd, he wanted to get on the story straight away. But where to go? St. Peter's Square was full of nuns praying for the Pope's recovery. The police were not talking beyond a terse statement and so Edwards thought he would go to where the story was still developing – the hospital where the Pope was fighting for his life.

Amazingly, when Edwards arrived at the hospital at one in the morning, he found that he was the only reporter there. More to the point, there were no police to bar his way. So in he went and after walking around for a while he found a waiting room where he could sit and watch and judge the situation. He dozed a little and then, at around 6 a.m. there was the sound of doors opening, footsteps and voices. He saw six surgeons, their gowns covered in blood, walk into the waiting room and go on to a balcony. As they smoked and took in the early morning air, Edwards could see they were smiling. He approached them and got lucky. These people had saved the Pope's life and several spoke good English. They were pleased with their night's work and talked freely. They even drew pictures in his notebook of the incisions they made and described each step of the operation in detail. Not surprisingly, Edwards later described this as the best story he ever wrote.

Knowing what is the best the story can be

Some of what the inexperienced thinks of as the mysterious instincts of good reporters are, in fact, quite straightforward calculations. One of the key ones used by successful journalists is the train of thought that runs something like: what is the best this story can be? If I considered all the possible scenarios and facts, what would be the strongest intro I could write? This calculation is often just as useful in telling you which stories are not worth pursuing, as revealing the ones that are.

Building trust with sources

Good reporters keep up a regular relationship with contacts and do not just ring when they need them. They cultivate them by going to meetings they would otherwise not attend and occasionally pass information to them. The upshot is that the contacts remember them when they have a good story. Less regular contacts also remember the reporters whose work has proved fair and accurate. And a source that trusts a reporter can assist in all kinds of ways. A governing party politician whom I knew was instrumental in smuggling into Iraq one of the *Observer*'s top foreign news experts so he could investigate reports the paper was receiving about atrocities committed against the Marsh Arabs by Saddam Hussein. Without my relationship with that politician, her trust in the sincerity of my paper, her contacts with rebel groups in Iraq and their bravery, we would not have been able to get inside southern Iraq and the world would not have heard about these atrocities. The reporter, Shyam Bhatia, won foreign correspondent of the year for his work.

Showing interest in the subject, not just the immediate story

People can sense, just as you can, when a journalist is merely interested in them for the sake of a one-off story. Good reporters have a sincere interest in issues and the people involved in them – and it shows. They profit from this. In 1968 after Soviet dissident Aleksandr Ginsberg was jailed following a closed trial, his wife Ludmilla called a press conference. The night before it was due to be held, all the nearly 100 Western correspondents in Moscow were contacted by the government press department and warned that 'severe measures' would be taken against those who attended. The following day only four had the courage to go to the Ginsberg apartment, among them Raymond Anderson of the *New York Times*. A few months later, in July 1968, Anderson was given a document by a friend, who had received it from Andrei Amelrik, a dissident historian.

Inside the package was the now-famous essay challenging the Soviet system written by Dr. Andrei Sakharov. After a few more adventures and inquiries, Anderson established that the document was genuine and he sent it out secretly for it to make headlines around the world.

Sensing which stories are not yet complete

The phrase 'follow-up' is not a terribly glorious one to many reporters, carrying connotations of being asked to tidy up a few loose ends or dress up some hand-me-down story into something that appears fresh. As applied by a lot of papers, this is true. But there are also many stories which when followed up, bear richer fruit than the original. Good reporters sense these by thinking what is – or may be – missing from the whole story. An old lady, for example, once died unnoticed in her home in the north of England. The coroner, remarking on the contrast between the visible signs of this (milk bottles on the doorstep, etc.) and the indifference of her neighbours, said that the old lady might still be alive if neighbours had paid attention to her or taken the trouble to visit.

The *Daily Mirror* sent Derek Lambert to investigate for a possible piece on the woman who died ignored by her comfortable neighbours. He went from house to house, collecting a few scraps of information, but mostly finding blank looks and shrugs of the shoulders. Finally he came to one neighbour who talked a little. Just as Lambert was turning to go, the man said, 'Mind you, that coroner's got a right cheek, hasn't he?' Lambert asked him what he meant (always a good question). 'Well,' said the man, 'the coroner only lived up the road.' He had been one of the woman's neighbours he was criticising. Lambert knew then he had a good story – the tale of the coroner who criticised himself in court, but didn't realise.

Looking at things another way

Comedians and good journalists have a lot in common. Both find productive ideas by turning things on their head, by inverting a situation (or a phrase) in order to examine it and so deliver the unexpected. Successful reporters get a lot of good ideas by looking at things from an unusual perspective. When John Tierney of the *New York Times*, for example, was sent to do a piece on women who sign up for self-defence classes (a pretty tired idea at best), he did an article not on the women, but on the 'model mugger' – the pretend rapist in a padded suit who took all the punches and kicks.

There are, however, limits to reporters' inventiveness. There was, for instance, once a reporter called Maurice Fagence on the *Daily Mail*. Never the best timekeeper, he was so spectacularly late one day that the newsdesk punished him by sending him to cover a story they assumed would be a long trip for very little copy – a pigeon show in Birmingham.

Not to be outdone, Fagence smuggled into the show a cat under his coat so he could write an intro about who put the cat among the pigeons.

Making connections

Making connections is what good reporters do when they take a couple of hitherto unassociated stories, or facts, and make a link. This is what Willi Gutman, a newspaper librarian who fled Hitler's Germany, called 'scoop by interpretation'. It is one of the reasons why those who criticise newspapers for 'feeding off each other' are wrong. Many good stories come from a journalist spotting a small item in another newspaper, investigating and finding there is a lot more to the subject or issue than the first paper thought. And many important stories have only been fully revealed because individual papers working on them independently found different pieces of the jigsaw which *collectively* completed the picture. The investigation of the Watergate scandal in America in 1973–74, which led to the resignation of President Nixon, was a classic case of this.

Not relying on the summaries of official reports

It is difficult to stifle a yawn when you see the cover of most official reports. But in some of them, perhaps buried away on page 94, is the real story. It may even have been put there deliberately, in the confident expectation that most journalists cannot be bothered to read that far, or that closely. Too many reporters, when confronted with a thick report, will look only at the summary pages. If you have time, read the whole report; if not, then look in the places most likely to produce good material – the submissions from criticised parties, the evidence given by the aggrieved and the case histories section.

Reading reports thoroughly can repay enormous dividends. In the early 1990s, Eileen Welsome, neighbourhood news reporter for the *Albuquerque Tribune*, was leafing through a declassified document about radiation experiments on animals towards the end of World War II. In an obscure footnote at the bottom of one page, she found a reference to 18 people who had been injected with doses of plutonium so that scientists could study the effects of radiation on the body. She began researching and in November 1993 published a three-part series. A month later the US government called a press conference and admitted all. President Clinton ordered an inquiry and lawsuits from victims families came in. The following year, Welsome won a Pulitzer Prize.

Not pre-judging people

The most successful intelligence agent I have ever met was a big, fat, jolly, apparently simple-minded soul whose cover was that of a professional wrestler. Large amounts of foreign travel aside, he was almost the last person you would expect to be a spy; which was why I had no idea of what he really did until after his death. I thought he had taken one too many sizable bangs on the head.

Successful journalists know that judging people by their appearances and occupations is a good way to make mistakes and miss stories. Some of the least reliable sources look the toniest, and some of the best ones look like bums. This does not mean you have to spend hours with the parade of lunatics, paranoids and obsessives who regularly plague newspapers with their tales of being followed, transported to outer space or persecuted by the government. But it does mean making a judgement based on what they say, rather than on how they look. After all, a journalist at the *Daily Mail* in the early 1930s once returned to the newsdesk from attending to a shabbily dressed visitor in the lobby. He said the man was an obvious lunatic who was muttering something about transmitting moving pictures. Three days later several rival papers reported the invention of television by a man called John Logie Baird – the name, of course, of the 'shabbily dressed lunatic' in the lobby.

Keeping an ideas file

This is hardly a devastating insight, but it is commonly overlooked. The quality and range of ideas is one of the things that makes the difference between news pages crackling with interest and those that are so limp and wet you could not use them to start a fire. You should therefore have a file where you can jot down ideas, plus cuttings from papers and magazines that might make a future story. If nothing else, it should encourage that other habit of successful journalists – reading a lot of newspapers and magazines. Apart from keeping them up to date and in touch with what the opposition is doing, it also maintains their general knowledge – something else they are conspicuous for.

News editors

On some papers, the control is so centralised, or the news editor so smart, that most good stories are originated by the news desk. So maintaining good relations with the desk is essential if you want your share of the good stories they have available. Good reporters soon learn what the desk wants, and give it to them – at least until they are sufficiently senior or highly thought of to start contesting the desk's decisions. Yet, as junior reporters soon realise, dealing with some news desks is not easy. News editors are a demanding breed. While some of us have tried to combine news editing with being a halfway reasonable human being, the fact is that the pressures of the job encourage news editors to play up to the feisty, snarling, never-satisfied, sharp-tongued caricature.

For the benefit of reporters who think their boss is uniquely psychopathic, let me tell you briefly about Charles Chapin, in many ways the original model for the hard-bitten news editor. At the *New York World* in the early years of the twentieth century, he stood out for insisting on hard news intros and factual reporting that answered the who-why-where-what-and how of a story, pioneered the use of the telephone, and a network of 'leg-men' (local correspondents) who collected information which they sent back to the office to be shaped into stories by 'rewrite men'. He loved nothing better than a good disaster, and, when a steamboat called the *General Slocum* caught fire on New York's East River and 1,021 people lost their lives, Chapin was to be found whistling and singing his way round his newsroom, reading out the choicer bits of copy as some of his staff openly wept at the tragedy. It will come as no surprise, then, to learn that Chapin kept for himself all free tickets sent to the paper (those he couldn't use he tore up in front of his staff), and he claimed to have fired no fewer than 108 reporters in his time (including Joseph Pulitzer Jnr., the son of his proprietor). This highly skilled, but monstrous, item might have a more elevated place in journalism history had he not, in 1918, become something of a news story himself when, in a moment of madness over money troubles, he blew his wife's brains out. He was sent to Sing-Sing where he so aggressively transformed the prison newspaper that he was removed even from its editorship for upsetting so many of its inmate contributors. Thereafter he devoted himself to gardening, with such success that *Homes and Gardens* ran features on his flower beds and visitors would always ask to see his roses. The one-time snarling city editor went to his grave known as 'the Rose Man of Sing-Sing'.

Non-obvious sources

Most journalists think too narrowly when it comes to sources. But if you look at national quality newspapers, which have the pick of all that is available on any day, you find that the sources of their stories are not nearly as conventional as people imagine. The *Independent*, for instance, would have in a typical issue 33–38 domestic news stories, not including briefs or Parliamentary reports, sourced as follows:

Government depts or agencies	10
Off-diary (contacts, observation)	5
Courts, inquiries	5
Universities	3
Pressure groups, unions, etc.	3
Political sources	3

Specialist press	2
Commercial companies	2
Consumer magazines	1
International organisations	1
Police	1

Other issues of the paper show slightly more police and political stories and fewer from courts, but otherwise these proportions do not vary markedly. This means that half the stories consistently come from unofficial sources. If the government stories include only those which are official announcements, as opposed to stories obtained by personal contacts, then unofficial sources regularly account for something like 60 per cent of stories. This shows the importance of building up contacts and, in particular, of opening up your mind to unconventional sources and subjects. Here are some suggestions of the less obvious places where good stories can be found.

Universities and research institutes

Whether it is pioneering medical research, a study of your region's wildlife or an investigation into why men wear certain colour ties, academics undertake studies that no novelist would dare make up. Some of them are highly specialised, but a lot will have general interest. For example, a space research institute outside Moscow has been studying for years what personality types are truly compatible so that the people they put together in the Mir space station will not begin fighting as soon as they leave Earth. Written for the general reader and applied to how people get on inside homes and offices, rather than a space ship, you would have a story that should interest anyone.

Specialist and underground press

If you have the expertise to read specialist journals, they can be a lush hunting ground for off-diary stories. Your country's underground press is also worth reading regularly. The reporting in such publications is often unbalanced, but it is often the product of contact with unconventional sources. Some of the best stories first surface in such papers.

Books

In 1998, Maciej Zaremba, a Polish-born journalist writing for Sweden's largest paper *Dagens Nyheter*, uncovered the full story of how Sweden had forcibly sterilised more than 60,000 women between 1935 and 1976. Working with a researcher called Maija Runcis, who had access to the archives of the State Medical Board, Zaremba discovered that, contrary to common belief in Sweden, the sterilisations had never been voluntary. Girls who fell behind at school, were labelled promiscuous or had otherwise fallen foul of authority, were defined as 'undesirable', removed from their homes by state officials, placed in institutions and were only released if they would be sterilised. The story was published all over the world and the Swedish Government set up an inquiry. And where did Zaremba first stumble upon this story? In an obscure book written by two Swedes but published only in the US.

Esoteric magazines

These are not magazines written for an academic audience, but for ordinary people with special interests. Reading such magazines allows you into worlds (like that of the treasure hunter or vegetable grower) which you would never normally enter. And in almost every issue you can be sure that there is a story which, properly handled, would be of interest to the newspaper reader. A computer magazine might have a story about a new computer virus that is threatening commercial data systems; a car magazine one about a new auto-theft racket; a sex newspaper might have an advertisement that leads you to investigate child pornography; a gardening magazine a story about how used bank notes are being pulped to make fertiliser.

International organisations

There are thousands and thousands of international organisations pumping out reports, statistics and data, holding conferences and seminars and staffed by experts – yet they never hear from a general newspaper reporter from one year to the next. This is a great shame. Organisations like these are one of the great untapped sources of stories. And not just stories about global problems. Much of their work involves studying or working on specific problems in particular countries. Go to a library, look up the organisations covering your area of interest and make contact or visit their website. The United Nations, for example, has bodies dealing with women, disasters, children's welfare, health, disarmament, training, economic development, human settlement, the environment, oceans, trade, refugees, peace-keeping forces, population, food aid, food growing, atomic energy, civil aviation, labour, shipping, telecommunications, industry, copyright, meteorology – indeed almost every subject under the sun.

Blogs

These, for the few who remain uninitiated, are online diaries or logs. They range from entries of a few words linking to sites the blogger thinks interesting to self-obsessed ramblings of many paragraphs. The skills (and time) needed to set up a blog (as opposed to make it interesting) have now been reduced to next to nothing, which is why something like 12,000 are begun every day. Most of these will perish, and only a tiny handful of those that survive contain anything worthwhile to anyone who is not related to the blogger or their therapist. But blogs can be valuable. Ones keeping an account of a developing story (such as that by Salam Pax in Baghdad in 2003, or kept by scores of people during the 2004 Tsunami or the 2005 destruction of New Orleans by Hurricane Katrina) are a rich source for off-beat angles on a major story. And there are a few 'citizen journalists' investigating where the mainstream press cannot, will not, or has not got the time to tread. Bloggers also seem to often have a single-mindedness in examining source material in more detail than print journalists, such as the 2005 revelations found by Bologna blogger Gianluca Neri in the official US report on the killing by American troops of Italian agent Nicola Calipari.

Classified advertisements

Journalists who do not read the classified advertisements in any paper they can get their hands on are missing one of the best sources of human interest stories there is. After all, this is where the parts of the human race that are not journalists often communicate with strangers. For instance, on 2 May 1962, the following ad was placed in the *San Francisco Examiner*'s classified columns by a Mrs Gladys Kidd:

> I don't want my husband to die in the gas chamber for a crime he did not commit. I will therefore offer my services for 10 years as a cook, maid or housekeeper to any leading attorney who will defend him and bring about his vindication.

One of the city's most famous lawyers, Vincent Hallinan, saw the ad and contacted Mrs Kidd. Her husband was about to be tried for the murder of an old antique dealer after his fingerprints had been found on an ornate bloodstained sword in the victim's shop. During the trial, Hallinan proved that the dealer had not been killed by the sword. He also established that Kidd's prints and blood found on the sword got there because he once fooled around with the sword while out shopping with a friend. The jury found Kidd not guilty and Hallinan refused Mrs Kidd's offer of servitude. There are countless lesser examples of stories found in the classified sections: from the woman in Russia so poor that she was trying to sell her son to the exotic animal smuggling ring that was advertising rare pets, and so on.

Anniversaries

These are an endless source of stories. The anniversaries can be simple births and deaths, major historic events or more unusual, social anniversaries like inventions of household objects, or other landmarks of everyday life. Nor do anniversary stories have to be light. Researching the five-year anniversary of a major news story for a background piece can often turn up some buried report, neglected group or something else that makes a good hard story.

Other productive areas are: specialist branches of police and other emergency services (especially those dealing with fraud, computer crime, art and antiques); obscure government bodies (such as ones dealing with public access to landed estates in return for lowered death duties, managing the assets of the mentally infirm, etc.); investments promising very high yields; any get-rich-quick or 'can't fail' business scheme; loan companies (especially those which target the less well-off); newly released public documents; and pressure groups or self-help groups operating in unusual areas. You come across many more if you keep your eyes and ears open. Look for the incongruous, the things which don't seem to add up, the things which need explanation. My first major story was about homeless people on the streets of the city in Britain where I lived. It was the result of noticing them late at night in doorways and parks and asking the basic reporter's questions: who? why? etc. The series I wrote led to a great number of people approaching me with stories and to my news editor giving me better assignments.

Stories that good reporters avoid

If successful reporters have a trick, apart from hard work, it is knowing the stories that are unlikely to be good ones and staying well away from them. They know that good stories don't, except in very rare circumstances, come from commercial press releases, routine press conferences, most of the mail that arrives at your news desk, or from people who call you up and say 'Have I got a story for you!' Neither do they come from surveys with small samples, surveys that dress the blindingly obvious in the language of science, surveys purporting to identify new social groups, stories that are purely about what people are saying, or from events concocted purely for the benefit of journalists, like photo-calls, press launches or stunts. And, above all, they know they don't generally come from row stories.

Row stories

These have become the great contagion and con-trick of journalism. Legitimate when reporting serious criticisms of official action, genuine or sharp disagreements among those who can influence an outcome, row stories are more commonly seen in a form where the 'row' is nothing much more than a figment of the reporter's desire for some phoney drama. Something happens, or something is said, and a reporter phones some known and convicted loudmouth who obliges by condemning, deploring or calling for an inquiry. This journalistic equivalent of shooting fish in a barrel is then topped off with a headline about 'Row over...', 'Fury over...', or even 'Furore as...'. The result is stories that are blindingly predictable and have reality only within the pages of a newspaper.

Another common form is when a 'row' angle is written onto a story in an attempt to 'freshen up' something that has happened or been announced earlier in the news cycle. The predictably opposed are asked for a comment and their disapproval is then reported in the intro as 'A furious row last night erupted over...'. This, quite apart from the hyped-up language of 'erupted' and 'furious row', is a complete non-angle. As an intro, it weakens the story rather than strengthens it.

The ultimate test of 'row' stories is, however, this: have you ever heard readers discussing a 'row' story in the terms as presented in the paper?

Celebrity Stories

These have got a lot more common, even on quality newspapers, as staffs have been cut. They are cheap stories, in every sense. Most of them are hardly news at all, often generated by the public relations industry, and quite a few not true but dreamed up by the celebrity's management to get a few column inches to go with the inevitable picture. Such is the desperation on some papers for celebrity stories that accuracy seems of little account, and normal news values are forgotten.

If you work for a mass-market paper that specialises in stories related to TV, film, music, and fashion, then celebrity dross, even if true, is very difficult to avoid. If this is not your idea of journalism, then the best bet is to find another, more intelligent newspaper to work for. But, even here, the desire to get famous faces into the paper (on the spurious grounds that readers love 'people stories') is having its corrosive effect, as editors demand celebrity involvement in news stories. I remember, a few years ago, that I could not persuade an editor to give much space to a story about how the area of a planned national park in Scotland was being reduced until, many weeks later, a celebrity or two took up the cause. The final result was a story, complete with large pictures of the celebrities (and not, as it should have been, maps of the shrunken area), which made it look as if it was a story about celebrity Scotsmen rather than that nation's landscape and heritage.

There are two kinds of journalism. There is the journalism that is trying to tell the truth and there's the journalism that treats the news as showbusiness.
Max Hastings

5

Research

When the call comes in the middle of the night, a fireman only has to put on his pants and extinguish the flames. A correspondent must tell a million people who struck the match and why.

Mort Rosenblum of Associated Press

Let's start with the basics, and you can't get more basic than the physical tools needed to do the job of research. Time was when the only supplies a reporter required was any old notebook and any old pen. Not any more. Today, you need a mobile phone, lap-top computer, a digital camera (useful for recording a person or scene you may later want to describe in your story), and, maybe an electronic organiser or Blackberry. You will also want to have the following old-fashioned items:

Notebooks: You need two: one, as small as will slip discreetly from pocket or handbag when out working face to face with people; the second, as large as possible for working on the telephone from your office. The big size will mean you can take notes a lot better and will not have to keep pausing to turn the page. And get a spiral-bound one, not a stapled or gum-bound one. The pages turn, lie flat and can be torn out without the whole thing falling to pieces.

Tape recorder: Tape recorders are at their best for face-to-face interviews and, with the right leads and connections, for recording telephone interviews, the contents of which may be contested later on. (In all but the most special circumstance – like investigating criminality – you should tell the person they are being recorded.) But even in interviews with a tape recorder, a notebook should be used as well: to jot down your observations, and to record the highlights of what is said, consulting the tape only for confirmation of detailed facts and precise quotes.

Contacts book: Every reporter should maintain a detailed book of contacts' phone numbers. It can be a ring-bound notebook or an electronic organiser – but make a copy of its contents. One day you will lose it; I guarantee that.

And also one piece of practical, mental equipment:

Shorthand: Unless you are the only human being on the planet who can write as fast as people speak, you will find shorthand invaluable, if not essential. Tape recorders break down, their batteries suddenly fade and there are a lot of circumstances, like press conferences, street interviews, etc., where it is simply not possible to get a usable result. There are also an awful lot of people who will say far more to you if they are not being intimidated by a recorder. An even greater number will soon tire of the reporter who keeps asking them to repeat things so they can be taken down in longhand.

So much for the means of research; now for the finding out.

You don't have to edit and judge news stories for very long before one thing becomes apparent: the most common reason why stories fail is not bad writing, duff quotes or poor construction, it is inadequate research. In reporting, no amount of fancy phrases will disguise that. You either have the raw material, or you don't.

If you do, then you have the means to write a clear account, free of any gaps, with a strong original angle, some lively examples or anecdotes and a sense of perspective. Your story can be tight and solid, with no loose writing because there is no need to pad it out.

If you don't have the raw material, then your story will be fuzzy and uncertain, with some holes where information or explanations should be. It will be waffly, stale and lifeless. At best it will be what news executives call 'a trot round the block', meaning that it is a mere tour of the story's more obvious and familiar points. And too many stories are not merely 'research lite', they also lack any kind of intellectual depth. This is not just because of a failure of ambition by the reporter or news desk, but a failure to apply intelligence as well. To do good research, you should be constantly asking yourself: what is the real story here? Try and find out the why, as well as the what, where, who and how.

So what do you have to do to get that good material? First you have to know, broadly, what you are looking for. Second, you have to know where to get it, or at least where or who to ask. Let's assume you're going to research a substantial news story for your paper.

What you should be looking for

You start with the basics of who, what, where, when, how and why – but you don't stop there. What is needed above all is the detail and anecdote that illuminate the basics. This extra information is what generally makes the difference between an ordinary version of the story and a good one. Just take any big story on any given day and examine different accounts in different papers. It will be the richness of some compared with others that strikes you.

Detail

Collecting detail is crucial to good research. If you are reporting an incident you need to build up a detailed chronology of what happened, so that you can run a 'video' of it in your head. It can never be as complete as frame-by-frame, but that should be your aim. You will not use all of these details, but, until you come to write the story, you never know which are the telling ones. Almost no detail is too small to collect, for even the tiniest fragments can add worth to the story far beyond their nominal weight. An account of a murder, for example, can say that it was committed in the countryside and even name the date of 1 May. But if you report that it was committed at Sunnybank Farm on May Day, it immediately becomes more evocative and powerful. Better still, get to the scene and describe it – the cottage garden where the weapon was found (abandoned by the runner beans), the pink walls of the kitchen, the flowers in the jamjar by the backdoor, etc., etc. On many occasions, sections of the report, or even the whole thing, can be hung on even the smallest detail. And the details that are most valuable are the unexpected ones, either the apt or the particularly incongruous.

In some ways, and in a lot of cases, the detail is the story. For instance, a body has been found in a public park, but police have no idea about its identity, and can't tell the cause of death yet. With no more facts than the name of the park, and the gender, approximate age, and obvious features of the body, it's not much more than a paragraph or so. But with some assiduous questioning, the story can become something more. What was the victim wearing? How tall? Any birthmarks? What was in his or her pockets? Any tattoos? Did he or she wear a watch? Did it have an inscription? Any prescription medicines found in their pockets? Was there a wallet? What state were the shoes in? Any make-up worn? Was this in any way distinctive? The potential questions are almost limitless. And some answers to such questions will not only make a potentially intriguing mystery story, it may also produce results. In June 1983, Edna Buchanan, crime correspondent of the *Miami Herald*, began a story: 'He wore a flower tattoo on his shoulder and he died violently. That is all police know about a man whose murder they are trying to solve.' Five weeks later she was reporting: 'The unknown tattooed man, dumped by his killer into a drainage ditch just off a rutted and remote dirt road, had been identified by relatives who recognized a newspaper description of the intricate flower design on his right shoulder.'

Detail is especially valuable when you are writing a report, or news feature, after the basic story has been around for a day or so. The great Bill Connor ('Cassandra' of the *Daily Mirror*) once based the opening of his piece about the death of Stalin, written several days after the event, on the detail that the old monster who had sent so many of his fellow-Russians to a premature death, died in his bed at the age of 73, 'between the comfort of his sheets'.

Anecdote

The same applies to anecdotes and examples. They should not be long (otherwise they will overwhelm the main thrust of the story) and indeed the best kind of anecdotes in news reports are often incidents or episodes summarised in one or two sentences. A story about an eccentric decision by the council of a small town is going to be a lot more lively if you can include some tales from its past. They may be not much more than a brief incident or two from history, mention of a couple of the town's most famous natives, or even something as simple as an inscription on a grave in a local churchyard. But you can be sure they will be a lot more interesting and informative than the predictable quotations from one of the protagonists that would otherwise take their place.

Background

This is something you should collect for any story, even the briefest ones. You should be looking for the setting, context and relevant parts of the history of the subject or issue. It might be a paragraph or two of 'the story so far', or a potted history of the subject or issue. It might even be some wider analogy or comparison. A story about attempts by your country or city to limit car use in cities, for example, will be all the better for some idea of what policies have been adopted (and what worked and did not) in other places or countries. News stories are rarely unique eruptions of fate; they belong in a continuum.

Perspective

Context can sometimes be *the* vital part of the story, putting facts or developments into a proper, even far less dramatic, perspective. This is particularly vital where someone is issuing blood-curdling warnings about health or public safety. Stories about health risks in the environment, for example, can often be preposterously overstated unless some perspective is given. Would you think it a good story that a sample of sea water contained 6,000 molecules of poison? You might be thinking front page until you learnt that this is what would be produced if you took a pint of poison and tipped it evenly into the world's oceans. And many stories about the dangers of pesticides might be a little more intelligent and accurate if they also compared the risks to the amount of naturally occurring pesticidal chemicals found in basil, peanuts and mushrooms.

There are journalists who think it is our job to dramatise everything, but a little reflection will tell you this is a fairly dumb route to take. Think how we react to the people in our own lives who always put the most melodramatic construction on everything. In the end we regard them as gullible, unreliable and a pain in the butt. Why should readers think differently of us if we omit context and perspective to ham up every story?

Where to get it

Research is about knowing where the bodies are – or might be – buried. You should therefore be as insatiable about collecting potential sources of information as you are about the information itself. These sources fall into three categories: online, human and printed.

Human sources

These are the most familiar sources, covering everything from the official spokespersons, officials and politicians contacted regularly, to the person spoken to once and maybe never again. They also extend to people that the inexperienced would never dream of contacting. If there is a golden rule of successful research it is: never be afraid to ask. The worst any one can say to you is no and you will often be amazed at the help you get. Other hints are:

Collect phone numbers obsessively

The most basic tool is obviously a well-maintained, detailed book of contacts, with their addresses, phone and fax numbers. When you are the only person in your office, it is late at night and you need some vital information, you will find out just how good your contacts book is. You should be ruthless at entering every name and number you are given or can get hold of and use every possible means of getting hold of more. Scrounge them from colleagues and rivals and when you read papers and magazines note down the names of useful-sounding experts and try to get their numbers. And don't, like me on many occasions, fall into the trap of thinking you will not need that person's number again and fail to transfer it from notebook to contacts book. You can be absolutely sure there will come a time when the lack of it will be a real problem.

An awful lot of people are paid to help you

There are more people than you might imagine who have been put on this planet to assist journalists. They may not know it, but they have been. How many lakes does the Lake District have? How deep is that ocean? How high is that mountain? There is someone in an embassy, tourist board or visitor centre who can give you an instant answer. If you want quick, uncontroversial, factual information, go first to those who are paid to promote, or help the public with, the subject in question. In a country like Britain there are literally tens of thousands of them. Make them earn their wages.

Whatever the subject, there's an expert somewhere

There are a surprising number of people and places who can speedily put you in touch with experts on some of the more obscure aspects of life. Professional institutions, trade associations and specialist museums often have an in-house expert and if they don't, they can refer you to one. For instance, suppose you want to speak to someone about marine salvage in a hurry. You can call the national maritime museum, a trade association for divers, a marine insurance company, navy press office, a journal of marine history, even the library of a local council on the coast – and that's before you've gone online, or searched the cuttings for experts named in previous stories on the subject, etc. Certain organisations, such as local libraries and museums, maintain a database of experts on even the most arcane subjects.

When you have a choice, think before deciding who to call

A common mistake in research is to ask the wrong person. A lot of information that you want will be known to a variety of sources, but some are more likely to help you than others. If, for instance you want to find out the sort of profit margin that shops charge on imported fashion shoes, don't ring a store's press department. They will be nervous at the very mention of the words 'profit margin', especially as it is theirs you are investigating. Go instead to a wholesaler or manufacturer. Then go to the stores for a comment.

Try other media

On one occasion in Moscow I heard of a Russian professor who was being held by the immigration authorities in San Francisco in the United States, pending deportation in unusual circumstances. It looked like a good story. The problem was that I had no telephone numbers for her representatives or the American authorities; the US embassy in Moscow was closed, there was nothing yet on the wires and the story was needed within the hour. After a couple of false starts I got the number for the Associated Press office in San Francisco, called it and immediately got numbers for everyone I wanted, including that of the professor's American husband and, from him, those organising a campaign on her behalf. Local newspapers are always worth a call in such circumstances. You can offer to trade information, or free publication of your final piece.

Be cheeky

The most pathetic words a reporter can say are, 'I can't find out. I've tried everywhere.' Oh really? In 99 cases out of 100 you can be certain they have not and that there are several more places they could try, for there is nearly always somewhere where you can get the information you want. Imagine this situation: you are in your office at 10 p.m. at night and hear that one of your nationals has been arrested for armed robbery or gun-running in Florida. What do you do? The US embassy in your city is closed, your consulate in Miami is not answering the phone, the FBI office in New York knows nothing about the case and neither does the Associated Press office in the city. When that happened to me, I called the American Express office in Miami, claimed to be a card holder (which was true, but need not have been – they would never have checked) and asked if they could give me numbers for the local police, district attorney's office and prison. I soon had my story.

Researching online

One day in 2006, I asked a journalism trainee to research the brown bear for a sidebar to a story we were running. One of the 'facts' she presented us with was that each bear eats 10,000 moths a day. I asked her if this was likely, given that moths do not congregate, and that a bear would have to catch each one individually. Even if they could do this each day, would the food value in the average moth make this worthwhile? She looked at me as if I was mad. 'But it was on the web,' she said. A discussion about how the Net was not entirely infallible ensued, during which she told me that Wikipedia was reliable since it was fact-checked by experts. 'Oh yeah?', I said, 'what experts? And who pays for them?' My explanation that Wikipedia is a non-profit, open-source operation came as devastating news to her. As did, somewhat later, my discovery that the bear's moth appetite related to an entire year, not one day. For the benefit of such trainees and journalists, here are the things I think every reporter should know about the Net:

Treat web pages like any other source

In other words, be suspicious. The Internet is not an opportunity that has been wasted on the unhinged, exhibitionist and boring. Seeing credibility flaws in the websites of the slightly mad is not difficult. Nor is it hard to spot the hopelessly biased offerings from activists and single-issue obsessives. The problem comes with sites that look plausible, but which aren't. You have to develop the radar to detect these, asking all the usual questions when approaching any source (Who is behind this? Why are they putting this out? What's included? What's left out?). My alarm bells ring whenever I come across: no highly visible date for the material presented; the need for excessive page-turning; and a site whose contact details contain no postal address, or phone number.

Be as specific in your searches as you can

You can search not just for words but for phrases; and putting double quote marks around them will ensure that the search engine delivers only the instances where those words occur together in that order. For instance, put East Timor militia into Google and you get 477,000 results. But put quote marks around those words and you only have 584 matches. You can combine phrases in a search, so if you add '+ "in 1996"', the results are further narrowed to 53. You can subtract words and phrases as well. Thus, if you wanted to find out about President Bill Clinton's relationship with Tony Blair, you might search for: 'Clinton' + 'Tony Blair'. This gets you 4.47 million results. But, the most detailed material is likely to have been written before Clinton left the White House. So make your search: 'Clinton' + 'Tony Blair' – George W Bush and immediately more than four million sites are eliminated.

Treat searches like a brain-teaser

When using a search engine, you are pitting your wits against a database with billions of entries. The smart researcher finds words or phrases that give them a manageable number of matches – not every site that has ever glancingly dealt with the subject in question. Thus, if you want to know about the life of, say, some dead politician, it is far better to search for 'name' + 'obituary' (or 'biography') than just the name. Better still, try and think of phrases that would be used in the kind of material you are seeking. In the case of an obituary, that would be something like 'he was born in' or 'he is survived by'. Good online guides to searching are: searchenginewatch.com or researchbuzz.org.

Use the advanced search facility

Whatever your favourite search engine, there will be a link on its home page that will lead you to the advanced search facility. This enables you to refine your search by date and other parameters.

Use the cached version

Sometimes, when checking pages produced by a search engine, you find the site no longer contains the material you were after. This is because the page in question has since been updated and your material archived or deleted. The answer is to click on the 'cached' version of the page. This is the page the search engine logged, and therefore will contain the information you searched for. Cached pages (a link to which you will find next to the url under the page title on Google) have another advantage. The terms you searched for are colour-coded, so, in a long page of close type, the needle you searched for will stand out in the haystack.

Consider subscribing to an online archive

These are pretty comprehensive libraries of articles, academic journals and books, and are immensely worthwhile if you write lengthy magazine stories or books. Ones I have subscribed to when researching books are eLibrary, and Questia. The latter is the world's largest and has an enormous number of books you can download and search. There are also newspaper archives like that of the *New York Times*, which has a database of all articles going back to 1851. You can buy articles individually or in bulk.

Be aware of the limits of search engines

Search engines can't penetrate beyond the front or search pages of databases. Since a lot of good content (like newspaper or magazine articles) are archived in a database, anything other than the most recent cannot be found via a search engine. A very good guide to these more recessive parts of the Net is The Deep Web, run by the University At Albany, New York.

Use online tutorials

Turn yourself from a basic Internet user into a relatively expert one by spending some time with one of the online guides to searching and using the Net. A good starter one is internettutorials.net. If you prefer books, the best is *The Net for Journalists* by Martin Huckerby, (published by UNESCO), which comes complete with a CD.

Newsgroups

These are the forums on the Internet, open to anyone. There are more than 17,000 of them, covering everything from classical music to previously unknown species of pornography. Many are frivolous but there are more serious newsgroups than you might imagine. Some, like alt.disasters.aviation, are occupied by conspiracy theorists, but there are enough groups with informative, sensible postings to make regular visits worthwhile. Many newsgroups are regularly used by academics and others with serious credentials. Generally, specialised newsgroups are more likely to have useful postings. Overall, it is worth half an hour of any journalists' time to download the full list of groups supplied by your ISP and go through it, noting any which cover your interests.

Newsgroup postings can give you: a general feel for the current issues in an area; potential stories (particularly contributions from qualified experts); and, since posters leave behind an email address, potential sources, to whom you can send questions or a request to talk.

An archive of newsgroup postings can be found by searching Google Groups.

Blogs

These range from online diaries (most commonly the ramblings of cranks, obsessives and bores), or daily logs of web links of interest (the most useful to journalists), to serious articles by professional (or non-professional) journalists. There are enormous numbers of them. As Guy Chapman wrote on a BBC website: 'The great thing about blogs is that anyone can set one up. The only problem is that anyone can set one up.'

Most numerous (but with the highest drop-out rate) are personal journals of the 'Dear diary' variety. These can chart experiences at work (earning some of their writers the sack), everyday emotions, trips, parenting, and living with an illness or a crisis. A few are newsworthy, like SaveKaryn.com, which recorded a New York woman's battle with credit card debt – and raised, via donations, the cash to clear it. Others contain writing of a more sustained fictional or autobiographical kind, and a few of them begun in lone hope have ended in a publisher's contract, among them: 'Baghdad Burning: Girl Blog From Iraq', 'Straight Up & Dirty', memoirs of a divorcee in New York, and 'Girl With a One-Track Mind', the sexual experiences of a thirtysomething single woman in London. Then there are those which have political or religious axes to grind, whose collective, if generally unco-ordinated, highlighting of writings they dislike can constitute a raucous lobby.

More directly useful to the researching reporter are links blogs that direct, with or without comments, readers to sites deemed interesting. Metafilter is a classic example, and I doubt a week goes by without me finding on it an idea for a news story or feature. There are also single subject blogs, which track news and developments within that field. Some, especially in technical areas, now attract enough audience to be courted (or quietly sponsored) by manufacturers, others are journalism by another name, and specialist ones have exposed product faults or stories that mainstream journalism has failed to spot. Bloggers also seem to examine source material in more detail than print journalists, and can research the Internet with more skill than 999 out of a 1,000 print reporters.

Printed sources

There are two basic printed sources: books, and newspapers and their cuttings.

Books and directories

Reporters can sometimes spend hours chasing down a fact which is sitting innocently in a readily-available reference book just an arm's length away. As with human sources, the job is to know what is available and where it might be found. And that includes being aware of which librarians will know if you don't. You will be surprised how often such people will look something up for you for the sheer pleasure of proving they can do it.

For journalists, books have four uses – to check spellings and dates, give you basic facts, supply names of potential sources from yearbooks, etc. and provide historical facts or brief anecdotes to enliven a story. The only precaution is, with the first three categories, to make sure you are consulting an up-to-date edition.

In practice, time pressure means that trips to libraries are not always possible and your use of printed sources normally depends on what is to hand at home or in the office. That, plus my natural appetite for trivia and so-called 'useless information' (which is often very useful) is why I have over the years assembled a good collection of books of odd facts. On the shelves above my head as I type these words are books of days, chronologies, books about wills, sex lives and obscure origins of the rich and famous, eccentric lives, origins of sayings and slogans, originals of famous characters in fiction, odd classified ads, firsts, inventions, encyclo-paedias of crime, stories behind the songs, etc. All of them have supplied golden little paragraphs to stories and columns and have sometimes provided the entire piece.

Other newspapers' stories as sources

It is common to be given a story from another paper and asked to stand it up. You should try to match it, not merely regurgitate it. If you are unable to get any new source of your own to substantiate it and your editor is insisting on a story, then quote it with attribution to the original paper. Better still, get an acceptable source to comment on the report.

The written source that should be treated with the most care is newspaper cuttings. Just because it has appeared in print does not mean it is correct. It may have been subsequently corrected or the subject of legal action – something that applies just as well to computerised press cuttings and other databases.

And beware the statement that 'everyone else is reporting that, so it must be true'. It is often correct, but don't rely on it. In the autumn of 1989, when then-Czechoslovakia was on the brink of what was to become the 'velvet revolution', a young woman told reporters that state police officers had beaten to death a student called Martin Smid. The story was reported locally and people began to visit the spot where Smid died, which soon began to acquire the aura and status of hallowed ground. Reuters wrote the story and Agence France Presse said that three young men had been killed.

The Associated Press failed to have the story. Its desk chiefs were not happy with their Prague bureau and demanded they catch up fast. Their local man was Ondrej Hejma, a guitarist who combined journalism with rock music at the expense of neither. Taking none of the earlier Smid reports at face value, he began investigating. He and his wife, a doctor, toured local hospitals and mortuaries trying to find someone who had treated Smid, dealt with his body – anything. He found not the slightest shred of evidence for the Smid story and several days later the rival agencies were forced to report that Smid, whoever and wherever he was, had not died on that Prague sidewalk.

Research as a foreign correspondent

Reporters in an area of extreme difficulty or danger often need assistance not just to research, but to survive. The people who will help you do that are the real unsung heroes of journalism. They are fixers, reporters' sidekicks who translate, drive, have contacts, know whom to bribe, which roads to use and which to avoid, have cousins in visa offices, old school friends among insurgents, or brothers-in-law in the security service. Without them, many more reporters would be killed, and a lot of valuable stories would be missed.

They range from security service informants whose helpful pose disguises (often not very well) a desire to lead the reporter away from 'inconvenient' stories, and charlatans who crowd lobbies of hotels like the Pearl Continental in Peshawar, Pakistan offering their services to newly arrived western reporters, to sharp young journalists who will often act as 'stringers', or local correspondent after the big-time reporter has left. They are paid well by indigenous standards (Alpha Koromah, who assisted the London *Evening Standard*'s Alex Renton in Sierra Leone, was paid 75 times the pay of a private in the national army), but it's a risky business. Those helping correspondents write stories that reflect badly on regimes can find themselves threatened, jailed (as was Khawar Mehdi Rizvi, who fixed for magazine *L'Express* in Pakistan), or killed. In 2004, nine died in Iraq and six more world-wide. In places of extreme danger, like Baghdad, the fixer can indeed become the reporter, going onto the streets to collect information and quotes and bring them back to the correspondent safe in the Green Zone who will then write the story.

The egos of foreign correspondents make many reluctant to give credit to those who help them, but some do, like the *Independent*'s Robert Fisk and Ann Leslie of the *Daily Mail*. To reporters like her, fixers are not just people you hire, use, pay, and leave, but long-time colleagues. She stays in touch with them and their families long after she's moved on, and, judging by her stories, it's obvious they repay her loyalty handsomely. There was Mr Massamba, who obtained a whole book of vital phone numbers for her in Zaire so she could uncover the story of the corrupt Mobutu, a president worth £6 billion who built, among the direst poverty, a residence twice the size of Buckingham Palace; 'Mr Zhou' (not his real name), her brave guide in China, through whom she met survivors of the Tiananmen massacre; Igor Kuzmin in Moscow, who, when Leslie flew straight from her holiday in the Swiss Alps to cover the attempted 1991 coup against Gorbachev, had sufficient pull with his old KGB colleagues to arrange her admission to Russia despite the lack of a visa; and Wiebke Reed, her fixer in East Berlin, in whose spluttering little red Wartburg, she crossed through Checkpoint Charlie on the night in 1989 the Berlin Wall fell. Not for nothing did I dedicate my book *The Great Reporters* to fixers.

> *No intelligence system, no bureaucracy, can offer the information provided by competitive reporting; the cleverest secret agents of the police state are inferior to the plodding reporter of the democracy.*
>
> Harold Evans

6

Handling Sources, Not Them Handling You

The fact that a man is a newspaper reporter is evidence of some flaw of character.

Lyndon Baines Johnson, US President 1963–1968

Twenty years ago the normal source in the average city dealt with maybe a couple of papers, a radio and a TV station. Today news outlets have proliferated to the point where any local official source deals with perhaps two cover-price papers, several freesheets, a specialist local business magazine or two, maybe two radio stations, a TV station, three cable channels and a rapidly rising number of news or community websites.

This growth has hugely accelerated the tendency for official organisations to hand press relations over to dedicated professionals. It has also meant that there are a lot more journalists hunting for information where once only a few roamed. These days you are far more likely to be one of many and will find yourself dealing not with the person with the expertise, but with their mouthpiece. All the more reason, then, to know how to deal professionally with sources and how to make the best of, and occasionally subvert, the channels down which officialdom would prefer you to go. For although most dealings with sources are routine, straightforward transactions where both sides gain, there are times when you are in a highly competitive game of wits with sources to make sure that the strongest and most complete version of the story hits the streets and not the self-serving one they would prefer.

Guidelines for dealing with any source

Before considering the specifics of dealing with official sources, news management techniques, contentious sources and some of the other perils, here are a few key guidelines for dealing with any source:

Always make your identity as a reporter plain

To do otherwise is to trick people into giving information, which is not only dishonest but also unsafe. People are often very free with talk until they realise you are a journalist. Then they become a lot more guarded and start to qualify their information. This is because instead of merely shooting the breeze, they now have to take some responsibility for the quality of these facts. Not telling them you are a reporter is a good way to get them to exaggerate in a way people often do in informal conversation. The chapter on investigative journalism (Chapter 10) deals with the very rare times when concealing your identity is justified.

Be fair with sources

Believe it or not, journalism is quite a lot like real life. From this flows the devastating truth that if you want sources to help you, then being friendly, honest and treating them fairly works a lot better than bullying, trickery or intimidation. Being fair is especially vital. If they are being criticised or accused of wrongdoing you should not only put these claims to them, but also give them time to reply. Ten minutes before deadline is not good enough.

Copy approval

Showing a source the finished article before publication is soliciting censorship. The usual reason given is that this is a chance for factual errors to be corrected – and if you believe that is the real motive, you will probably believe anything. Showing someone what will inevitably be described as 'the draft' of a story encourages the idea that it is being given to them for approval and, hence, possible alteration. It is the journalists' job to produce accurate copy, not something that is the basis for negotiations with the subject. But sensible checks do not constitute copy approval. If you have written a story about complex, technical matters with which you are unfamiliar, I see nothing wrong – and everything right – with emailing your story in whole or part to an expert. I have been saved on many occasions by doing this. You are not giving them copy approval, but ensuring your story is as error-free as possible.

Retraction

Many times a source or subject will say something to a reporter that they subsequently regret. There is not a lot of point in journalists training themselves to question good information out of people if they then offer them a subsequent opportunity to withdraw it. However, if sources want to correct what they told you, then you must let them, unless you have very good grounds for thinking some subterfuge is afoot – in which case, report both their earlier and later statements. Sources' appeals for a retraction on the grounds that they will be fired are another matter. Handle these by questioning them closely, then passing the matter on to an executive. It is not a reporter's job to play God; leave that to editors.

Payment

This is another issue reporters can kick upstairs to editors. It is the executives' decision whether they can afford – financially or morally – to pay for information. The dangers of the practice are obvious. First, it establishes a market and encourages people caught up in stories to demand payment. Second, paid informants have an unimpressive record of reliability. They know that the stronger the story, the higher the fee and so have a direct inducement to invent or embroider. A few years ago the *Sun*, Britain's most popular newspaper, had to pay out £1 million libel damages to Elton John because they believed, and printed, a fictitious story sold to them by a gay male prostitute. It is not a lone example. Neither, however, are the instances of cheating public figures exposed solely through a paid-for story. If you are a mass-market tabloid, the temptations to pay for stories are understandable.

Official sources

These are ones authorised to give you information – from the owner of the corner store commenting on how trade is, to the chief press spokesperson for the head of government making a statement about why she has resigned. They span the full range of human helpfulness, cussedness, expertise and idiocy. Most, if approached in the right way, are helpful. But make sure your official source really is in a position to know what he or she is claiming to know. In 2006, I wrote a story about the Iraq Museum and the thefts from it that occurred in the immediate aftermath of the invasion three years before. In 2003, reports had gone around the world that more than 170,000 objects, many priceless antiquities, were stolen by looters. I was able to report that only 13,864 objects were stolen, and that there were three separate thefts, only one of which was looting. The other two were the work of professionals, and an inside job. So how come I was able to get it right, when journalists the world over got it wrong? The answer is that they were writing their stories days after the thefts occurred, and I was writing a cool piece of hindsight several years later. They got their information from a 'museum official' who turned out to be an ill-formed ex-member staff, I got mine from an academic journal article written by the US Marine colonel who investigated the thefts.

When it comes to dealing with PR and press departments, authorised does not always mean well-informed. Some have good knowledge of their organisations and can answer detailed questions. Others are mere go-betweens, transporting your questions to the official concerned and ferrying back the answers, with an inevitable loss of freshness – and no opportunity to ask follow-up questions. For this reason, try to cultivate officials who will give you information directly, rather than it being filtered through their PR person.

In recent years, there have been big changes in the way large commercial, political and government organisations handle the media. There has been much bleating from journalists about the iniquities of 'news management' and 'spin doctors'. All that has happened is that these bodies have started to employ press spokespersons who are rather more of an intellectual match for journalists than hitherto. The result is a more sophisticated, although rarely subtle, approach to handling the media, the chief feature of which is to be proactive, rather than merely reactive. The following should be borne in mind.

Spin doctors

Often applied wrongly to all PR people, this term originally described people working on a political campaign whose job it was to shmooze journalists after new polls, candidate debates, etc. and give an interpretation that was favourable to their party. It has gradually been applied, wrongly, to almost anyone in the PR or image business. A true spin doctor is someone in the political trade who is a chief press spokesman or senior aide. Apart from routine statements and press conferences, they interpret events to the press on behalf of their boss, try to anticipate bad news (and divert attention from it) and also attempt to manage expectations in a way that helps their cause.

This last situation is where most journalists are led astray by spin doctors. Fearing, for instance, that bad news is in the offing, they brief journalists that results verging on the disastrous are expected so that when the real outcome is known they can smilingly report a veritable triumph. The frequency with which this ploy is tried on journalists does not seem to impede its success.

True spin doctors do, however, have one great advantage over lesser fry in their trade. They are close, often very close, to their boss and anything they say on the record has serious authority. They also spend much of their lives dealing fairly straightforwardly with routine questions and the best of them are invaluable sources. Just make sure you protect yourself by constantly asking: why are they telling me this? It is a question, too, you should ask yourself every time you receive a press release. And the answer, if you can get to it, may surprise you. That innocuous little release telling you of a new appointment may well have hidden behind it a tale of firings and mayhem at the most senior level. Ask the questions you need to establish whether this is the case. People may accuse you of having a nasty, suspicious mind, but then it's your job to have such a mind. Consider this: one of the most successful early uses of the press release was by the Ohio Bell Telephone Company in the first decade of the twentieth century. They discovered that if they handed out pre-digested information in this way, then reporters would stop attending telephone charges hearings to get the information. That had one great advantage – they would not be there to ask difficult questions. Don't get suckered in.

News management

Organisations, be they public or private, commercial or political, routinely have a great many reports and statements that they wish, or are obliged to, release. The idea that they should choose the most advantageous way and time to do this is not particularly shocking. Indeed often this 'news management' is helpful, making sure journalists have enough time to write for their editions, or avoiding a clash between a report's release and a major event.

Skullduggery, however, there is. It comes mainly in three forms and is nearly always connected to information that the organisation fears will play negatively. First is the dodge of timing the release of the information to coincide with the least convenient moment in the news cycle – say late at night, or towards the end of a Friday afternoon. The chances of it being ignored or meekly treated are then fairly high. Second is to leak the main angle of the story to a sympathetic news outlet in the hope that by the time the others have caught up or received the information through the official channels, the story will either be stale or its 'agenda' already set. The third trick is to sugar the pill with some fragment of good news which is then spun as the main angle.

The British government in 1999, for instance, was scheduled to release new hospital waiting list figures. Knowing that these were not good, and seeking to avoid adverse headlines, the figures were released on the same day as the annual school exam results (confident that this rarer story would overshadow the hospital data). The government also tacked news of the hospital figures on to a release about a grant of £30 million to help the situation. It worked. All papers ran the story small, and my paper gave it just three paragraphs in early editions. When we rumbled what was going on (the figures showed waiting lists had risen by 64 per cent in two years) we elevated the story to a page two lead. Your only protection against this and other forms of news management is to use your wits.

Withholding access

Sometimes organisations are so displeased by press coverage that they simply cut off access to their information. Crude, and rare, this practice is generally only seen in arts journalism, where an unfavourable review so irks a theatre or gallery that they simply ban the critic concerned. The film industry seems especially prone to this branch of censorship. In the US, according to a study by the University of Southern California, journalists have been banned from screenings or blackballed by a studio for the tone of their coverage or for breaking embargos. Judy Gerstel, for instance, wrote a report about poor audience response to *Hook* for the *Detroit Free Press*, was promptly ex-communicated by the studio and soon found that two other studios (Warner and Universal) had dropped her as well. Ultimately there is no solution. It is the studio's information and they have a legal, if not a moral, right to do with it what they want. The response should be to tell readers of the attempted manipulation and to encourage 'if she goes, then so do we' support from other papers. After all, it might be them next time.

Handling unauthorised sources

These are sources not authorised to give you the information they are passing on. They may be whistleblowers well-placed in an organisation, or someone with no official connection to the information. They could be passing on documents, or a mere suggestion to go digging in a certain area. Invariably their information will be contested, at least initially, and almost always they will not wish to be quoted in the story. It is from such sources that some of the best stories come – and the most trouble if they are wrong. In dealing with these sources, you should bear the following in mind.

Ask yourself what their motives are

People are rarely helpful to newspapers because they are saintly. They want to damage political, commercial or personal opponents, advance some cause (or harm a rival one), take revenge or simply cause trouble. While someone else's revenge mission can be useful, it is best to know what they are about from the start. So ask yourself (and occasionally them) what their motives might be. Their unattractive calculations may not disqualify the story, but they are a good reason to tread carefully.

Ask yourself, and them, what the other side to the story might be

The stories given to you by contentious sources are rarely as black and white as they would have you believe. Save time by asking them if there is another side to the story, or if there is any qualifying information you should know. Crazy, horrendous, absurd things do happen; but not as often as most sources claim. Under the front-page headline 'Shame On

The City – Shocking Story of New York At Its Worst', The *New York Post* once carried a story of a man who raped a three-year-old girl on a grass verge by a busy Manhattan highway while passing motorists parked and watched. Does that sound likely? What actually happened was that three motorists saw a man attacking a girl, leapt from their cars to give chase and other drivers were then caught in the resulting jam. A clear case of a single-source story that was not checked.

Are they in a position to know what they claim to know?

A lot of named sources frequently claim to be 'in the know' when they are in fact only marginally so. The classic case of this is the coverage by the Western press of the Soviet Union in the two years following the 1917 revolution. Western correspondents were barred from Russian soil and so papers sent them to Riga where, 300 miles from Petrograd, their only sources were former Tsarist generals and officials and deposed politicians. All claimed to be 'in the know'. Virtually none of them was. The results for the *New York Times* were, according to the famous study conducted by Walter Lippmann and Charles Merz, surreal. Between 1917 and 1919 the paper reported: the Bolshevik government had fallen or was about to fall (91 times); Lenin and Trotsky were preparing to flee (four times); Lenin and Trotsky had fled Russia (three times); Lenin had been imprisoned (three times); Lenin had been killed (once).

Insist on documents where possible

Always ask sources if there is any documentation to support what they are telling you. If they will not let you have it, ask for a photocopy; if they refuse that then ask if you can at least read it in their presence. If they still refuse, forget the story. And if you do get documents, be suspicious until you are satisfied they are genuine. Chapter 11 on mistakes and hoaxes describes what can happen when documents are false. Sometimes even photographs are suspect. Ed Behr tells a cautionary tale in his book *Anyone Here Been Raped and Speaks English?* of the agency given photographic evidence of atrocities by one side in an African civil war. The pictures are of a woman being raped by soldiers. All very convincing until the local bureau chief had the sense to ask for the contact strip. They showed the harrowing rape scenes and then, in the final frame, the 'victim' with her arms round her 'attackers', smiling and posing for a group photograph.

The more passionate the source, the less they should be trusted

Passion does not guarantee unreliability, but it helps. The more strongly someone feels about something, the less good they tend to be as a witness. Question such sources very carefully. They often fit facts to their theories and are blinded by those attitudes into ignoring key information. Beware especially the committed activist, fired employee, ex-wife, former husband and spurned lover. Ask them if anyone can confirm what they are telling you. An instant modification of their original account will often follow.

Unattributable sources 'off the record'

The sensible motto is: use 'off the record' as sparingly as you can. If you don't, you will end up with a lot of sources you cannot name. And if you are discussing some species of unattributable information, get it absolutely clear with your source what you have agreed. That way there will be no subsequent argument. Are they, for instance, giving you material which you will have to confirm and source with another party (background)? Or are they giving you the information on an unattributable basis, in which case you can use it, but not their name? Make sure that when an interview subject uses a phrase like 'off the record' it means the same to them as it does to you.

Above all, don't be intimidated when seemingly impressive officials tell you something and then add that it is off the record. In 1997, President Bill Clinton ruptured a tendon while staying on the Florida estate of golfer Greg Norman. A White House aide rang Ron Fournier of the Associated Press and said that Clinton was in hospital with a minor injury but added: 'That's off the record'. Fournier told the aide that he could not possibly accept that such information was off the record. He went ahead and wrote the story. Quite right. Do not accept their reluctance to be quoted without a fight. Keep on at them to go on the record. Argue that the importance of the story depends on verification from named sources. If they persist in wanting to talk 'on background', continue the interview and then, at the end, try to find something they might be happy to be quoted on and then edge them towards attribution. Negotiate. And do not let people say to you at the end of the interview: 'Oh, by the way, that was all off the record.' The rule is: it is only off the record if you have both agreed that in advance. And once you have an agreement, don't go back on your word. Do not name them in the story and, if they wish to be on deep background, tell no one except your editor who they are. Ever.

One of the main problems with 'off the record' is the way it has been picked up by politicians and their advisers and used for their own, sometimes shady, purposes. To illustrate this, here is an example given at a Harvard University seminar on journalism in Moscow:

> You have been called in for a rare personal interview with a senior government adviser. He tells you that everything he will say is off the record. During the interview he tells you about a major change in

economic policy. You are excited by the story and rush back to your office and write it, quoting 'well-placed government sources'.

Well, it turns out that the government intends no such change, that the adviser knew that when he spoke to you and was feeding you the story to deflect attention from some other problems the government had. More common is for politicians to use off-the-record briefings to float an idea, which, if attacked, will be denied. In both cases you look a fool. If you suspect you are being set up, get a second source.

Getting too close to sources

Finally, here is a story that illustrates the dangers – to reporter and paper – of a specialist getting too closely involved with sources. It concerns one Alfred 'Jake' Lingle, who was a police reporter for the *Chicago Tribune* in the 1920s. Lingle was highly regarded at his paper. A lot of well-informed stories about organised crime in that city came from him and his contacts and he built a legendary reputation with readers and colleagues. Lingle prospered and, thanks to what he said was a bequest of $50,000 from his father, the $65-a-week reporter dressed well and maintained several homes. His fertile supply of crime stories, however, was suddenly stopped on 9 June 1930. As he entered a train station on Randolph Avenue, Lingle was gunned down in the street in broad daylight by a man dressed as a priest.

The killing had all the marks of a gangland professional hit. Lingle's paper was outraged.

> The meaning of the murder is plain. It was committed in reprisal and in an attempt at intimidation. Mr Lingle was a police reporter and an exceptionally well-informed one. ... To the list of those who were killed in the St Valentine's Day Massacre [when seven died in a gangland feud], the name is added of a man whose business was to expose the work of the killers. *The Tribune* accepts this challenge. It is war.

The *Tribune* backed these fine words with a $25,000 reward for information about the killers, other papers followed suit and Lingle was accorded a civic funeral, complete with military bands and guards of honour. Tens of thousands of Chicago citizens lined the streets and bowed their heads in respect as the cortège passed.

But not long afterwards, some hitherto unknown details of Lingle began to emerge. It turned out his father only left him a few hundred dollars, not $50,000. When Lingle was shot he had over $1,000 in cash in his wallet and was wearing a belt-buckle encrusted with diamonds. It was, apparently, a gift from Al Capone, the most notorious of the city's organised crime bosses. Moreover, his bank account showed deposits of more than $60,000 in the previous 18 months.

One of his joint accounts was with City Police Commissioner, William F. Russell, who resigned in disgrace immediately. He and Lingle had been friends since their youth and the crime reporter had been selling his influence over Russell to other policemen wanting transfers and promotion, to politicians, hoodlums and major gangsters like Capone. He was a frequent guest at Capone's retreat on Palm Island, Florida, and had day and night access to this, the most feared man in the United States at that time.

But Lingle liked to gamble and gambled heavily. Despite several successful attempts to fix dog races, he was soon losing $1,000 a week at the tracks and at Capone's illicit casinos. By the summer of 1930, his gambling debts with the organised crime boss totalled more than $100,000 – worth more than $1 million at current values. His attempt to extort money from members of Capone's own gang was, for the crime boss, the final liberty that Jake Lingle was ever going to take. The killer in priest's clothing was hired.[1]

Three weeks to the day after Lingle was shot, his paper was forced to admit:

> Alfred Lingle now takes on a different character, one in which he was unknown to the management of the *Tribune* when he was alive ... He was not and could not have been a great reporter.

All day long, Hollywood reporters lie in the sun, and when the sun goes down, they lie some more.

Frank Sinatra

7

Questioning

Newspapermen ask you dumb questions. They look up at the sun and ask you if it is shining.

Sonny Liston

Asking someone questions for a newspaper story is a special skill. It may at times resemble a conversation, but it is not one; it may at times be entertaining to overhear or participate in, but that is not its point. Questioning people for newspapers has one purpose: to collect information, especially detail, and not – as so many poor reporters think – to get 'a few quotes.'

Interviews, whether in person or over the telephone, are not scripted and you should be prepared for unexpected answers, to follow their implications and ask follow-up questions. They will often be long, pedantic affairs, as you persist with a question you want answered or something you want to understand. They are not opportunities for you to tell that official what you think of him, show off your knowledge or engage your subject in heated debate.

A lot of interviewing is perfectly straightforward. But there are two particular situations that give trouble: questioning those who are uneasy and reluctant to talk, and questioning those who are positively elusive, evasive or even hostile. These situations are looked at later and some of the techniques involved apply to all questioning. But first, here are some guidelines that apply to talking to any source.

How to approach people

Before starting to question someone, you first have to get them to agree to talk, and then do all you can to get (and keep) them in the right frame of mind. Here are some pointers:

Don't call it 'an interview'

To most people, the word 'interview' conjures visions of being questioned by the police or formally interrogated for a job. Either way, it's one that makes them feel uncomfortable. So don't, when trying to get someone to talk to you – and especially with those not used to speaking to journalists – use the 'I' word. Say you'd like a chat, you'd like to pick their brains, hear their experiences, learn something from them – but don't say you want to interview them. It makes a lot of people very nervous.

Get them to want to help you

You're at a party, meet someone who seems your kind of person, and start talking. You're open, sunny, interested in them and what they have to say, and you are careful to do more listening than talking. I can think of no better analogy of how you should be when questioning people as a journalist. In fact, unless you are cornering some villain at the end of a lengthy investigation, the last thing you want to do is to come on with the 'I-am-a-reporter' attitude. Remember: your job is to get people to want to help you – and that nearly always means being sunny, open, and interested.

How to get past the gatekeepers

Gatekeepers are those, like secretaries, assistants and PRs, who control access to the people you want to speak to. PRs are dealt with in 'Handling Sources', but sometimes the secretary/PA who is determined to protect his or her boss from the outside world can be a real hurdle. What doesn't work is 'I am Melissa Bloggins from the *Inquirer* and I insist on talking with ...'. Open and friendly is better, as is using Christian names. Get their first name, and use it when calling back. If you use yours, the gatekeeper will begin to see you as a human being, not 'that pest from the paper'. And intrigue them. If you are very specific about the subject you are researching, that will give the gatekeeper an excuse to say: 'Oh, Mr Fantini doesn't really deal with that any more', or 'He's not answering questions about that'. Then what do you do? Instead, be fairly vague about your purpose. Say you're just making a few inquiries about his work, or that someone else (and name them) suggested you speak with him.

Know what you want from an interview before you start

You should always have a good idea of the basic information you want from a source before you start asking questions. Think of the final shape that the story might take and therefore the information you will need. During the interview you should continue to think of your report and how the new information you are getting is changing it. Above all, be aware of where the information gaps are in your story, and try at all times to fill these holes. This may sound very complicated but in fact becomes second nature after a while. And do not be afraid to write one-word reminders to yourself on the flap of your notebook. This helps to avoid having to contact the person again for things you forgot to ask in the interview. That is sometimes not possible and you may have to try to write the story without this information.

Do as much research as you can before the interview

You should never be afraid to show ignorance, but that is not the same as being proud of not knowing. Before interviewing someone, find out as much as you can about them, the subject and any other relevant thing. Apart from anything else, this helps to prevent you being hoodwinked or blinded by science. It will also let them know they are talking to someone who takes them and their subject seriously. They are then more likely to give you a slice of their time, as opposed to a quick couple of questions over the phone.

The simple questions are the best

There is not a single example in journalism where so-called trick or clever questions produced results. Asking questions like that is normally the sign of inexperience or someone more concerned with making an impression than getting the best story. Normally the simple questions are: Who? What? Where? When? How? Why? If you have satisfactory answers to those questions you will be well on the way to having completed your basic research.

In stories about events, build up a chronology of what happened

Your job, when questioning people about an event is to build up a step-by-step, or, in the case of disasters and accidents, a minute-by-minute or even second-by-second account of what happened. The way to do this, especially with sources at the scene of a disaster where they are shocked, if not actually traumatised, is to take them slowly through the event as they saw it. In such circumstances, people tend to dodge about all over the place, telling you a little of the aftermath, then about something they saw at the start, then a cry they heard in the middle of the sequence. So here's what you do: you take them back to the last moment when things were normal, then get them to tell you in as much detail as they can, the sights, sounds, and even smells *in the order they occurred*. By the end of your questioning, you should be able to run a video of the event (as experienced by your sources) in your head. If you can't, how are you going to explain to readers what happened?

Check names and positions

Obvious, boring to do, but essential. Ask sources to spell out names, titles, ages and addresses if you need them. Sometimes, if it is an awkward or foreign name, get them to write it in your notebook. You may think that makes you look silly – but not half as silly as you will when you get back to your office and find you do not know how to spell their name. And, when you do check spellings, verify both Christian name and surname. There is the story of the reporter who interviewed a Bryan Smith. As he left, he asked: 'Do you spell your name with an I or a Y?' To which the answer came: 'With a Y'. Sure enough, Bryan Smith appeared as 'Brian Smyth'.

Get as many telephone numbers as you can

This is as basic as getting your subject's name right. Get the phone number for their office, home, mobile, bleep – whatever they will give you. If their office number is printed on the phone, discreetly help yourself. If not, then ask.

Get too much information rather than too little

Most of the time you get only one chance to interview an important source. Take full advantage and ask every question you can. The answer to that extra question is often what makes the story. And remember that it is often details that lift a story out of the ordinary. Ask about them.

Do not be afraid to look stupid

We have all been in that situation where someone is talking to us and we sit there nodding and agreeing, even though we do not have the faintest idea what they are talking about. We are afraid that if we ask them to explain we will look stupid. And then we come to write the story and realise that we don't understand what we have spent the last few hours pretending we knew.

Never, ever, be afraid to look silly by asking basic questions. First of all, people, even in press conferences, will rarely be so rude as to snigger at your ignorance. And, if they do, so what? Who is the most stupid: someone who pretends to know, or the person who does not know and admits it? Nearly every source is prepared to explain specialist concepts to reporters and most will be flattered that someone is interested in their subject.

If in doubt, describe your understanding of a situation

If you do not understand an answer, or if the situation you are reporting on is confusing, then describe your understanding to those you are questioning. Never be afraid to say: 'Can I just go over this. It all began when ...', or 'Can I just see if I understand you correctly ...', or even 'If I wrote that ... would I be right?' This is a standard technique. It does not imply that you are slow-witted. And even if it did, so what? Better that than an ambiguous, or wrong, report. The same applies to motives. Do not assume motives. If someone does something and their motive appears to be relevant, ask them, don't assume it. Reporting is not a parlour game.

Ask questions to get information, not opinions or reactions

You are talking to sources to get facts and each question should be designed to do that. It is very easy to start asking questions about their reactions to something. But reactions are rarely surprising and so you will not have collected anything that is useful to your story. The knowledge, for instance, that a right-wing politician disapproves of liberal reforms is hardly news. The only exception to this, of course, is when the story is about opinions.

Try to avoid asking clichéd questions

To ask someone who has just been involved in a tragedy 'How do you feel?' is to invite a clichéd answer at best, or a flat refusal to answer any more questions at worst. If they have just lost their only son in an air crash how do you expect them to feel? Thrilled? Yet every day you can see in news stories the most predictable emotions ('I was excited to win this money', 'We are very upset to be sacked without compensation') paraded as if they were devastating insights.

Probe for anecdotes

Good anecdotes can add a tremendous amount of life to stories. Collect them at every opportunity from the people you are questioning. But remember that getting people to discharge amusing, ironic, telling anecdotes is a matter of chatting in a relaxed way, not sitting bolt upright opposite them and saying, 'Now tell me the funniest thing you ever saw/experienced.' They won't. Their mind will go blank. Instead try to get some feel for the areas of their life/work/activity which are likely to provide humour. For instance, if you are interviewing airline cabin crew for a story about a new service and you want a couple of yarns about passengers' crazy behaviour, then don't say, 'Tell me the silly things travellers do.' Instead, naturally edge the conversation around to drunkenness, fear of flying, luggage, complaints about food, kids, strange requests and so forth.

Don't let them bullshit you

You should obviously ask for all jargon to be explained. But a lot of phrases that sound like technical talk are, in fact, euphemisms. Each industry, company or bureaucracy evolves phrases to camouflage reality. An airline will talk about 'passenger underflow', when what it really means is that not many people want to fly with them. An investment fund might issue a statement about a 'net liquidity export situation', when what they mean is that their investors have finally rumbled them and are taking all their money out.

Institutions which deal with dangerous materials, like the nuclear industry and the military, are especially adept at developing this kind of bullshit. In America, following a famous accident at Three Mile Island in 1979, the nuclear power industry came up with a potentially bewildering series of euphemisms to describe bad things. Statements talked of an 'abnormal evolution' at a plant which had led to an 'energetic disassembly' and then a 'rapid oxidation', perhaps followed by 'plutonium taking up residence'. What this meant was that there had been an accident at a plant which led to an explosion and then a fire, followed by plutonium contamination – all of which straightforward words and phrases were banned. Unban them. Ask what they mean.

Listen to the answers

It is easy to be so concerned with rattling off the next question, or taking down the answer, that you fail to appreciate the significance of what is being said. Ten minutes after questioning someone is often too late to realise the importance – or absurdity – of what they have said. This is especially true when people make extraordinary claims in interviews.

The French novelist Georges Simenon once told a reporter from the Swiss newspaper *Die Tat*: 'I have made love to 10,000 women.' The paper duly reported the claim without comment. However, even the least numerate of brains should be able to calculate that, to reach this total, Simenon would have had to have made a new conquest every other day for about 65 years – no mean feat for a man of 73 who also found time to write nearly 100 books. The real total, according to his tolerant wife in a subsequent interview, was nearer 1,200.

Dare to ask the cheeky question

Providing you've built up to it, and don't pop an outrageous question right at the start, there is much profit in asking a blunt, and possibly even personal one. It might provoke a black look, or uneasy silence, but it's just as likely, if done in an open and spontaneous way, to produce a telling answer, or even outburst. Nellie Bly, perhaps the greatest woman journalist of the nineteenth century, made something of a career of asking cheeky questions. Once, when researching a series called 'Our Workshop Girls' about Philadelphia's abysmally paid female factory hands, she was talking to a girl who said she went to bars and drank with strangers, then an almost unspeakably shocking thing to do. Bly asked: 'Why do you risk your reputation in such a way?' To which the girl replied with the kind of quote any reporter would cherish: 'Risk my reputation! I don't think I've had one to risk. I work hard all day, week after week for a mere pittance. I go home at night tired of labour and longing for something new, anything good or bad to break the monotony of my existence. I have no pleasure, no books to read. I cannot go to places of amusement for want of clothes and money and no one cares what becomes of me.' And that's a pretty good quote by any standards.

Stop people rambling

When time's short, as it often is, there's nothing more destructive of a useful interview than someone droning on and on about some irrelevance. And it happens more often than inexperienced reporters think. You can, of course, tell them you're short of time and that you need to ask them other questions, but that is not going to endear you to them. Instead, try something that John Brady recommends in his excellent *The Interviewers' Handbook*: interrupt them with something trivial – parking, something you see in the room, or the weather – and when they've responded to that, ask them a question you want answered.

Review the answers at the end

If at all possible, go back over your notes with people and double-check figures and anything of which you are still unsure. Apart from these overt purposes, this process has two covert ones. First, to see if you can discover any holes or 'information gaps' that have escaped you, and second, to see if you can squeeze a bit more information from the person. Ask them at this stage if there is anyone who can support their contentions.

Never make promises to sources about how stories will be treated

Only the editor is in a position to know how a story will be treated and appear in the paper. A lot of the people that you question will ask this question, but you do not need to answer it. Tell them you are 'just a reporter' and give them your editor's name and number.

The most useful questions in journalism

We all know that what we're after is the who, where, when, how and why of things. But there's good ways and bad ways to try and get those answers. Top of the unwanted list are lengthy questions. If there's one infallible rule about interviewing it's this: the longer the question, the shorter the answer is likely to be. Equally dumb is that cliché enquiry, especially beloved by television reporters: 'How do you feel?' It's normally asked of lottery winners or the recently bereaved, eliciting the astonishing news that the person who has just collected £12 million is feeling 'terrific', or someone who has just heard that their entire extended family has been wiped out is 'devastated'. Well, no shit. Now, if the new millionaire was 'appalled', or the grieving relative was cracking open the champagne, that would be a story.

But that's enough of bad questions. Here are some better ones:

And then what happened? – A lot of people, when questioned about a sequence of events find it very difficult to tell you of things in a chronological order. So take them back to the start and keep asking them: 'And then what happened?'

How do you know that? – Sources often make remarkable claims. Asking them how they know that will either get you some reassurance that they know what they're talking about, or, rather more likely, a back-tracking or admission that some unnamed person told them it. Either way, you're making progress.

Do you know anyone who can confirm that? – If they don't, then you need to ask yourself a question: how come this person is the only one in the world who knows this?

What do you make of it all? – This is a good way to collect opinions, and less intimidating to some people than a question like: 'What do you think?' And it is far, far better than questions like: 'So you think the company has been negligent?' This is putting words into people's mouths, which some journalists think smart, but which the world in general, and law courts, tend not to.

What it's like … – A lot of reporters, if they're trying to get someone to characterise an experience, will ask them a question like: 'Was it difficult doing X, Y or Z?' To which a one-word answer can too easily be given. Better to ask them: 'What was it like doing X, Y, or Z?' Then they've got to try and explain things in their own words. These may not be as conventionally 'punchy' as your words, but they're likely to be more original and will certainly be more natural.

And? – Not really a question, but a good way to get people to elaborate, or to keep the flow of their conversation going. With some interviewees, interrupting even with a nine-word question will stem the flow of their revelations.

Questioning uneasy sources

A lot of people are rather intimidated by journalists. This is not because they find them frightening as people (although some are), but because they are not used to dealing with the press. Even if they are, they may be reluctant to talk because they fear losing their jobs or some other repercussion. As one who has several times been involved in a news story, I know that it can be unsettling to be interviewed. You worry about what you might say, or be quoted as saying.

Often the reporter's first job with people who are uneasy is to persuade them to talk at all. When doing this, you can be friendly, light-hearted, talk about the public's right to know, etc.; in fact, whatever you may think will work. Often, however, you do not have the chance to negotiate first. You are 'cold calling', that is, visiting them without any preliminary telephone call. In these circumstances, just getting past their front door is a problem. The important thing here, as the following quotation illustrates, is to get inside their living room or office. Once you are there, it will be a lot more tricky for the subject to refuse to answer any of your questions. Once inside, the trick is to find ways of staying as long as possible.

This story comes from the book *All The President's Men*, written by Carl Bernstein and Bob Woodward of the *Washington Post* to describe an investigation they mounted which led, eventually, to the resignation of President Richard Nixon. Their reporting, and the story behind it, is looked at more closely in the next chapter. Here, Carl Bernstein is convinced that the woman he is trying to interview is a potentially important source of the activities of her employers. This, and her anticipated reluctance to talk, is why he visited her in her home and did not telephone her first:

A woman opened the door and let Bernstein in. 'You don't want me, you want my sister,' she said. Her sister came into the room. He had expected a woman in her fifties, probably grey; it was his image of a Bookkeeper, which is what she was. But she was much younger.

'Oh, my God,' the Bookkeeper said, 'you're from the *Washington Post*. You'll have to go, I'm sorry.'

Bernstein started figuring ways to hold his ground. The sister was smoking and he noticed a pack of cigarettes on the dinette table; he asked for one. 'I'll get it,' he said as the sister moved to get the pack, 'don't bother.' That got him 10 feet into the house. He bluffed, telling the Bookkeeper that he understood her being afraid; there were a lot of people like her at the committee who wanted to tell the truth, but some people didn't want to listen. He knew that certain people had gone back to the FBI and the prosecutors to give more information ... He hesitated.

'Where do you reporters get all your information from anyhow?', she asked. 'That's what nobody at the committee can figure out.'

Bernstein asked if he could sit down and finish his cigarette.

'Yes, but then you'll have to go, I really have nothing to say.' She was drinking coffee, and her sister asked if Bernstein would like some. The Bookkeeper winced, but it was too late. Bernstein started sipping. Slowly.

The woman talked, gave Bernstein some very useful leads, later spoke again to both reporters and proved to be a valuable contact. This may have had something to do with the fact that Bernstein did not immediately pull out his notebook and begin taking down every word the Bookkeeper said, while pulling faces of delight and amazement. He waited, maybe ten minutes, before slipping the notebook out of his pocket and starting casually to make notes.

If, however, people have agreed to talk, the next thing to think about is how to make them feel at ease. This will help you to get the most information from them. Here are some tips.

Think carefully about where and how to speak to them

Will it be on the phone or face to face? What will be best for them? If it is face to face, where will it be? In a bar? In their office? At your office? Over a meal? In their home? In other words, in which environment are they least likely to feel threatened and, will therefore, be most co-operative?

Adapt to them

Your aim when interviewing someone is to make them feel relaxed and helpful. This means not intimidating or annoying them. You may have to adapt your behaviour and appearance a little. You do not have to undergo a personality change for each interview, but you should consider your subject. For example, if you are going to interview homeless people on the streets, you would not wear your best suit or dress. That would make your subjects feel uncomfortable. Similarly, if you were going to interview the Prime Minister, you would not wear jeans and a T-shirt. They would probably be offended and think you were more concerned with making a statement about yourself than in getting a good interview – and they would probably be right. With people with whom you would have no natural rapport, you may even have to act a little to feign interest in them or adapt to them. If they are a formal sort of person, be more formal than your usual self; if they are very easy-going, then you can be too.

Make a judgement about them

What will get them on your side? Flattery? Friendliness? Jokes? Serious talk? Whatever it is, if they are an important source, do it. What interests them? Whatever it is, take an interest in that too. This is always easier if you are meeting them, especially in their home or office. People surround themselves with what is important to them – pictures of their family, paintings of their favourite places, ornaments and mementos. Use these things, ask them about them. Make the person want to help you. Try to find something you have in common with them, even if it just owning a dog or being a parent.

If you have time, try the 'life story' ploy

If your subject is shy, or antagonistic towards you, but seems to have time, try asking questions about their life story. These are basic resumé questions – where they were raised, educated, trained, where they first worked, success, achievements, overseas experiences, etc. It may give you some promising avenues for questioning. If not, it will almost certainly put that person more at ease and more on your side. Almost everyone warms to someone who seems interested in them.

If the interview is in person, don't get out your notebook immediately

There is nothing that will unsettle the uneasy interview subject more than a reporter marching into the room, notebook open, pen poised over it, ready to take down every word they say. Instead, gradually slide it out of your pocket or handbag when they are relaxed. You can even say something like, 'Do you know, I have a terrible memory, do you mind if I make a few notes?' Occasionally your judgement is that any appearance of the notebook will immediately stop them talking. In this situation, commit the important things they say to memory and make an excuse to leave the room (such as to go to the toilet or wash your hands). As soon as you are out of their sight, you can write down the highlights of what they have said.

Be honest about your intentions – but don't tell people everything

You should never fail to declare yourself as a reporter. Neither should you misrepresent your interest in talking to someone. However, you do not always have to explain precisely why you are calling them. If you have a controversial issue or question in mind, you would often be wise not to spell this out when you start talking. Just say: 'I am just making some general inquiries about this subject.'

Do not come straight out with your main question

Ask some general questions first. These could be questions to which you already know the answer. If nothing else, the subject's answers will tell you what they know and how honest they are. Only when you think they are ready should you ask what you are burning to know. When you do, it may be better to feign indifference to the answer. Dropping your notebook in amazement and exclaiming 'My God! Do you realise what you are saying!' is not the way to react. The thought that they have just given you the story of the decade is liable to produce an almost immediate retraction.

Use the words they do

There's nothing that sets up barriers in any conversation – never mind a reporter's interview – faster than two people using very different kinds of language to describe the same thing. You may be far more educated than the person you find yourself questioning, but this is not a good time to prove that. Instead, echo the terms people are using, unless, of course, they are using wrong ones. And if you need to query the phrases they're using (in order to establish that you're both talking about the same thing), do so gently. You're there to educate yourself, not your source.

Use the pregnant pause

If the person you are questioning does not fully answer the question, try a pregnant pause, accompanied by an expectant look. Sometimes they will respond by adding the extra information you need or giving a far more lively answer. It is especially useful when questioning personalities, politicians and officials who are frequently interviewed and feel they can get away with the same old standard answers. One of the masters of this strategy was the great American broadcast journalist, Ed Murrow. In *Edward R. Murrow: An American Original*, Joseph E. Persico quotes him on the subject:

> If you put a direct question, the interviewee will answer it as he has probably answered the same question dozens of times before. Then begins the waiting game. He thinks he has given you the definitive answer. You manage a slightly uncomprehending, puzzled expression, and you can watch his mind work. `You stupid oaf, if you didn't comprehend that, I'll put it in language you can understand' and proceeds to do so. Then, in the course of editing, you throw out the first answer and use the second one.

There is, of course, a limit to the length of time you can try to out-wait them. Delays of more than a few seconds are liable to be construed as idiocy or the onset of some serious disorder of the nervous system.

If all else fails, throw yourself on their mercy

Tell them that you will be in trouble with your editor if you do not get this information. Ask for their help. It often works.

Keep the conversation rolling

When faced with 'I can't comment', don't attempt to deal head on with their anxieties. In almost every case you will lose that argument because their reasons are to do with their position or organisation and they obviously know more about that than you do. Instead, keep the conversation going and try several other tacks. First, reassure them that talking to you is no shocking departure, many other people have spoken to you. Then, without pausing, say, 'What puzzles me is ... Can I ask you if ...'.

Questioning elusive, evasive and hostile sources

Some ways of dealing with uneasy subjects also apply to dealing with the evasive or hostile subject. But, more often, a different approach has to be taken with the potential source who is avoiding you or difficult to get hold of.

Be persistent

Getting hold of such subjects is sometimes extremely difficult. Never give up. Keep calling them, visit their offices. Make them realise that the only way to get you off their backs is to agree to talk. When US freelance Larry Miller wanted to interview Diane Sawyer, then co-anchor of 'CBS Morning News', he rang her 28 times until he got through, according to John Brady's *The Interviewers' Handbook*. Knowing her working day started at 3.15am, he would set his alarm and call her around this time. That is persistence.

If telephoning, do not be fobbed off with, 'He will call you back'

Many people have no intention of doing so, despite what they or their secretaries or colleagues say. Do not accept this. Say you will hang on, say you will ring them back or, in a few cases, agree to be rung back – but fix a time for them to ring you back. If they do not do so, ring them back. Better still, ring them back an hour before the set time. Many people will say they will ring you back at 4 p.m. because they know they leave their office at 3.30 p.m.

If someone is stonewalling over a factual answer, put options to them

If, for instance, you need to know how much the government paid for a certain contract and the person who knows is refusing to give you the answer, try putting sums of money to them: 'Is it $6 million?', 'Is it as much as $12 million?' Such questioning often produces results, or good hints. Yet be careful with this technique, make sure people understand what it is they are being asked. It, and similar verbal games, can lead to confusion.

The most notorious occasion of this was during the *Washington Post*'s Watergate investigation referred to earlier. The reporters had a very good story, but only one source for it. Their editor insisted on two before he would publish. So, late at night, one of the reporters rang the only other person who might be able to support the story. He would not do so directly; so the reporter said:

> 'I am going to count to ten, if the story is wrong, hang up. If it is correct stay on the line.' He then began counting, 'One, two, three, four, five ...' His voice was now getting excited. '... Six, seven, eight, nine ... ten.'

He put the phone down and excitedly told his waiting colleague and the editor that they had confirmation and the story ran. The only problem was, it was not true. The late-night contact had misunderstood the instructions from the reporter and thought if he stayed on the line, he was letting him know the story was not right.

Occasionally, try pretending that you know more than you do

If you strongly believe something to be true, but cannot get confirmation of it, ring a source and say you are just calling for a comment. For instance, try asking the official *why* something happened, rather than *whether* it happened. He or she will often then start explaining rather than denying. This, however, is something only experienced reporters should do.

Watch out for non-denial denials

A non-denial denial occurs when an accusation is put to someone and, instead of denying it, they make a statement which insults the person who is making it, or the reporter, or both. Asked, for instance, if the government contract has been unsupervised and millions of dollars over-spent, the subject would reply: 'Your sources do not know what they are talking about.' That is not a denial of the claim. It is often the classic ploy of the person with something to hide – and it's your job to find out what they're hiding. The classic non-denial denial came from President Richard Nixon's Attorney-General John Mitchell during the Watergate investigation. *Washington Post* reporter Carl Bernstein rang him to put allegations that he controlled a secret fund that paid the burglars of the Watergate building. Mitchell replied: 'All that crap you're putting in the paper. It's all been denied. Katie Graham [the *Post*'s publisher] is going to get her tit caught in a big fat wringer if that's published. Good Christ! That's the most sickening thing I've ever heard.' All bluster, of course, and Mitchell, like his president, was brought down when these claims, and others, turned out to be true.

Watch out for uninvited denials

Unlike the situation described above, people with something to hide can sometimes go further than your question requires them to go. When asked for a comment, for instance, they deny things you never put to them. Be alert to this, it sometimes comes out of the blue and is the first indication that they have something to hide.

Do not use 'set-up' questions

These are the questions that try to trap someone, not with information, but with a verbal trick. The fact that the trick is not very original does not stop it being used. It is a variant on the old 'have you stopped beating your wife?' question, to which the unwary might answer 'yes', implying they used to beat their wife but have now seen the light, or 'no', meaning that they still beat her.

One of the occasions when this was used most flagrantly was when rumours were flying around Britain's national papers that Prince Edward, the Queen's fourth child, was gay. The *Daily Mirror* pursued him to New York and, at a public event, shouted out the question: 'Are you gay.' The Prince was naïve enough to say 'No', and the next day's *Mirror* appeared with the huge front-page headline: 'I'm Not Gay Says Edward'. The impression readers were left with was that Edward was indeed gay, but was now strenuously denying it. Nasty reporting.

Ask them to imagine how 'no comment' will look in the paper

If an official is refusing to comment, ask him or her to visualise how this will look in the paper. But don't make it sound like a threat. Make it sound like you are trying to save them from a public relations disaster: 'You know the readers will see 'X declined to comment' and they will think you have something to hide. Now I know that isn't the case, so can I just get your answer to ...'.

Finally, remember that a person may refuse to talk to you one day but be more amenable a few days later. If they are an important source, try again.

Questioning by email

Occasionally, if a source is very busy, or in a significantly different time zone, it is worthwhile offering them the option of asking questions by email. It will be stilted compared to a conversation, but, if this is the only way to get a response, it's better than nothing. But make sure you ask questions that are snappy and unambiguous; after all, you are not there in person to elaborate.

Press conferences

Press conferences are obviously a special case when it comes to questioning. You are not alone, you are not face to face and you often have little time. If that is the case, and you have to file a story immediately after the conference ends, make sure you or other people ask the questions you need answered. That can sometimes mean being aggressive, shouting your question so that you are sure it is heard, or standing up to ask it.

A lot of people who call press conferences seem to imagine that the event is one where they can hold court before a group of docile note-takers. No reporter should ever let that idea take root. These events may be organised solely for the purpose of generating publicity, but that does not mean you have to play their game. You decide what the story is, not them. Never mind what they think is the significant message, is there another, better story?

Just as common as spokespersons handing out spoon-fed drivel they expect you to swallow is the press conference which has been called under duress, or because the host organisation feels obliged by some turn of events to face journalists. The problem here is a lack of information, and a marked reluctance to answer questions. In this situation, remember the action of the great *New York Times* reporter, David Halberstam. The year was 1963, the place Vietnam, and he and other journalists were at a press conference convened by the US military, supposedly there in merely an advisory, and not combat, capacity. Halberstam and a colleague suspected US troops had actually gone into battle, and asked questions to try and establish this. These were not answered, and the general running the press conference said the reporters were 'bothering' the officials, and would not be allowed to do so again. Halberstam, then only 29 years old, rose to his feet. He was apprehensive, but felt the general should know something. 'We are not,' he told the general, 'your corporals or privates. We work for the *New York Times*, not the Department of Defense.' He said the American people had a right to know what had happened, and he would continue to ask questions. As he later wrote: 'Never let them intimidate you. Never.'

If the person giving the press conference is not too grand, and you have some time, you can save your own questions for after the event. In that case, do not let the person who can answer them leave the room until you have cornered them. That can sometimes mean standing between them and the door. Don't be shy of doing that. Any person who regularly gives press conferences will be used to this. You are not there to make friends but to get a story.

Another tip is to watch and try to note if there is another reporter there who seems to know a lot more about the subject. After the conference, engage them in conversation. Most reporters cannot resist showing off what they know, who they know and thereby passing on some valuable leads. Don't take other people's reporting on trust, but you will often pick up some good ideas to follow up from such conversations. This is a reminder that often the real benefit you derive from press conferences is meeting people and making contacts rather than the ostensible story.

Celebrity interviews

The bigger the personality, often the less time you will have. Don't waste it by asking questions that can easily be verified by a little pre- or post-interview research. Very big stars often have press agents in attendance, who try to set limits to the subjects you can ask about. It is your job to evade such controls where possible, and, if you can't, to tell readers about them. You are a reporter, not a courtier. Don't allow yourself to be flattered that this big star is talking to you; alternatively, don't allow your dislike of them or resentment of their wealth, beauty, brains or success to tempt you to write what you think will be a definitive demolition job. When printed, it will invariably say more about you than it does about them.

Above all, do your research. If time's short, read the cuts or a few online biographies; if it's not, then read their autobiography. All but the biggest names will be tickled by this, and you then don't have to waste interview time asking where they were born, etc. If you doubt the value of research, consider the case of the reporter sent to interview actress Vivian Leigh in 1940, then at the peak of her fame thanks to her starring role in 'Gone With The Wind'. At the time, this film, perhaps the ultimate blockbuster, was showing at virtually every cinema in the western world. 'Tell me, Miss Leigh' the idiot began, 'what part did you play in "Gone With The Wind"?' The interview was terminated on the spot.

And attempts to be clever will probably end with your subject speedily proving they are smarter than you, as the following shows: Reporter: 'What are all your great rock songs really about?' Bob Dylan : 'Three and a half minutes.' Instead, keep it simple. Describe them as precisely as possible and concentrate on questions that will enable you to compare their personality with their public image. As leading British interviewer Lynn Barber says, 'All you have to do is be punctual, be polite and ask questions.' She recommends, and most would agree, that the questions should be as short as possible. The following are often useful probes for unexpected answers, or areas of life that the subject may be willing to open up about. They are based on a list filed by Jeremy Martin to the CompuServe Journalism Forum.

- What is your first memory?
- What was your mother's/father's best advice?
- Who has had the most impact on your life?
- What was your first job?
- What was your worst job?
- What was your first car?
- Who was your first love?
- What do you do when you are nervous?
- What are you compulsive about?
- Have you got a bad temper?
- What do you eat/not eat?
- Who is your best friend?
- What is your worst habit?
- What makes you angry?
- What do you study?
- How often do you read?
- How many hours a night do you sleep?
- What do you do if you wake in the night and can't get back to sleep?
- What is your ideal day off?
- When do you plan to quit?
- Who would be your favourite party guests?
- Do you like Christmas?
- What is your favourite song/book/film/singer/artist?
- Who do you admire most?
- What is your favourite drink?
- Where is your favourite vacation place?
- Where would you live if you had total freedom of choice?

If those don't appeal, you can always try the element of surprise. Just before Canadian supermodel Krista Griffith met a reporter from *Stuff* magazine, she asked her agent what questions she should expect. 'Well,' the agent replied, 'he's probably just going to ask you what your favourite colour is.' Instead, she got this: 'We recently ran a review of vibrating nipple clamps, and I was wondering... Is that something you would ever try?'

The most guileful among the reporters are those who appear friendly and smile and seem to be supportive. They are the ones who will seek to gut you on every occasion.

Ed Koch, Mayor of New York

8

Reporting Numbers and Statistics

A journalist is a grumbler, a censurer, a giver of advice, a regent of sovereigns, a tutor of nations. Four hostile newspapers are more to be feared than a thousand bayonets.

Napoleon

Quite a few journalists have the idea that numeracy is a kind of virus which, if caught, can damage the literary brain, leading to a permanent loss of vocabulary, and a shrivelling of sensitivity. This is nonsense and dangerous nonsense, because so many stories are statistically based these days. Journalists are bombarded with surveys, opinion polls, PR people, businesses, pressure groups and politicians all quoting what seem to be, at first glance, impressive figures. Far from innumeracy being some badge of literary worth, it is, for the modern journalist, a fatal weakness. If you don't know enough to question data then you really are impotent as a journalist. Sources play tricks with numbers all the time. Without the rudimentary knowledge to sniff out the bullshit figures, you will have to swallow what sources tell you and faithfully reproduce it. The result? Your readers are misled and misinformed and you look – and, indeed, are – foolish.

Happily there is protection and that is to arm yourself with enough knowledge to understand day-to-day statistics. If that thought intimi-dates you, then be assured that what follows contains no maths that a child of 12 could not understand. If you are still intimidated, then maybe it's time to find another job; for, whether you like it or not, you will be dealing with statistics in some form or another every day of your working life.

Questioning data

Statistics, like any other source, have to be questioned. That means interrogating those promoting the figures, the data itself and any conclusions drawn from it. The starting point is:

Does the story sound likely?

It is surprising how often it does not. In 1999 I was confronted with a story that said that 50 per cent of personal loans advanced by banks to women were for cosmetic surgery. In the plusher parts of Los Angeles, California that might just be plausible. In London, it was not. When checked, the statistic was really: half the personal loans given to women for health purposes were for some kind of non-essential surgery. That sounded a lot more likely – and far less newsworthy. The story was killed.

Then there is the kind of story which requires a slightly quicker wit to spot. In the US, a newspaper published a story saying that 50 per cent of the residents in Itapum, Brazil use tranquillisers. It could be true, but a little reflection tells you that it is not. Towns must have children and teenagers. In small towns in Brazil under-18s make up at least half the population. So does this mean that the other half – every single adult, even the 90-year-olds – are all taking tranquillisers? Unlikely. Soon after the story was published a correction was made. The true figure was 16 per cent – of the adult population.

Many numbers abuses are the result of willful spinning by pressure groups or governments, and then numbers-phobic reporters taking the data at face value. I recently stopped a story appearing which would have informed readers that 'stress and depression cost the UK economy nearly £5bn a year'. When questioned, the reporter said the figure came from campaigners who calculated that when people are off sick, their employers immediately hire a temporary replacement. Yeah. Right.

The antidote to this, and most other numerical nonsense, is the question: does it sound likely? Mostly, it will not. A few years ago, a survey said that 11.5 million American children were at risk from hunger. But it turned out they were judged to be at risk if their parents answered yes to any one of eight questions, which included such catch-alls as: 'Did you ever rely on a limited number of foods to feed your children because you were running out of money to buy food?' Does that sound to you like starvation – or life as it is in millions of households just before pay day? Further evidence for my motto: Beware any story which involves a survey.

If the main thrust of the figures at least seems believable, then the next question is:

What is the source of the data?

Is it a university, private company, polling organisation or pressure group? Are they qualified to collect or understand this data? Or is research by a reputable source being used by some third party? If the latter, then go back to the original researchers, ask what they think of the use to which their data is being put and invite comments on the conclusions being drawn from it. This can result in a better story than the original.

Where did it come from?

If someone can't tell you where the numbers came from – often the case with second-hand surveys and surveys of surveys – alarm bells should ring.

Why are they putting out this data?

Why are they telling me this? Do they have an axe to grind or an angle to promote? A study of the effects on rural employment of a ban on hunting has rather diminished credibility if it comes from researchers hired by the pro-hunting lobby. Deliberately falsified research from pressure groups is, however, rare. They are far more likely simply to not publish research which conflicts with their cause, or analyse figures in a way which supports a pre-conceived idea. The myriad ways of fiddling statistics are dealt with later in the chapter.

Why are they putting it out now?

Timing is rarely an accident, even among academic researchers. What may seem a haphazard date on which the unworldly academics completed their labours in the ivory tower and handed down their wisdom, will probably prove to be rather more closely linked to the need to reapply for government grants, pitch for some new sponsorship or put some published research on the departmental CV just in time for the next government assessment. With commercial and pressure group data, you can rely absolutely on there being some strong rationale behind the timing. Businesses are animated by a new product launch, word of one by a rival, the imminence of a shareholders' meeting, etc. Nor is the reason behind the timing always obvious. It should, however, invariably be part of the context of the story.

Is this data a product of the Chinese whispers effect?

This is where figures are presented by campaigners, or some otherwise biased source, as if they are well-known and established fact. Thus the assertion that 200,000 people were stalked every year in the US turned out to be a distortion of a survey that 200,000 people exhibited stalker's traits. And an estimate of 150,000 young women suffering from anorexia in due course became '150,000 are dying from the disease' – three times the number of Americans killed in Vietnam.

Are the numbers taken out of context?

Data can sometimes seem superficially remarkable only because the context has been left out. In 1997, the Associated Press reported that 29 per cent of former employees of the Rocketdyne Santa Susana Field Laboratory were reported to have died from cancer. Cause for concern? Not really. Cancer is the cause of death among all people aged 44–65 in 35 per cent of cases – six per cent more than among the former laboratory workers.

Is the data comparing like with like?

Not using comparable statistics to reach an apparently newsworthy conclusion is a recurrent pitfall, too. In 2002, it was reported that 'more African American men are incarcerated than enrolled in college'. It's a shocking statement, but a misleading one. Prisoners can be anything from 16 to 96 years old, but college students are nearly all from the narrow age range of 18–23. Among black Americans of college age, nearly three times as many are students than convicts. So no story there, then.

How are the terms used being defined?

It is not uncommon for campaigners to adopt a very much wider definition of a common term in order to boost the numbers of people suffering from a certain condition. Thus, surveys of domestic violence can include 'raised voice' or 'walking out on an argument', both of which can be unpleasant, but neither of which fit what most think of when we hear the words 'domestic violence'. The Statistical Assessment Service (a wonderful online resource of numbers abuses found in the media from which many of the examples above are drawn) says that, in 1996, a report from the US National Center for Health Statistics 'received wide coverage for its finding that nearly 100 million Americans have "chronic diseases or disabilities"'. And what was the largest category in this 100 million? It was the 32 million Americans who have sinusitis or hay fever, which few of us would define as 'chronic diseases or disabilities'.

Yes it may have doubled, but what's the base?

A headline that the number of people killed by wasps has doubled may catch the eye, but when you read further down the story that the wasp victims per year have gone up from four to eight (in a population of 60 million), the game is given away. And it is a game that is being played all the time in the media. The facts of the story are true, but have been manipulated in such a way to give an unduly shock-horror treatment. As former BBC political editor Andrew Marr writes in his book *My Trade*: 'BBC journalist Roger Harrabin has pointed out that if the cancer-causing risk of a useful drug is estimated at 0.01 per cent and then upgraded to 0.02 per cent you are still only talking about two patients in 10,000 being affected; yet the emotive headline "Cancer risk doubles" would be factually accurate.' But still a con.

Are the figures all round numbers?

This is invariably a sure indication of something less than rigorous science. A good rule is to presume that any source claiming '50 per cent think this' or '60 per cent do that' is guilty until proved innocent.

Are the graphics honest?

Graphs have vertical and horizontal scales and these can be adjusted to give the desired impression. A small rise can be made to look like a large one, or vice versa. Bar charts or graphics can also be deceptive. The old trick is a graphic representing income as money bags. If one income is twice another, then a bag twice as high as the base one is shown. But this is misleading because the resultant money bag is four times the area, and eight times the volume, of the original.

The uses and abuses of statistics

So far all that has been needed has been a dose of common sense and healthy journalistic suspicion. That will get you so far. But in properly reporting any story involving statistics, a little rudimentary maths is needed. Without it, you will get taken for a ride. For example: a firm in the middle of a pay dispute tells you that their staff's average salary is £28,000. So you report that – and look silly. What they've just told you is the mean, calculated by adding up all the salaries of all their staff – including the four family directors who are paid in excess of £200,000 a year. If the firm had given you the fairer figure, the median salary, it would have been £14,500. But if you don't know that the median exists, never mind what it is, how on earth can you prevent yourself from being taken in? So here is a journalists' guide to the uses and abuses of the most common statistics.

Averages

There are three kinds of average:

Mean

This is what most people mean by average. You add up all the values, divide by the number of values and that is the mean. Its weakness is that it disguises as much as it reveals. A mean says nothing about the range of values in the calculation. It will not, as in the case of the salaries above, show that a few high (or low) values completely distort the results and so give a misleading 'average'. Unfortunately, this falsifying kind of average is the one most commonly used. 'Unfortunate' because, when you write about 'the average father' or 'the average student' you want to refer not to some fictitious 'mean', but to the father or student in the middle. Which brings us to the median.

Median

This, in a set of values, is the value in the middle of the data. So for salaries ranging from £9,000 to £23,000, but with most at the lower end of the range, the salary in the middle might be £14,500 – a more accurate reflection of what most people are paid than a mean distorted by the high pay of a handful of directors. The confusion between the two most common types of average probably comes from people thinking of sets of values like the numbers 1–20. Here the mean is ten, and so is the median. This is because all the values are evenly spread and rise by the same increment each time. Data from the real world is rarely like that.

Mode

Put simply, this is the most common value in the set.

Distribution

What is often just as relevant as the median is the range the values cover and you often need to know this to begin to make sense of the data. For example, the mean temperature for two regions might be 61 degrees, giving the impression that their climates are similar. Wrong. They may share the same mean temperature but the range for the former is 45 degrees and for the latter, 130 degrees. Their climates are very different.

The range of the values is called the distribution. Most social data has a normal distribution with values close to the mean, plus a few at either extreme. For example, statistics for the average (mean) hours that people aged 21–40 sleep would be normally distributed. Few people regularly get by on five or fewer hours a night and not many need more than nine. Most of the values would be around the 7.5–8 hours mark, with a steep decline in either direction. Plotting such a distribution on a graph results in a bell shape, hence the statistical term 'bell curve' to describe a normal distribution. On the other hand, the mean disposable income for 21–40-year-olds would vary tremendously – some existing on state benefits, others being millionaires. The distribution here would be much more spread out.

Percentages

It is amazing how often reporters, when fooling around with a few figures on a story, make mistakes when calculating percentages. So, for the benefit of anyone who played truant from maths classes, here's how to work it out: you take the old value from the new value, divide the result by the old value and then multiply the answer you have by 100. Or, to get a percentage increase or decrease, take the old figure from the new figure, divide by the old figure and then move the decimal point two places to the right to get the percentage. A decrease will be a minus figure.

Such a simple thing and yet a cause of so much confusion. It is, for instance, by no means unknown for mathematically impossible decreases of more than 100 per cent to find their way into stories. Nothing can fall by more than 100 per cent, because once it has, it has gone. If you doubt that, go back over the method in the paragraph above and try to make it result in more than 100. If something is reduced to a quarter of what it was, it has not fallen 400 per cent, but by 75 per cent.

Other pitfalls of percentages are:

Base figures

This is the old value, the value to which the new one is being compared. Always watch base figures. All but the most pathologically honest source will choose the base figure that, when compared with the new number, gives results that support their case. Always think – why was this base chosen?

Don't get the wrong base

If something is cut by 40 per cent, then raised by 20 per cent, many journalists would report that half the previous loss has been restored. Not so. If the original base is 100 and 40 are lost, then the new total is 60, and a 20 per cent raise of that is 12, leaving a new total of 72, well short of the 80 you would get if half the original loss had been restored.

Watch out for no base

Politicians and advertisers love slipping in claims that the unquestioning find impressive. 'We are now investing 25 per cent more in schools.' 25 per cent more than what? Than last year? Than the previous government? Than is invested in defence? Without the base, this kind of comparison is useless – and is probably being trotted out more to conceal than reveal. And watch out for sources giving out percentages on their own, unaccompanied by the raw figures they are based on.

You can't add percentages

Well you can, but not if you want to remain accurate. For example, if an industry's labour costs have gone up by 4 per cent, insurance costs have risen by 20 per cent and raw material costs are up 2 per cent, then the overall increase in costs is not 4+20+2= 26 per cent. A little reflection will tell you that insurance costs are unlikely to be anything other than a tiny fraction of labour and raw material costs. You have to add all the raw cost figures to arrive at a new total and then recalculate the percentage increase over the old total.

Don't forget the difference between percentage and percentage point

Percentage is a part of a whole where the whole is thought of as 100, while a percentage point is 100th of that whole. To get a grip on this, think of a market for a certain type of good. Various products will have a share of that market, each expressed as a percentage of the total market and adding up to 100. So, if Product A's market share falls from 5 per cent to 4 per cent, it has gone down by one percentage point but fallen by 20 per cent (or one-fifth), from five to four.

Per head

When comparing two communities, cities or countries, percentage changes on their own mislead as often as they inform. To compare things like social changes you need to know the populations of both places so that you can work out the rates per head.

Let's say, to paraphrase an example in Darrell Huff's excellent *How to Lie With Statistics*, you are writing a story about rape in two cities. Aville and Beeton both have 50 rapes a year. That makes them sound similar, until you ask how things have changed recently. Now you learn that five years ago there were 42 rapes in Aville and 29 in Beeton. So Aville's rise is 19 per cent and Beeton's is 72 per cent. Based on this data, hasty journalists might make plans to write a story about the rape crisis in Beeton, asking what is going on there and what is being done about it. But big cities tend to have more crime than little ones. You need to know the rate per head. Calculate this by dividing the number of crimes by the population and then, to avoid dealing in miniscule figures to several decimal points, multiply the answer by 100,000 to give the rate per 100,000 people. Now things look a little different. Five years ago Aville had a population of 550,000 and a rape rate of 7.64 per 100,000. Beeton had a population of 450,000 and a rape rate of 6.44 per 100,000. Now Aville has 600,000 inhabitants, giving a rape rate of 8.33 per 100,000, and Beeton, which has expanded hugely, has a population of 800,000 and a rape rate of 6.25. So in fact, Beeton's rape rate has gone down by almost three per cent, while Aville's has gone up by nine per cent. Now you have the information for a more informative, balanced and less hysterical story.

In making any comparison, you need to know the rate per unit, whether it is per head, household, or miles travelled. For example, travel safety can only be assessed by accidents or deaths per passenger miles. The greater number of people killed in the air in 1998 compared to 1952 might suggest planes are more dangerous now. Looking at the figures per miles travelled quickly corrects that error. And remember to compare like with like. The death rate in the British army is lower than in the sleepy village of Lower Piddlington. Hardly surprising, one is a group of healthy young men, the other mainly the old and poor.

Surveys

Of all the types of news stories, surveys are consistently the most suspect. Every two-bit publicist has long since realised that here is an easily-concocted way of getting coverage for their cause, product, policies or organisation. They think of some controversial issue, or newsworthy subject, ask people questions about it and then construct a press release revealing that X is the nation's favourite breed of dog, Y its favoured policy or Z per cent are now doing this or that. And every day newspapers swallow such unscientific trivia and print it. Even worse is the social trend survey, which reports the discovery of some new sub-species of society based on a few speedy answers to a few unscientific questions.

Most of the surveys that try to seduce journalists come not from academics, but from businesses and activists. Neither group has much of a track record in producing dispassionate research. So when confronted with a survey the first issue is: who is telling you this – and why? Nor do the pitfalls of surveys stop there.

What is the sample?

Times without number, stories given high prominence fall apart when the question is asked: how big was the sample? Even experienced national newspaper journalists have been known to write 700 word stories based on surveys which turn out to have samples numbering only dozens. Such samples, unless they constitute a sizable fraction of the total being measured (a sample of 20 in a class of 40, for instance), stand only a small chance of being representative. Their conclusions might be eye-catching (hardly surprising given how inaccurate they probably are) but that is no reason to publish them. The responsibility of journalists goes beyond finding a source for a story. It extends to bringing some intellect to bear on the material. And sometimes that means deciding there is no story.

How big should the sample be?

Obviously, the bigger the sample, the more likely it is to be representative. But, providing the sample is chosen intelligently, it does not have to be that big. Surveys of 1,600 people can, if carried out properly, be a very good guide to the division of opinion within a nation of 50 million. But that's all they are – a guide. How good a guide is indicated by the margin of error.

What is the margin of error?

This is the likely range of accuracy. Say a survey has a margin of error of 2.5 per cent. It finds that 45 per cent support the governing party, so the result has a range of 42.5 per cent to 47.5 per cent. Margin of error is calculated on the number of people in the sample (and not with any reference to the overall size of the population being sampled). The sample size dictates the margin of error, regardless of what it is a sample of. A sample of 1,600 has a margin of error of 2.5 per cent, and a sample of 400 has a margin of error of 5 per cent. A sample of 100, not untypical in surveys done for a quick bit of PR, has a 10 per cent margin of error. This means that a finding of 50 per cent in favour of X could in fact be 40 per cent or 60 per cent, or anything in between – not exactly precision work.

How was the sample chosen?

There is a huge credibility gap between a survey sample chosen at random and one that is self-selected. Self-selected polls are normally answered by those with a motive – either activists with a strong opinion (and thus far from being representative), or those who have been given an incentive to respond ('Just complete this simple questionnaire and be entered in our prize draw').

Who's in the sample?

A good random sample makes sure everyone has an equal chance of being included. Even for statisticians this is not easy to achieve. After all, where would you go to find a 'representative' sample? The street? And miss all those working, housebound and driving cars? Door-to-door? And miss all those out working, shopping, visiting, clubbing, wining and dining? And would you go out during the day, or at night? This is why reputable surveys are carried out by stratified random sampling – dividing the population into several groups and sampling them in proportion to their part of the whole. Even then, the accuracy depends on who goes out and finds their quota of, say, 25–40-year-old women with a certain income. The truth is that any method has problems of bias, conscious or otherwise.

Who's not in the sample?

This is often as important as who is in it. Darrell Huff quotes the case of a large survey carried out many years ago into the salaries of the Yale class of '24. The result was $25,111, the respondents being contacted via industry yearbooks, etc. In other words, they were senior executives and company directors. Yale graduates of that year who were unsuccessful would not have been easy to trace, and, if they had been, would probably have refused to reply. If a survey is done by sending out questionnaires, ask what percentage did not reply? And why not?

Are the results for the whole sample or just those who respond?

A press release says that in a survey of business attitudes to interest rates, 80 per cent of firms said high interest rates was a problem. Oh really? Ask how many forms were sent out. Answer: 2,000. How many responded? Answer: 160 – 80 per cent of which found interest rates a problem. In honest words, then: 'A survey of business attitudes to interest rates, found that 80 per cent of those responding saw them as a problem, but 93 per cent of the 2,000 businesses surveyed did not reply.'

Is self-reporting involved?

If it is, be alert, especially if the survey requires people to report on their behaviour rather than their beliefs. Is there a stigma attached to one answer rather than to another? In a survey on personal hygiene or honesty, for instance, people are unlikely to tell a stranger about their unpleasant or illegal little ways. The most blatant example of this is sex surveys. These are doomed from the start to be answered disproportionately by exhibitionists or boasters. The prim, less adventurous and private are far less liable to take part.

Are the questions fair?

In surveys which seem reputable yet produce startling results, ask to see the questions. Blatantly leading ones ('The colour red has been linked to low income groups. Now can you tell me what is your favourite colour?')

are rare. More common are a series of questions which gradually lead the unwitting respondent in a particular direction. For instance, in an article by Laurie Ouellette and Harry Goldstein for the Utne (Understanding the Next Evolution) Reader Online, they wrote:

> When the Yankelovich polling organization asked respondents the question 'Should laws be passed to eliminate all possibilities of special interests giving huge sums of money to candidates?' 80 per cent of the sample said yes, and 17 per cent said no. But when the same organization reposed the question as 'Should laws be passed to prohibit interest groups from contributing to campaigns, or do groups have the right to contribute to the candidate they support?' 40 per cent said yes while 55 per cent said no.

Do the people being surveyed have the knowledge to reach a valid verdict?

This may seem like a highly elitist question to ask, and for any general opinion survey, it would be offensively pompous. But what about surveys that require, as many do, some knowledge of the subject? Consider, for instance, a school science project carried out by Nathan Zohner of Eagle Rock Junior High, Idaho in 1996. He approached people and explained to them the scientifically proven dangers of dihydrogen monoxide (can cause excessive sweating and vomiting; is a major component of acid rain; causes severe burns when in a gas form; can be fatal if inhaled; and has been found in cancerous tumours). He then asked 50 pupils at the Greater Idaho Falls Science Fair if they would favour a ban on dihydrogen monoxide, and 86 per cent said yes, 12 per cent were unsure, and only one person said no. He knew that dihydrogen monoxide is ... water.

How accurate are respondents' answers?

People, especially in surveys of attitudes and behaviour, tend to give the answers which they think will make others regard them more favourably. Hence the famous survey conducted for the *News of the World* when people were asked which features they liked and disliked. Most said they liked the leading article and the religious feature; few confessed to reading the sex crime reports. These were dropped and circulation plummeted.

Opinion polls

Reputable polling organisations are rarely guilty of the more spectacular flaws described above. As long as their results are accurately reported (and that means giving the margin of error somewhere in the story) and some context is given, there is little chance of badly misleading readers. After all, it is up to them what faith they put in polls.

The danger with opinion polls comes with interpretation. Several key points should be borne in mind:

The trend of several polls is more important than a single poll

A lone poll can be a rogue and no great reliance should be placed on it. But if the polls mostly head in the same direction, there is a high chance that the trend indicated is accurate.

Watch the sample carefully

With political polls, especially as election day draws near, the media often commissions polls at short notice. These are likely to have small samples and be less reliable.

Watch the margin of error if comparing polls

The classic error in reporting polls is to compare two polls and see significance where there is none. If the first poll finds support for the government of 45 per cent and that for the opposition of 42 per cent, and a second poll then finds them both at 44 per cent, has the government lost support? It all depends on the margin of error. If it is 3 per cent in the first poll, government support was then in the range of 42–48 per cent and the opposition's between 39 and 45 per cent. If the second poll also has a margin of 3 per cent, then support for both government and opposition is 41–47 per cent. The second poll's result is well within the margin of error of the first and so nothing, statistically, has happened. You would need further polls tracking movement out of the original ranges to draw conclusions.

Correlation

One of the most dangerous words in journalism is 'link'. A great many misleading stories appear because those with an axe to grind announce a relationship between two things and journalists fail to ask enough questions. The result is confusion between a statistical correlation and a causal relationship. They are not the same thing. A correlation could be, and probably is, a coincidence. A link is when one thing causes, or helps to cause, the other.

An association between two factors is not proof of a relationship. There may be, for instance, a close correlation between the spending power of Catholic priests and sales of condoms, but there is not a link.

All kinds of more plausible (but equally false) economic links are peddled to journalists when the most likely explanation is simply that, in a period of growth, all kinds of data will rise and many unrelated ones will rise at precisely the same rate. Chance is the best explanation here, as it is for so many correlations.

Health stories

The stories where 'links' are most freely asserted are those dealing with health. You are told, for example, that there is a clear correlation between wine drinking in moderation and lower cancer risk. Before reporting a link, stop and think. It may well be that those who drink wine in moderation do something else that lowers their cancer risk – they are wealthier, in better health, have more check-ups, smoke less, can relieve stress more easily, etc. This is a classic example of where a little intelligent, balanced context can put a 'link' into context. Then there are stories which compare disease rates between countries. These often produce results which are surprising. Cancer rates in developed countries, for instance, are normally well above those for significantly less wealthy countries. Does this mean the poorer nations have some dietary or other secret to tell? It's possible; but, on the other hand, the explanation could just be that, since cancer is mainly a disease of middle and late age, countries with wealthier populations live long enough to get more cancers.

In reporting health or safety stories, remember that death statistics are always more reliable than injury data. There is a legal obligation for cause of death to be recorded, so such figures are far less prone to misdiagnosis. They are also totally free of self-diagnosis, which, in the case of injuries, can be distorted by a financial incentive to exaggerate e.g. insurance or compensation claims.

Cluster studies

Another type of story where a superficially convincing 'link' catches the unwary are studies of illnesses in areas near power lines, toxic-waste dumps, farms where pesticides have been used, etc. Such studies are normally carried out by campaigners or lawyers acting for victims and have been invaluable in raising the alarm on environmental threats. But false 'links' are often obtained because researchers, anxious to prove a case, start cherry-picking the data, selecting what suits them and moving the boundaries of the area in and out to produce the desired results. Always check the boundaries of such studies, for they often make no sense. The same trickery can apply to counter-studies produced by authorities trying to deny the existence of a problem.

Projections

Sources frequently exaggerate projections. The most common method is to take the highest possible growth rate and apply it way beyond the time when early rises (necessarily high in percentage terms) would fall away. The following is another abuse.

'We are losing £7 million a month'

Firms often make such a statement during a strike. Question how they arrived at this sum. More often than not it is calculated by taking the year's most productive day, multiplying by 365, and then adding on estimates for all other kinds of losses – increased insurance premiums, cost of customers' alternatives, etc. Respond by asking first what the turnover was last year and then why the firm's estimated losses per month seem to result in a turnover several times what was actually achieved.

Real versus apparent rise

Another source of deception, since increasing reports may not mean an actual rise. There may have been a sharp rise in awareness, the introduction of compulsory reporting or a new incentive to report. All these factors are important to context and are especially vital when a type of behaviour, usually a crime, becomes news flavour of the month. One of the first things that happens then is that the phenomenon acquires a catchy name. 'Road rage' is a good example. Suddenly instances seem to be everywhere. But when subjected to statistical test, the 'new rampant' phenomenon is rarely as 'new' or 'rampant' as the coverage indicates.

Has the definition of the survey subject changed?

A huge growth in nursery schools, for example, can be produced if what were formerly defined as 'playgroups' are now termed 'nursery schools'. To conclude from this that there had been an explosion in schooling for the under-5s would be wrong.

Reality is more interesting than hype or myth

First, because it is real. Second, because it can often surprise. In countries that can have bad winter weather a ritual story is the spate of road accidents caused by sudden snowfall. But if you check with those who keep such data then you find there are far more crashes on clear, sunny days – probably twice the rate as on snowy days. In good weather a lot more people are out on the roads, while, on bad days, only those who must travel (including a high proportion of those who drive for a living) are out. Hence there are fewer accidents. 'Snowfall saves lives' – not quite as sensational a story as 'Blizzard kills 13', but actually more accurate and original. And statistics can be an antidote to scare stories that do the rounds and which rarely get tested against real life. A hardy annual is the one around Halloween that warns of the terrible dangers faced by children going trick or treating being murdered by poisoned candy and fruit given them by homicidal householders. Yet a Californian study found that since 1958 only three children have died in such circumstances. One ate his uncle's heroin, another died of a seizure, and a third was deliberately poisoned by his father. Reality, again, proving less scary, and certainly more interesting, than widespread beliefs.

And finally, three thoughts.

- Remember that too many statistics can kill the flow of even the best story. Use what you must and put the rest in a box, graphic, sidebar or table.
- Use one of the many good statistical calculations pages available online. One of the best is: http://members.aol.com/johnp71/javastat.html
- Why not run your data – especially some of the more complex calculations – past a friendly local university statistician before publishing them?

Phoney science

At regular intervals, some politician, campaigner, renegade scientist or doctor will advance some cure, remedy, theory, or invention that becomes, for a while, a widespread orthodoxy. Scepticism is always the best response to such sudden enthusiasms. You don't need a particular reason for this, merely the knowledge that this is what good journalism demands. But let me tell the story of one bit of nonsensical science that caught on, was accepted, and whose consequences were still being felt years later. It is the tale of the Great Sparrow War of China.

It began, as did many of Mao Zeadong's more damaging schemes, with a rambling speech to a party congress. It was the time of the Great Leap Forward, and, with a determined drive under way to create an industrial – as opposed to agrarian – society, food supply was unlikely to be sufficient. Mao identified several scapegoats. There were, he said, four great pests: rats, flies, mosquitos, and sparrows. The latter ate grain which could otherwise feed people, he said, and officials computed that the average sparrow gobbled up 4lbs of grain a year. And so Mao instructed the nation to mobilise and kill them. Extermination days were organised, and wholesale slaughter followed. On one – 13 December 1958 in Shanghai

– no fewer than 194,432 sparrows were killed. Since the Chinese were not much given to bird-spotting, few citizens could detect the difference between the ostensible target, the Eurasian tree sparrow, and anything else with wings and feathers. Closely-related species duly suffered as well.

The killing spree did not last for more than a week or so, but was intense while it was on. Area competed with area to kill the most birds, and guns, catapults, stones, nets, and even poisoned birdbaths were all deployed to wipe out the sparrows. Photographs show piles of bird carcases 20ft high, and, in the course of the campaign, tens of millions of birds are thought to have died.

But what Chairman Mao did not know, until it was too late, was that sparrows' main food is insects. Invertebrates made up three-quarters of their diet, as a pair of Chinese scientists subsequently discovered. And so, without the busy flocks of birds to devour them, the insects became a plague. Locusts, especially, multiplied, and the harvest of 1959 duly proved to be a disaster. It yielded far less food – about 40 per cent, according to some sources – than the year before, and millions of people – estimates vary from 16 million to 30 million – died from starvation. And all, ultimately, because of official ignorance and a supine media which failed to challenge the authorities.

A thousand stories which the ignorant tell, and believe, die away at once when the computist has them in his gripe.

Samuel Johnson

9

Investigative Reporting

The image of the reporter as a nicotine-stained Quixote, slugging back Scotch while skewering City Hall with an exposé ripped out of the typewriter on the crack of deadline persists despite munificent evidence to the contrary.

Paul Grey

There is a school of journalistic thought that curls its lip and sneers at the very mention of the words 'investigative reporting'. It argues that, since all reporting is investigative, the phrase is meaningless. If only that were true. But some reporting is investigative only in the most basic sense. It is the journalistic equivalent of the single-cell creature and bears about as much resemblance to the subject of this chapter as amoebae do to humans.

What is investigative reporting?

Investigative reporting is substantially different from other kinds and there are four features that distinguish it.

Original research

Investigative reporting is not a summary or piecing together of others' findings and data, but original research carried out by journalists often using the rawest of material. It can be extensive interviewing, or matching and comparing facts and figures and discovering previously unknown patterns and connections.

The subject involves wrongdoing or negligence for which there is no published evidence

Often you have suspicions of wrongdoing or negligence but have no proof and neither does anyone else. You need to accumulate evidence and this requires far more time and prolonged effort than ordinary reporting. It may also involve more than one reporter.

Someone is trying to keep the information secret

This is true of a lot of reporting, but in day-to-day work, there is often a point at which you have to stop and report what you have found or not found. Investigative reporting starts at the point where the day-to-day work stops. It does not accept the secrecy and the refusal of officials to give the information. It finds out for itself.

The stakes are high

The kudos and pride you get when the story works out can be considerable, but so can the amount of dirt hitting the fan when it all goes wrong. Consider the *Cincinnati Enquirer's* experiences in 1998. In May of that year they published a front page story and an 18-page section devoted to a year-long investigation into the international banana firm, Chiquita Brands. Headlined 'Chiquita Secrets Revealed', the paper alleged that Chiquita secretly controlled dozens of supposedly independent banana firms, that it and its subsidiaries used pesticides that threatened the health of workers and nearby residents, that employees engaged in bribery in Colombia and that its ships had smuggled cocaine into Europe.

All, however, was not quite as it seemed. In the issue of 28 June, the paper carried a six-column apology to the company across the top of the front page, totally repudiating the investigation. It fired its lead investigative reporter and it agreed to pay Chiquita no less than $10 million.

The problem was not the veracity (or otherwise) of the evidence, but the methods employed to obtain it. These involved access to internal voicemail messages of the company and the issue was how this access was obtained. The company alleged that the reporter posed questions and then tapped into their mailboxes to eavesdrop on their internal discussion on the issues the reporter had raised. The paper, in making the apology and settlement, appeared to accept the thrust of these allegations. In a published statement, the paper said that the reporter had misled them over the source of the voicemail messages. It was never clear, however, if there was any substance to the published stories.

The loss of credibility, plus the $10 million, made this a very costly investigation. Fortunately, for every episode like this, there are many more which were rewarding. They range from Nellie Bly's exposure of appalling conditions inside asylums for *New York World*, W.T. Stead's exposure of child prostitution in the *Pall Mall Gazette*; and the unmasking of the violently racist Ku Klux Klan by Roland Thomas in the *New York World;* to the uncovering by Seymour Hersch of the My Lai massacre in 1968; the *Sunday Times'* campaign for the limbless victims of the drug thalidomide;

and Carl Bernstein and Bob Woodward's Watergate investigation in the *Washington Post*. They also include many more localised stories, which exposed neglect and so changed lives for the better. A classic case is the *Alabama Journal*'s investigation into the state's infant mortality record in 1987 – at 13 deaths per 1,000, it was the worst of any state in the union. The paper ran a 20-part series which led to the State Medicaid agency quadrupling funding for prenatal programmes and a determined drive to bring better health care to poor mothers. By 1994 Alabama's infant mortality rate had shrunk by 20 per cent. By the end of the century, there were nearly 1,000 children who owed their very existence to this series. It's difficult to imagine more productive reporting than that.

Finally, what is at stake can even include your personal safety. In countries where organised crime is widespread, investigative reporting is a potentially lethal profession. In Russia, the *Moskovski Komsolets* reporter, Dimitri Kholodov, was investigating army corruption. An anonymous source rang him one day in the autumn of 1994 and said that a bag of documents had been left for him at Kazan Station. Kholodov collected them and took the bag back to his office. When he opened it, the bag exploded, killing him. And in the summer of 1992, Peruvian reporter Adolfo Isuiza Urquia was investigating drug dealing for the daily *La Republica*. In August he named a major drug trafficker who was being protected by the armed forces. 'The army does not want to fight terrorism because it lives off drug trafficking', he wrote. A few days later, on 27 August, his body was found in the River Huallaga. He had been tortured and stabbed. Anyone considering digging around in these areas should carefully weigh any risk involved. Dead reporters can't report.

Productive areas to investigate

Investigative reporting starts with a sniff of a story, or the hunch that in some subject lies the seeds of one. The main thing at this stage is to think carefully about the 'best case' outcome and consider whether the story will be worth the effort and time required. If it is not going to be page one, forget it. Specialised investigative units in particular can easily get obsessed with a story that is far too narrow to be of importance to general readers. Submit your planned inquiry to the headline test: if the anticipated outcome does not make a startling headline, then you are probably going to waste your time.

Potentially, good investigations can be found in almost any area of public life. Two broad categories, however, are particularly fruitful: activities and organisations that do their work in remote places or otherwise away from the public gaze; and people and institutions that suddenly get thrust into the spotlight, appear to have 'come from nowhere' and around which a mythology has speedily grown. They are people and institutions which seem to have no background. But they will, and in that background there is almost sure to be a good story.

Companies and financial institutions, especially of the 'get rich quick' variety, are a highly fertile ground for some journalistic digging. Sink your spade into a newfangled and highly publicised investment scheme and you can bet your salary that there will be dirt there. The Romanian pyramid funds of the early 1990s are a prime case of a missed opportunity. One that was not missed, and a classic example of this type of reporting, was the story of Charles Ponzi, or, as he liked to call himself, The Great Ponzi.

A lot of people believed him. More than 40,000 Americans plunged their savings into his scheme, lured in by his pledge to pay them, within 90 days, $2.50 for every $1 invested. Despite warnings from financial experts that his sums did not add up, Ponzi was, at one point in 1920, raking in $200,000 a day. In 18 months, he collected more than $15 million.

It was all based on currency exchange rates. His company would take your investment, and send it overseas, where his agents would buy International Postal Union reply coupons at depressed rates and then sell them in other foreign outposts at a higher rate. That was Ponzi's story and thousands joined the rush to have their investment earn money faster than they could. The reality, of course, was that he was paying new customers with the money from old ones. In the whole life of his company it traded in foreign currency with only $30 of the original $15 million.

But the flood of people who crowded the sidewalks outside his offices, queuing for the chance to invest everything they had, did not know that. It seemed, in the words of one of these hopefuls, that he 'had discovered money itself'. He hadn't, of course. He had merely found that if you offer people a big enough return on their money, and wave a few libel writs around, you can postpone the day of reckoning for a long time.

But not indefinitely; for other things were being discovered. Reporters from the *Boston Post* newspaper were discovering his past. 'The Great Ponzi', it turned out, was better known to the authorities in Canada as prisoner no. 5247, the number he bore while jailed for forgery. He had also done time in Atlanta for smuggling aliens. The *Post* ran the story, Ponzi's company duly collapsed, and he went to jail for four years.

Investigative reporting skills

Investigative reporting can be undertaken by anyone with the determination both to see the job through and to handle all the inevitable frustrations. It requires no greater skills than those demanded by general reporting. But there are a few things that make the job easier and which will make you more efficient at it.

Knowledge of the law on public access to information

What is the law on this in your country? Do you know what public records and documents you are entitled to see? This is vital. Some investigations have resulted from secret documents being passed to journalists, but many more have resulted from reporters discovering that certain records or registers are kept and that they have a right to consult them. Most bureaucracies do not exactly advertise the existence of such information and they erect all kinds of barriers to prevent people consulting them – by making them available only at certain times, or by storing them in out of the way places.

A reporter who once worked with me in London discovered in the small print of a government report the existence of a certain register. It listed all the rights of access to private estates that had been granted in return for the wealthy owners of the estates receiving tax concessions. Neither the officials (because they had given tax concessions) nor the owners (because they did not want members of the public tramping all over their estates) were keen to have this register publicised.

Once the reporter learnt of its existence and established that we had the right to examine it, she went through the lengthy process involved and consulted it. She was then able not only to report what access could be gained to these estates, but also to investigate the deals done between the owners and the government. None of this would have been possible were it not for her finding out about the register in the first place and insisting on seeing it.

This was in Britain, which has a tradition of secrecy about official documents. It is not exactly alone in this, but there are other countries that now have freedom of information laws which have opened up a vast amount of records to citizens. Very few ordinary people will know of these records and even fewer will consult them. All the more reason for journalists to make it their business to know what is kept and what can be seen.

In the United States, the 1966 Freedom of Information Act, strengthened in 1971, has opened up all kinds of documents to journalists. As a result of their use in investigations, all manner of scandals have been uncovered by the press:

- Unreported accidents at nuclear sites.
- X-ray machines at cancer-detection centres which were emitting 25–30 times the correct level of radiation (within months of disclosure, all such centres in the United States had reduced amounts of radiation).
- Anaesthetic drugs routinely given during childbirth even though they could – and did – cause brain-damage to babies.

There was also the paper in Louisville, Kentucky which obtained federal inspection reports on nursing homes showing the abuse of residents. As a result, new state legislation was introduced, many homes were closed and the owners of several were charged with fraud.

There are many, many other cases that could be cited. They all show the value of journalists discovering what records are kept, examining them and using them in their investigations.

Knowledge of standard reference sources

In all but the most furtive of societies there is much more information available than the average journalist realises. A lot of this can be traced through standard, if not commonly available, reference sources: lists of official publications, reports from legislatures, lists of public bodies, company ownership reference books or registers of bodies receiving government funding. Any reporter intending to carry out investigative work should make it his or her business to know what information such reference sources hold.

Contacts

All reporters obviously need contacts, but investigative reporters more so. And they need a particular type of contact – not just those who can give them information or point them in the right direction on a specific story, but those who can be useful on a range of stories. People like lawyers, officials in telephone services, car registration centres and those who can give advice on, and access to, official records.

Computer literacy

This means not just the ability to search effectively online, but also the ability to use database software. Examples of the value of this in investigations now abound. One of the most instructive was that by the *Atlanta Journal-Constitution* in Georgia, which won a Pulitzer Prize in 1989 for a series analysing racial discrimination in bank lending.

This investigation, by Bill Dedman, repays study; not because its subject has any great global significance, but precisely because it hasn't. It is a piece of local city reporting, although a particularly fine example. It did not bring any governments down, reveal any criminal corruption or save any lives. To someone who is white and living a long way away from the United States, it might appear to be small beer compared to the problems that affect their country. But the *Journal-Constitution* series is worth looking at for its methods, organisation and attitudes. It is the story of a journalist determined to report a situation into print, rather than wish it there or just repeat the hearsay that was coming his way.

The investigation started with an off-hand remark by a white housing developer. He said he was having trouble building houses in the black areas of South Atlanta because banks would not lend money there (something that would be illegal, if done for discriminatory reasons). He added that he had been told that loans were hard to come by even in affluent black areas. It is the kind of remark that reporters hear every day – general, unsubstantiated and seemingly impossible to prove. But Dedman's curiosity had been aroused. He wanted to see if the charge could be substantiated.

First he talked to some academics who worked in this field, and they told him that banks and savings and loan companies must file to the government the location of every home loan, by amount and census tract. As Dedman later wrote: 'All we at the paper did, to put it simply, was to cross-index the federal computer tapes with a federal census tape, looking especially at comparable black and white neighborhoods.' This was easier said than done. The first three days were devoted entirely to putting spaces between the numbers on the computer so they could be read properly.

For the next five months, Dedman checked loans made by every bank and savings association in Atlanta over a five-year period – a total of 109,000 loans. There was also another study looking at real estate records. But the effort was worth it. Dedman discovered that banks and other institutions were making five times as many loans in white areas as in black areas. By examining bank policies and practices, he also found that they were not looking for business in black areas and were otherwise discouraging black borrowers. Blacks, in turn, could only resort to unregulated mortgage companies and loan sharks. As he says, 'Only then did I turn to anecdote.' He collected personal experiences, which gave his series real lives, and showed how the policies of banks affected people.

When he went to the banks, they were predictably reluctant to talk. One replied to Dedman's request for information thus: 'Some of the material you have asked for does not exist. Other parts of the material exist but are confidential. The rest of the material exists and is not confidential but is irrelevant to your subject matter.' It is the unmistakable voice of someone with something to hide. Another bank tried sneakily to combine an appeal to local patriotism with a thinly-disguised plea to the paper's publisher, Jay Smith, to kill the story. He wrote: 'I'm sure that Jay Smith would recognize any article alleging racial discrimination by Atlanta financial institutions as another unmerited potshot at our great city ...'. And he sent a copy of the letter to Smith.

Finally, when Dedman had enough material for a series (which he would call 'The Color of Money' after the Hollywood film), his editors came into the picture. As Dedman wrote later:

I think I know the key to the effectiveness of 'The Color of Money'. The editors took out what I thought were the good parts. When I wrote that Atlanta's banks were red-lining [a pejorative word for marking-off areas to be discriminated against], editor Bill Kovach marked through it. 'Just use the numbers,' he said, 'Let the facts speak for themselves.'

On Sunday 1 May, the series began with a story of several thousand words headlined 'Atlanta Blacks Losing In Home Loans Scramble'. It began:

> Whites receive five times as many home loans from Atlanta's banks and savings and loans as blacks of the same income – and that gap has been widening each year, an *Atlanta Journal-Constitution* study of $6.2 billion in lending shows. Race – not home value or household income – consistently determines the lending patterns of metro Atlanta's largest financial institutions, according to the study, which examined six years of lender reports to the federal government.

The story went on to contain the following: explanation and denial from bankers, details of the survey with further news points (including the fact that the only bank which specialised in lending to blacks had the lowest default rate in the whole country), explanation of the law relating to bank loans, etc. Elsewhere in that day's paper was a story about individual blacks who were well-qualified for a loan but had had trouble getting one. The rest of the series was as follows:

- *Monday 2 May*: Detailed story on bank policies, the history of discrimination by them, plus more case histories including the black Vietnam veteran who was refused a loan which would have cost him $100 a month less than his rent. The article also detailed the process of home purchase and how it related to blacks.

- *Tuesday 3 May*: Detailed explanation of the law on banking and its regulation and practice over the whole country, plus the history of efforts by black groups to change Atlanta's banks' policies. There were also follow-up stories which established that discrimination was being practised nationally.

The results of Dedman's series were immediate. Nine days after it ended, Atlanta's nine largest banks began pouring $77 million into low-interest loans into black areas. Some institutions also went positively into black areas looking for business, hiring black staff, advertising in black media and even taking their executives on a bus tour of the areas. Eleven months after the series was printed, the US Justice Department began investigating 64 Atlanta financial institutions for possible breaches of the discrimination laws.

How to run investigative operations

The subjects for investigations come to papers in all kinds of ways: tips from contacts; by accident; a seemingly routine story that subsequent information indicates is far bigger; a reporter's own observations; a run-of-the-mill story which escalates bit by bit, or one where every question you ask throws up other, increasingly important, questions.

This was the case with perhaps the most famous journalistic investigation of all – Watergate. It began in June 1972 with a break-in at the Democratic Party's headquarters in the Watergate Building in Washington. It ended just over two years later with the resignation of the most powerful man on earth, President Richard Nixon. The role of the President and his staff in the original burglary and much else besides (phone-taps, slush-funds and, most important of all, the cover-up of these illegal activities) would never been known had it not been for investigative reporters. The two main ones were Carl Bernstein and Bob Woodward of the *Washington Post*.

When they started working on the story, in a mood of mutual distrust, it was a routine crime story. Five men had been caught breaking into the Democrat's HQ to plant a listening device. Woodward went to the courtroom the following day and noticed a prominent lawyer taking great interest in the case. What was he doing there? Woodward also learnt at the court that several of the men had worked for the Central Intelligence Agency. They were also carrying large amounts of cash on them when arrested and two of them had notebooks, inside one of which was a telephone number for a man who worked at the White House.

From these slender – but promising – beginnings was launched a series of stories that were finally to prove the Nixon administration's complicity in a whole raft of illegal activities. Bernstein and Woodward were fêted, wrote a best-selling book and a Hollywood film was made of their investigation. But that was the final outcome. Before that were a thousand frustrations, abuse from Nixon supporters and officials who feared and suspected their reporting, wasted days, weeks and months pursuing false leads, mistakes (some of which got into print), countless hours searching records for that one vital piece of information, self-doubts, criticism and envy of colleagues, and late nights, all nights and weekends of their own time spent on the case.

There are valuable lessons to be learnt from their experiences. Their book, *All The President's Men*, is probably the best detailed description of reporting in the English language. It tells the story of two reporters edging slowly, and not always in a straight line, towards the truth by painstaking research and a healthy obsession with accuracy. The following guidelines on investigative reporting are based on their work, the study of other cases and my own limited experiences.

Find and file every document

The moral of every investigation ever mounted is to lay your hands on every document that you can and throw nothing away. You never know when documents, notes, reports – indeed anything you accumulate – will be useful. Months after you acquire that apparently innocuous report, something might give it sudden significance. Bernstein and Woodward, the Watergate reporters, filled four filing cabinets after just a few months.

Write up every interview and file the notes

This is especially important if there is more than one of you working on an investigation or if it is a lengthy one. It pays to swap notes of interviews to see if you have missed something of significance. Typed (and filed) notes are also a lot easier and quicker to consult. This practice also allows executives to participate better in the discussions of the story.

Be persistent

Read the story of any investigation and the persistence of the reporters is the thing that strikes you. During the Watergate investigation Woodward and Bernstein often spent days going through records, sat at their desks making phone calls all weekend, or waited outside lawyers' offices all day for the chance to see a perhaps vital source. On one occasion they obtained a list of the hundred-or-so people who worked at the Committee to Re-elect the President, the seat of much of the wrong-doing. Since they obviously could not visit these people at their offices, they spent many weeks calling on them at their homes after their normal day's work at the paper.

Re-interview 'old sources'

As long as an investigation is in progress, there is no such thing as an 'old source'. People working in the area you are investigating will often remember things they should have told you, receive new information, or are able to make sense of new information you get. Each one of these is reason enough to call them regularly. Woodward and Bernstein each kept a separate master list of phone numbers of contacts. This eventually amounted to several hundred names. They were each called at least twice a week, every week, for well over a year. As they wrote in their subsequent book: 'Just the fact that a certain source would not come to the phone or return calls often signalled something significant.'

Cultivate sources who really are in the know

During the Watergate investigation, Woodward contacted a man who worked at a senior level in the government to ask him if any word of the wrong-doing had reached him. It had. He knew an enormous amount and clearly regarded it as his duty to assist the exposure of the conspiracy. However, he had the bureaucrat's natural suspicion of the press and was also concerned lest stories based on knowledge only he and few others had was used without confirmation by other sources.

He therefore agreed to help Woodward, but only on certain conditions: he would only guide the reporter in the right direction, anything he told them would have to be corroborated by another source. Meetings between him and Woodward took place in underground car parks, late at night and were only arranged at his behest. Such was the quality of his assistance that Woodward agreed to these conditions.

The source revealed his identity to no one, and an executive at the *Washington Post* christened him 'Deep Throat' after the title of a fashionable pornographic movie which featured a woman whose speciality was oral sex. Deep Throat's identity still remains a mystery to all but Woodward.

It is an opportunity few reporters experience, to know and have the co-operation of such a well-placed source as Deep Throat. But the moral of Woodward's dealings with him is that if such a source sets certain rules, you should stick by them. That does not mean you should accept everything they say; Woodward argued with his contact frequently. But whatever is finally agreed should be adhered to.

Executive support

The news editor/editor must commit staff and other resources to the project. The editor should be prepared for the project to take a long time and possibly result in no story. Publishing something just because a lot of time has been spent on it is a sure way to have a disaster on your hands. When it is finally printed, the story should be watertight.

The executives and reporters will also have to make a decision early on about whether the investigation will be a series of stories published as they are written, or a 'big hit' operation printed only when all the research is complete. If it is the latter, a deadline should be set. It is easy for investigations to drag on for months, with the reporters always claiming that they need 'just one more week' to finish their research. You should also remember that interim stories can sometimes encourage people to come forward with more, or even the vital piece of, information.

Yet whichever way it is being published, the investigative operation should be closely monitored by an executive. A key part of this role is to ask questions continuously of the reporters about the story. Such executives should act as devil's advocates and also keep going over evidence with reporters. They should be the fresh mind on the case.

Going undercover

Most of the time there is a better way of collecting information than going undercover. But occasionally, very occasionally, it might be the only way to write the story. Investigating the situation inside some 'closed' world, like a secretive group, organisation or company is the most usual pretext, and there may be others. But the story had better be worth it, because it is very time-consuming and comes with a lot of risks, the least of which is the embarrassment if you are discovered.

The other hazards will take a lot more living down. First, undercover work always involves some deception, so the wrong-doing you are reporting needs to be serious enough to justify that dishonesty. Second, the physical dangers in such a situation can be immense and last long after you have surfaced to write your story. Third, if you are investigating criminal activities undercover you may well be drawn into participating, which makes your actions even harder, if not impossible, to defend.

There is an additional risk when you are investigating an illegal trade and posing as a buyer or seller, in other words as an *agent provocateur*. Apart from the dubious morality of that, you also become part of the story and so change it. This, to me, means that you have already passed beyond anything recognisable as journalism. The most flagrant case of this was in 1994 when stories began to emerge of weapons-grade plutonium being offered for sale on the German black market. A number of reporters thought they would make a name for themselves by probing this trade. Some posed as sellers, others as buyers with unlimited money. As if this was not bad enough, some journalists working undercover as 'buyers' then ran into others impersonating sellers. None discovered the true identity of the other and so their published stories were not of the 'trade in death' as they claimed, but of two over-enthusiastic journalists fooling each other – and themselves.

Yet there are instances of undercover investigations producing memorably good stories. At the end of the nineteenth century, *New York World* reporter Nellie Bly (real name Elizabeth Cochran) feigned insanity to get inside the asylum at Blackwell's Island and wrote a shocking exposé. Her findings were later published in her book *Ten days in a Madhouse*. The reward from her publisher, Joseph Pulitzer, was an assignment to beat the round-the-world journey time of 80 days set by the fictitious Phileas Fogg in Jules Verne's novel *Around The World In Eighty Days*. She did it in 72 days 6 hours 11 minutes and 14 seconds.

Less well-rewarded was the editor of the *Pall Mall Gazette*, W.T. Stead. He exposed child prostitution in Victorian London by 'buying' a 13-year-old girl from her mother and, under the strictest of supervision, spent enough time alone with her to prove that she could have been put to almost any immoral purpose. His campaign to change the law on child prostitution had the support of many leading figures, including bishops. They, however, could not prevent Stead subsequently being prosecuted. The authorities jailed him for three months on a technicality for buying the girl at the centre of his story. This strange, red-bearded and eccentric man (he sometimes caught mice, fried them and ate them on toast) went down with the *Titanic* in 1912.

Since then, journalists have gone undercover mainly to expose the treatment – or maltreatment – of various 'victims' of society like the homeless, mentally ill or drug addicts. This involves a degree of acting and perhaps the adoption of disguise. The master of this genre is a German called Gunter Wallraff. His aim is to enter worlds forbidden to a writer. He uses false papers, an invented life-story, new clothes, new spectacles or contact lenses, ways of disguising his hair and teeth. For, as he says, his task is 'to deceive in order not to be deceived'.

He styles himself 'the undesirable journalist' and, as far as his targets are concerned, not without good reason. He has played the part of an informer for the security services and the political police, tested Catholic theology and morality by posing as a man who had been making napalm bombs, led the life of a homeless man in a hostel, an alcoholic in a mental hospital, and impersonated a ministry adviser to find out how armed units are available to German industry for factory protection. As a 'German financier of the extreme Right' he discovered plans for a *coup* in Portugal, and, as a 'tabloid reporter', worked on and exposed the methods of the mass-market *Bild*.

Scrupulous about notes and records, he tapes everything and photocopies all documents that he wishes to quote. As he says: 'I decided to conspire in order to take a look over the wall of camouflage, denials and lies. The method I adopted was only slightly illegal by comparison with the illegal deceptions and manoeuvres which I unmasked.'

Most of his work is published, not in newspapers, but in magazines, booklets or books. Wallraff's investigations consume a great deal of time, more time, perhaps, than many newspapers would grant a staff reporter. But his results are impressive and his methods worthy of more attention than they get.

A newspaper can send more souls to heaven, and save more from Hell, than all the churches or chapels in New York.

James Gordon Bennett

10

How To Cover Major Incidents

Have you noticed that life, real honest-to-goodness life, with murders and catastrophes and fabulous inheritances, happens almost exclusively in the newspapers?

Jean Anouilh
The Rehearsal, 1950

There is an unwritten rule in journalism that the stronger the story, the easier it is to write. There is, after all, no need to spend hours chewing the end of a pencil wondering what the angle for the intro should be when the story is that 68 have died in a disco fire. But while the writing of major incident stories is usually straightforward, researching them to the point where a clear story has emerged is often difficult.

Major incidents are, by their very nature, chaotic. Even to the authorities it is often unclear, for many hours or even days, exactly what has happened. Disasters can happen in inaccessible places, in countries where communications are poor, or where authorities are badly organised and secretive. They can happen at night, or be the kind of natural disaster, like Hurricane Mitch in central America in 1998, where it takes some days for the full enormity to be appreciated. The death toll, which for our professionally ghoulish purposes is often the key indicator of how big the story is, can often be slow to emerge. First reports of it can be particularly misleading.

Then there are the witnesses, invariably traumatised and confused, and, as a result, sometimes giving highly inaccurate testimony. The authorities, too, can often mislead; most commonly because their first priority is saving lives and not assisting journalists; or because they have an interest in promoting one aspect of the incident, or disguising another. In both the Hillsborough stadium disaster of 1989 (when 94 soccer fans died in a crush) and the Dunblane massacre (when a lone gunman killed 16 pupils and three teachers at a Scottish school) the police forces concerned briefed to disguise their own share of the liability. These days, the threat of litigation, liability and insurance claims may make officials even more cautious, unhelpful and, occasionally, deceitful. Never underestimate the willingness of organisations involved, or representing those involved, in disasters to brief journalists to further some internal, hidden, agenda.

The classic case of this was the Strangeways Prison riot of April 1990, probably the most inaccurately reported major incident in living memory. It began on 1 April when prisoners, angered at overcrowding which meant they were locked in their cells for 23 hours a day, seized keys from officers, released up to 1,000 other convicts, set fire to the chapel and gym and took control of the jail. It was a major incident by any standards, made photogenic by the prisoners who hung banners from windows and sat on the roof wearing makeshift masks and hurling slates to the ground. And since the prisoners had barricaded themselves in the main blocks and held them for several days, there was no telling what was happening in there. There were strong suggestions that in the frenzy of the moment, the normally segregated sex offenders had been attacked.

This uncertainty of what precisely was happening was a vacuum that tabloid papers were not prepared to see unfilled. On 2 April, the *Daily Mirror* reported '11 dead in Jail Riot'; that day's *Evening Standard* said that 20 had died and two days later the *Sun* had a front page 'exclusive' that 'more than 30 might have died'. Not to be outdone, the *Daily Mirror* countered with 'Prison mob hang cop'. There were stories of hangings following kangeroo courts, castrations, prisoners thrown from landings, or impaled on furniture, throats slit, forced injections of 'cocktails of drugs' stolen from the prison pharmacy, batterings with iron bars and dismemberments.

There was not a shred of truth in any of these tales. Only two men had died and, as for the *Mirror*'s 'hanged cop', he turned out to be a convicted rapist, who was decidedly unhanged, having spent the days of the riot quietly serving his sentence in Armley Jail, 70 miles away in Leeds. What had happened was that several factors came together to make a heady cocktail of half-truths, false assumptions and lies – which the tabloids, and a few of the broadsheets, then swallowed.

First there was the chaos of the situation, the impossibility of knowing at the time what was really going on. (A prime source for the 'execution' stories was a solicitor who told Oldham magistrates court that his client had seen three bodies hanging from balconies. They turned out to be resuscitation dummies used in first aid classes.) Second was that many of the more lurid rumours came from men in uniform, prison officers especially. They had their own reasons for portraying the riot as 'an explosion of evil', as they put it. Official spokesmen spoke constantly of 'deaths', often in combination with off-the-record peddling of horror stories. The government department responsible added to this impression by, at one point, delivering 20 body bags to the jail.

But the press added hugely to their own subsequent embarrassment. They did not question what they were being told, and, in some cases, did not even report these statements as claims. but reported them as fact. They wanted to believe the worst, and, on this occasion, they found willing, official accomplices. They were told what they wanted to hear and believed it. The tabloids then excluded anything which did not fit with this thesis. On the morning after the riot started, for instance, a consultant at North Manchester General Hospital said in a press conference that he had not admitted any seriously wounded prisoners. Only the broadsheet papers reported it. And, crucially, most journalists did not ask themselves if what they were being told sounded plausible. They just reproduced it. They forgot that the responsibility of journalists goes beyond finding a source for a story. It extends to bringing some intelligence to bear on what sources say.

The other self-inflicted enemy of accurate, level-headed coverage of major incidents is the rush to judgement. It is far more common than the circumstances which undermined the Strangeways coverage, and journalists reporting disasters which involve human or mechanical failure are particularly prone to it. The modern need for an instant explanation, and immediate villains, pressures journalists into trying to point the finger of blame, sometimes long before all the principal facts are known. In May 1991, for instance, a Lauda Air Boeing 767 crashed in the Thai jungle, killing all 223 people on board. Among them was Don McIntosh, a 43-year-old British civil servant on secondment to the UN anti-drug programme. This fact alone was enough for the *Daily Star* to leap to conclusions. 'Sacrificed' read their front page headline over a story of how 'ruthless drug barons' (a knee-jerk cliché, straight from Central Casting) killed 223 people to assassinate one man. It was, of course, pure speculation based entirely on the coincidence of McIntosh's presence on the plane. Before the week was out, the black box had been found and its tapes later revealed that an engine suddenly going into reverse thrust had caused the crash.

Case history: Hurricane Katrina, 2005

With most disaster stories, like the 2004 Tsunami and 2005 Pakistan earthquake, the media gets it more or less right. But the way we cover disasters, and the sources of immediate information on them, are changing. The classic case of this was the Hurricane Katrina disaster in 2005 when the death toll was widely reported to be 10,000 (wrong by a factor of ten, as it turned out), and papers were full of accounts of multiple rapings, knifings and killings in the New Orleans Convention Center, all now known to be wildly exaggerated.

The errors were in part the result of pressures created by a 24/7 media of TV news channels and the Internet. These encourage journalists to build on each other's scariest death tolls and horror stories until everything is hopelessly exaggerated – a bit like that game you play as children where one lays a hand on another's, and, with hands being madly removed from the bottom and placed on top, you go higher and higher. There is certainly a fear, within a competitive media, of being slow to appreciate what is happening, and of not having the latest death toll. In those circumstances, would you want to be the editor who prints only official death tolls (which can often be days behind events), not the estimates of experts at the scene? The responsible thing is to report both, making plain ('feared dead' is the convention used for unofficial estimates) the source of each figure.

Too bad then, if the experts and local politicians get estimates badly wrong. They were the source of the 10,000 figure, and the media (some of whom grabbed too keenly at a stick with which to beat President Bush) reported it. After all, they didn't have any other answer to the pressing question of how many died because the usual, official channels had broken down. Into this vacuum rushed the 10,000. The same applies to the stories of violence from the Convention Center, and of sniper fire at helicopters. In the absence of official word, the testimony of shelterers and bloggers filled the gap. The alternative is waiting patiently for official word (by no means always true) and suppressing the word on the street. In the days of 'citizen journalists' you can't do that. When I wrote news reports on the Egypt, Bali and Delhi terror bombings, the wires had, in the first few hours, virtually no eye witness accounts. But blogs like the BBC's were full of emailed testimony from those at the scene, and I used them. I had no time to check if these were authentic or invented, I just asked myself if what they described sounded likely, and in my article – which is what Katrina reports should have done – made plain where they had come from. Journalists may not invent things like we used to, but these days we rely, in our first reports of a disaster, far more on 'unofficial' information than we used to and more than we often care to admit.

How to make sure your coverage of a disaster doesn't turn into one

Often the first reports of what turns out to be a major disaster arrive on agency wires as apparently trivial incidents and then build into something huge. Sometimes it can be the other way round, appearing to be a calamity of vast proportions, which later reports correct to a relatively mundane event. Experience teaches you not to rush to make a judgement, and it can give you an instinct for which incidents will blow big and which will stay small. A good guideline is that any incident not immediately downgraded should be treated as potentially big until you have proof to the contrary. No one's reputation has ever been ruined by making a few extra phone calls that prove to be wasted effort, but plenty of journalists have become the life-long butt of office folklore for missing the big story.

The first hint of a potential disaster would probably come in a one-line report over the wires, something like: 'Incident at Heathrow airport at 14.26, involving EuroAir Boeing.' You know the domestic news agency would not bother with complete trivia, but at this stage the incident could be almost anything, from a full-scale crash to merely a small fire which leaves no one injured. So you wait. Then, maybe ten minutes later, the agency reports: 'EuroAir from Frankfurt apparently crashed. No reports yet of fatalities.'

This is the point where a reporter and photographer get sent to the scene, and, if the news editor knows what he or she is doing, one of the better writers assigned to be the story anchor. This is the person who follows the story on the wires and creams off all the best material from the reporters in the field to write the main front-page narrative.

Further reports will now be coming in, making it clear that this is a major disaster. The plane caught fire on landing, over 100 people have died and there are many unanswered questions. As the day goes by, some of them are answered: a EuroAir Boeing 737 had some technical troubles as the plane approached Heathrow Airport. These grew worse. A fire started in one engine, which fell off in mid-air, another engine caught fire, the plane's electrics failed and the pilot had to land manually with only two engines. The engine that fell off landed on a school, which was fortunately unoccupied. More and more information comes in, not in the logical way that's represented here, but in confusing bits and pieces, with retractions and corrections flying in with ever more bizarre details.

The death toll starts at maybe three or four confirmed dead. Then a reporter rings in to say he has spoken to a woman who saw 'many bodies'. Then you learn that on board the plane were the German Trade Minister Dieter Boch, who died in the fire after the crash landing, and rock star Elton John, who helped in the rescue. A press briefing is held where the airline says that the fire started in the cabin after the landing and within ten minutes had engulfed the plane. Only 60 of the 210 passengers are known to have survived, many of them injured. If you are lucky, very lucky, all this will be known in time for your first edition. Normally, however, the incident will be played out over several editions and the first edition has to go to press long before the whole story is known.

And, of course, running alongside this is the uncertainty for most of the day about how bad the disaster is, how may pages should be allocated to it, and how to handle all the day's other news. However, in an ideal world, this is the coverage a serious paper should aim for, and how it should be put together:

- *Chronological narrative of what happened*: You, or the team you are part of, must build up a minute-by-minute, or hour-by-hour, account of what occurred, from the moment it started to its final conclusion. This means never tiring of asking the question: 'And then what happened?' Try to build up a frame-by-frame video of the event in your head. You should also be in regular contact with all emergency services, hospitals and authorities. The main narrative will almost certainly be written by the anchor person and be the core of their account. The bare bones of it can also be written as a 'tick-tock' – a sidebar where entries consist of a few lines on every part of the narrative, each with its precise timing.

- *Eye-witness reports*: These are gathered at the scene by you, wires, freelances and office-based reporters calling people who have been on TV and radio. Reporters sent to a disaster or hospital should make sure they get a precise briefing on what aspect of the story they are expected to file on – colour, quotes, narrative, causes, etc. Without this, you often find several people filing what is essentially the same piece. And don't be upset if your job consists of collecting information and filing it in bits and pieces back to the office. The most common fault with most disaster coverage involving several reporters is that everyone stops reporting too early in order to get down to writing some purple-prosed version of the tale.

- *Cause*: Both the narrow, immediate cause of mechanical failures and, perhaps, the wider cause(s) are vital parts of the story, but it may take time to get hard information on them. Beware, especially, being in a rush to apportion blame. Concentrate instead on reporting the fullest picture of what happened and treat even official theories as speculation until proven. There is a long history of officials thinking aloud – sometimes wildly – about causes of disasters. Papers that report these ideas as established truth subsequently look very silly. Any unsubstantiated theory which involves terrorism or suicide should be treated with particular care, clearly attributed and any lack of proof made plain.

- *The safety record of Boeing 737s*: How many accidents have they been involved in? What were the causes?

- *Profile of EuroAir*: Full details and history of the airline involved, plus possible effects of the crash on the company, share prices, etc. If the airline's headquarters are within reach, a reporter can go and speak to staff about the company and its policies. It may, for instance, be that the airline has been economising recently, cutting back on the regular maintenance of planes in order to try to save money.

- *Profile of the pilot*: According to the information we have, he played a heroic role in landing the plane manually and without two engines. People will want to know about his background and experience.

- *Dieter Boch obituary*: This may not be worth a separate piece, but when anyone prominent dies in a disaster, you should always put a reporter on to researching their life story.
- *Casualties*: Until the dead have identities, they are merely statistics. When you do learn their names, you will want to know who they are, what they did, etc. There are nearly always stories about the person who only caught the plane at the last minute or something similar.
- *The rescue*: What happened on the ground once the plane had crashed? How did the emergency services react? Who were the heroes and heroines of the rescue? How was it carried out?
- *Elton John*: His role in the rescue and the reason for his journey, etc.
- *Chronology of recent crashes*: List of the fatal crashes in Britain in the last ten years, or the major air crashes around the world in the last two years. News agencies routinely supply this.
- *Description of the scene*: Colour from the airfield and inside the airport will be invaluable material for the main anchor piece. Look for detail, and avoid the impressionistic and predictable.
- *The black box*: What is a black box flight recorder? How do they work, what do they record and what do they look like? The black box is one of those objects people always refer to, but know little about, beyond the fact that they are an important part of any crash investigation. It is, for example, not black. A sidebar on the black box could stand on its own or be part of a piece on the investigation that follows.
- *Expert's view*: With many disasters, especially those which are rare, you suddenly need experts to explain technical matters. Plane crashes are not infrequent events, but, even so, an expert on air safety could be interviewed at length or write a piece for the paper. There may, for instance, be a retired former crash investigator who could give some fascinating insights. If you do get hold of experts like that, try to bring them into the office. After all, if they are in your office, other papers cannot get to them.
- *Anchor piece*: All the best information from these above stories (and other enquiries such as the effect on flight schedules and telephone numbers for anxious relatives to ring) would be pulled into the anchor piece. This would be the page one account of the crash and would be long and comprehensive. Normally the best approach is a simple one, with a straightforward, unemotional 'It all began when...' narrative construction, topped off with a few paragraphs of intro. Never try to be tricky, especially with a story that is still unfolding as you write. Report only what is certain and don't leave any hostages to fortune when further and better particulars are known.

Not all of these elements would run as separate pieces, but many would. Some people may think that such coverage would be over the top in scale and scope. But on a story of this size you have a chance to report in depth on a matter of great public interest. Television will bring the immediate news and pictures to people first, but they cannot offer anything like the depth that papers can. A half-hour news programme contains only about as many words as does the front page of the average broadsheet paper. And, although this is not the first consideration, newspapers are judged by their staff and peers on how they cover the big stories. The most common regret in most editors' lives is that there is a big story that they underplayed.

Death tolls

There are two aspects of reporting disasters which often give trouble – death tolls and contacting the relatives of victims. In the first few hours, death tolls are an incessant source of confusion. With natural calamities like floods, the uncertainty can last for days, and, even then, the official toll can prove to be wildly inaccurate. In the Tokyo earthquake of 1923, for instance, newspaper reports of the number of dead went from 10,000 to 500,000, and then to more than one million in just three days. The real figure was about 150,000 and by the time papers had reported that, they had also stated that Mount Fuji had erupted (it hadn't), an island in Sagami Bay had disappeared beneath the tidal waves (not so), and that the Japanese Prime Minister had been assassinated by a frantic mob (also not true).

Early estimates of death tolls are as often a serious undershoot as an overshoot. The trouble is, you never know which until sometime later. However, with luck, there will be sufficient common agreement among the authorities for a reliable round figure to be confidently used. If not, then either take the lower figure from a source that is usually reliable and say 'At least X people died when ...', or take the highest figure that seems educated and say 'Up to X people are feared to have died when ...'. No prizes for guessing which method papers normally favour, but the latter course should not be used as a licence to hype the story. And make sure you know what figure you are being given. Is it the bodies counted, or an estimate of the final toll? And the figures for those injured: is that people hospitalised? Or all wounded, however slightly?

Even the most cautious authorities make big mistakes with death tolls. The Paddington train disaster in London in 1999 was a classic case. Two trains collided in the morning rush hour and it was immediately apparent this was a big incident. Within hours, the main sequence of events had been established, together with a death toll approaching 70. Lurid reports then began to circulate of the 'fireball' that had whipped through the instantly notorious Carriage H at the front of the train. Anyone inside, said officials, would have been instantly incinerated. By the day after the crash, some papers were reporting a death toll of 70-plus as fact and then this grew, on the back of briefings by the fire and police services, to 'perhaps as many as 170'. But when the teams were sent in to search the wreckage in detail, it became apparent that, far from finding Carriage H littered with charred remains, there were no bodies in it at all. What no one – police or journalists – had bothered to do was to talk to the known survivors of Carriage H and ask them how many people were sitting in it. It turned out that, instead of the scores assumed from its capacity, there had been only a dozen. And they all escaped. Within a few days, the death toll had been reduced to 35.

The death call

Calling the relatives of victims is the job that every reporter dreads. You would have to be wired up pretty strangely to think otherwise. The difficulty, at least in the reporter's mind, has a lot to do with the time that has elapsed since the family received the news. It always seems a lot worse to be asked to call or visit the bereaved within hours of the accident, rather than to see them days after their husband, son, wife or daughter died. In the US and other countries, where the police have less control over when names are released than in Europe, you can even find yourself speaking to a family that does not even know their loved one is dead. No wonder that some reporters, when asked to do this job, simply pretend to go through the motions and report back that no one was talking. We've all done it.

The death call is one of the many areas of the job where there can be no hard and fast approach. At one extreme is the idea that the public has a right to be told all details of an incident (including the minutiae of a victim's life). Anything less is regarded as pussyfooting around. If that means bothering the newly bereaved, goes this argument, then so be it. The most insensitive case that I know of involved *Los Angeles Examiner* City Editor, Jim Richardson. According to the autobiography of sportswriter Jim Murray, Richardson once ordered reporter Wayne Sutton to call the mother of a murder victim.

'Don't tell her what happened,' he instructed, 'tell her that her daughter's just won a beauty contest at Camp Roberts. Then get all the information on her.' Sutton did as instructed, and the mother happily confided her daughter's life history. Then Sutton put his hand over the mouthpiece. 'Now what do I do?' he wondered. Richardson looked at him wickedly. 'Now tell her,' he purred.

As a technique (further details are on p. 144), it belongs in a journalistic chamber of horrors. At the other extreme is the idea that any approach to the bereaved is an unjustifiable intrusion and therefore should not be made. Reporters, goes this line, should stick to information that can be gleaned from public sources or those with knowledge but not intimate involvement (such as colleagues or neighbours).

The most intelligent, professional attitude is, I think, to make a sensitive approach to the family, and to offer them a chance to speak. After all, who are you to deprive them of seeing the life of their loved one told, perhaps for the only time, in some concrete way, rather than being a mere name on a list of victims? And a thoughtful approach will often be surprisingly welcomed. Many bereaved want to feel that their relative had a life worth recording, and speaking to the media is also a way they can connect with the outside world and share their grief. In their situation, even talking to a reporter is part of the therapy. *Daily Mirror* reporter, Derek Lambert, wrote in his memoirs:

> Whenever I visited a grief-stricken parent or grieving widow, I was welcomed into the home. Out came the scrap-books – a boy in knee-length shorts, a serviceman grinning fiercely and self-consciously in his best uniform – and out poured the memories. By the time I reached the garden gate, it was I who felt like weeping.

The golden rule is to empathise, an attitude that is central to the excellent advice proferred by the Victims and Media Center at Michigan State University's School of Journalism. Their tips to reporters on death calls are:

- Give victims' families a sense of control. Ask them to tell you when they want to say something that they do not want in the paper. Give them your phone number and tell them that they can call to discuss the story.
- Discuss issues of privacy and confidentiality at the outset. Explain what you need, with whom you plan to talk and for how long.
- Prepare for the possibility that you will deliver bad news – if not the actual death message, then some aspect of it they had not known.
- Approach them without your notebook in hand and then ask if you can take notes. Ask if you can use a tape recorder.
- Acknowledge their loss. Say something like 'I'm sorry this happened to you', 'I'm glad you weren't killed', 'It's not your fault' or 'I'm sorry for your loss'.

If you do follow the last tip, then for heaven's sake never catch yourself saying: 'I know how you feel'. It's highly unlikely that you do. Professors at Michigan State University were once told about a young reporter's interview with a man whose daughter had just been raped and murdered. 'I know how you feel,' the reporter said, 'I remember when my dog died.' Not much comfort to someone who has just lost their only daughter.

Finally, if your contact is by phone, here is a tip on how to handle the angry or upset reaction. It comes from Edna Buchanan, the Pulitzer-Prize winning former crime reporter of the *Miami Herald*. In her 18 years on the paper, she covered more than 5,000 violent deaths and frequently had victims' families slam the phone down on her. Her policy was to wait 60 seconds, then pick up the phone and call again. Often, the person would have changed his or her mind or a more receptive family member would answer. 'This is Edna Buchanan at the *Miami Herald*,' she would say. 'We were cut off.' Buchanan adds:

> It's really important to give them the chance to reconsider because they might immediately regret hanging up or someone in the room might say, 'You should have talked to the reporter.' If they hang up again, I don't give it a third chance. But more than half the time, they'd do it again on a second try.

All reporters are tough, aren't they?

Finally, how well do you think most reporters would handle being part of a disaster? Everyone thinks that reporters are as hard as flint. Cynical, cold, calculating and maybe even a little cruel. The sort of people who can look a corpse in the eye – and smile. A person, in fact, like Ben Hecht, co-author of 'The Front Page' and a reporter with the *Chicago Daily News*.

In the late 1910s and 1920s Hecht covered every low-life, sordid kind of story that this roaring city of gangsters had to offer. His beat was the mortuary and the police raid, the courtroom and the condemned cell. His daily conversations were with killers and freaks, psychopaths and perverts. He had seen everything Chicago's dregs had to offer and always managed to keep his head and stomach from turning.

Until one day, when he attended the trial of a man who had slaughtered his entire family. It seemed like just another case to Hecht as he sat in the crowded reporters' gallery watching the murderer, a great giant of a man, stand impassive before the judge for sentencing. The judge calmly pronounced death by hanging, and, at this, the giant came suddenly to life. Shouting 'Hang me, will you?' he produced from his jacket a long butcher's knife and plunged it into the judge's heart. The judge fell forward gasping out his life.

Stunned silence gripped the court. Everyone, including the hardened Hecht, was frozen. Everyone, that is, except a little reporter from a rival paper called the *Inter-Ocean*. Hecht could see him writing furiously, the only reporter out of 30 who had nerves strong enough to not be diverted from his task. He scribbled on a moment more, filling several small pages, then yelled 'Copyboy!', and a youth sprang forward to take the scoop off to the telephones.

Hecht later recalled: 'None of us in the courtroom had the presence of mind to write a single word, paralysed as we were by the attack. Yet here was this guy from the *Inter-Ocean*, who had nerves of steel, who had never paused in doing his job. I just had to find out what he had written.' Hecht ran after the copyboy, caught him by the arm, and grabbed the pages. On them, written over and over again in a shaky hand, were the words: 'The judge has been stabbed, the judge has been stabbed, the judge has been stabbed ...'.

> *When you hear something described by a journalist as disturbing, you know you cannot take it seriously.*
>
> Kenneth Robinson

11

Mistakes, Corrections and Hoaxes

Perhaps an editor might divide his paper into four chapters; heading the first,
Truths; the second, Probabilities; the third, Possibilities; and fourth, Lies.
                                                                Thomas Jefferson

Once upon a time, newspapers did not make mistakes. If that reads like
the beginning to a fairy tale, that's because it is one. Newspapers did make
mistakes; it's just that they did not admit them – or at least not unless
forced to do so by lawyers. For decades, the Press preferred to be confident
liars than seekers after the truth.

This pretence of infallibility was absurd. Inaccurate reporting produced
(and is producing) millions of wrong details, false accounts and not a
few spectacularly duff stories. On the 15 April 1912, for instance, the
Baltimore Evening Sun ran a story headlined 'All Titanic Passengers Safe'.
On 3 November 1948, the *Chicago Daily Tribune* proclaimed 'Dewey
defeats Truman' and on May 1983, *The Times* declared all over its front
page 'Hitler's Secret Diaries to be published'. As contemporaries knew
very soon after each of these stories appeared, 1,500 died on the Titanic,
Harry Truman beat Dewey and the diaries were not written by Hitler but
by a little German crook called Konrad Kujau.

These days, newspapers of quality do admit mistakes and they put
them right as soon as they can. They recognise that stories are written
by fallible human beings under great pressure and without access to all
the sources. Inevitably, some errors will creep in. They fall into one of
six categories:

- Errors of detail – names, ages, addresses, etc.
- Errors of narrative – false part of an otherwise true account.
- Hoaxes and inventions – where the entire story is fiction.
- Errors of context – incorrect or missing background causing a false
  account.

- Errors of omission – an account made misleading by a missing part.
- Errors of interpretation – adding two and two and coming up with five.

The better papers such as the *Chicago Tribune* also have a system for recording and tracking mistakes, and attempting to put right any part of their processes that caused the error. Such papers have learnt a great deal about how mistakes arise, and who makes them. And the truth is that no group of journalists produce more errors than reporters. According to surveys carried out at The *Guardian* and the *Fort Worth Star-Telegram* in Texas, reporters made half the errors that were published. (Copy editors were responsible for about one mistake in five.) This is an important insight for the papers and even more for individual writers; for nothing destroys a reporter's reputation faster (or more comprehensively) than a record of generating errors.

Reporters serious about not falling into this category should realise two things. First that the accuracy of their stories is their responsibilty and is not something that can be passed up the production chain to a news editor or copy editor. Second, train yourself to be so aware of how errors creep in that checking for these potential ambushes becomes second nature. Learn not just from your mistakes but also from those of others. When you see a correction in a paper, think of how it might have occurred.

Mistakes

There are 13 main causes of errors in stories:

False information from sources

With simple facts like names, dates and ages there is said to be not a lot you can do about wrong information. I disagree. You can double-check, ask yourself if the source is in a position to know what they are telling, listen out for the tell-tale clues to uncertainty ('I think...', '...probably...', '...or so I was told...', etc.) and ask if the information sounds plausible. Often a little reflection will tell you that it does not. A related source of error is to take information given to you (perhaps in the midst of an as-yet unclear situation) and present it as unattributed fact, rather than a sourced contention. This was where the *Titanic* error was made, because the papers took on trust assurances from the ship's owners, the White Star Line, and did not attribute them when reporting the passengers were all saved.

Poor note-taking

Shaky notes – from an uncertain shorthand outline to a long-hand word that could be this or could be that – often make shaky stories. Time to brush up on the short-hand or handwriting. And don't guess what sources meant – ask them again. Few will mind as much as you imagine, if at all. And learn to ask them to spell out, or write down, names.

Failure to double-check 'facts' with sources

Often one source tells you something that contradicts an earlier source. Check it, double check it and triple check it, if necessary. The same applies to working from documents. A few seconds checking that you have copied figures and names correctly will save untold grief.

Wishing something is true

There is, probably, no finer example of this than the events described in a correction published by the Warren, Ohio *Tribune Chronicle* in 2008: 'It was incorrectly reported in Tuesday's *Tribune Chronicle* that Sen Hillary Rodham Clinton answered questions from voters in a local congressman's office. Reporter John Goodall spoke by telephone with Hillary Wicai Viers, who is a communications director in US Rep Charlie Wilson's staff. According to the reporter, when Viers answered the phone with "This is Hillary", he believed he was speaking with the Democratic presidential candidate ... The quotes from Viers were incorrectly attributed to Clinton.' Oh dear.

Reluctance to check 'sensational' facts or developments

There is a smirking part of the culture of journalism which discourages reporters from checking too closely the more outrageous parts of stories, lest someone deny them or water them down. Such perilous idiocy flies in the face of generations of experience, which is that few stories are as straightforward, black and white, or outrageous as they first appear. If you were not born with healthy scepticism, acquire some.

Failure to read a story once written

We all make typing errors when working quickly, and we also have 'facts' in our heads that are not borne out by our notes. A read for accuracy (apart from one for style and possible cuts) stops a lot of these errors.

Trusting websites too much

Until the early 1990s, getting a news story published required its approval by an editor or two. Not any more. Now, anyone can start a website, post an item on a blog or message board, and watch it take off into global circulation. Thus has been created the biggest hoax and false information machine in history – a 24-hour trap for gullible, desperate, or lazy journalists.

It was a combination of this – plus ignorance of the nature of the source – which led, in 2002, the *Beijing Evening News* to reproduce as true a story from The Onion, the well-known American satirical news site. Unaware that The Onion specialised in concocting such stories as 'Apollo 13 Astronauts Drown as Ted Kennedy Flees Splashdown Site', and 'Nagasaki Bombed Just For The Hell of It', the Beijing paper took as fact an item that the US Congress – dismayed that there are not enough places to entertain lobbyists in the old Capitol building – intends to move to Memphis, home of Elvis Presley, where a new seat of government will be built, complete with luxury hospitality boxes.

Many internet hoaxes stay largely confined to web news sites, like the story a few years ago about the prosecution of Irishman Thomas McCarney for bringing a donkey into a Galway hotel room. The tale went that the donkey swallowed the room key, ran amok in the corridor, and Mr McCarney was arrested still wearing his latex nightwear and handcuffs. He was duly charged under the Unlawful Accommodation of Donkeys Act of 1837. It was all nonsense, of course, but beautifully constructed, and websites all over the world carried it with no hint that it might be baloney. This despite the fact that the hotel receptionist quoted was a Ms Irina Legova – something of a clue.

Failure to listen to your own anxieties about a story

Any experienced reporter knows the feeling of having a 'sensational' story, which will make big headlines, but about which they have some anxieties. It does not quite ring true, it does not fit with what you know of the world, etc. The mistake is to charge ahead, afraid that caution will rob you of front page glory. Instead, listen to those doubts. Most of the time they will prove correct. Many of the errors I have made were when my show-off ego would not heed the wise doubts of the sensible little journalist in my head.

Omission of facts not fitting with a pre-conceived (or too-rapidly conceived) theory

Making your mind up about a situation before knowing all the facts (although you can never know *all* the facts) is one of the great traps a journalist must perpetually fight to avoid. It is an ever-present danger on major incident stories, for there is then great pressure to deliver both a seemingly all-knowing account and a pat explanation for the incident. A classic case was the riots at Strangeways Prison in Manchester, described in Chapter 10 on Disasters.

Rushing into print too early

This was the mistake with the Hitler Diaries. The anxiety to protect an exclusive property (exacerbated by the belief within News International that, ultimately, entertainment and not truth was the object of journal-ism) meant that the story was published before all the scientific checks were made. This fear of being scooped rushed Murdoch into sanctioning publication, despite strongly expressed misgivings by some of his most senior *Sunday Times* journalists. The pitfalls of dashing into print with a story that is far more emphatic than the evidence warrants is a frequent cause of major errors on stories large and small. The moral is obvious – publish only that of which you are certain.

(Note the absence of fatigue and inexperience from this list. They are not causes of errors, but excuses for them.)

Failure to clear technical material with experts

A young, inexperienced reporter interviews a leading expert about a complex issue in medicine or science. Does she email her copy to the expert before publication to check it is right? Not in Britain she doesn't. There, taking this elementary precaution is seen as a sign of journalistic weakness, and on the first paper I worked for showing your copy to a source was actually a sackable offence. I was always uncomfortable with this 'don't show the sources' policy. And so, in recent years I have taken to emailing a finished story to whoever was its most helpful expert source. (If time was short, I telephoned and read part of it.) The result? A source so pleasantly surprised they became a helpful contact for ever more, the elimination of errors, and the placing of a correct version on the record. Most of the top specialist reporters follow the same policy.

Over-reliance on cuttings

Journalists use cuttings files as a crib more than they admit, and an error made by one reporter can reproduce down the years like a persistent virus. Consider this: in 2003, the *Virginian-Pilot* newspaper carried a light-hearted correction of its original story on the first flight, by the Wright brothers. That 1903 story contained no fewer than 33 errors, quite a few of which, I would guess, have been reproduced down the years by writers going to the *Virginian-Pilot* cutting. Journalists even make mistakes when reporting their own colleagues. For my book, *The Great Reporters*, I researched a well-known reporter before interviewing her, and took extensive notes from a recent newspaper profile. Before our meeting, I went to a library where her past stories are lodged, and there found a copy of this profile. Attached was a letter from her itemising 12 errors. I noted these, and, after meeting her, sent her a copy of my piece. She spotted four more mistakes, which I duly corrected. Why should that show weakness? You are not letting the source have 'copy approval' – the demand made by, and often shamefully granted to, film stars – you are merely, and sensibly, letting them in on the process of information gathering. And, of course, you, not they, have the final say.

Production errors

Not all errors are due to bad reporting. Copy editors, page editors and news editors can all introduce mistakes. For instance, a couple of years ago, the Berlin correspondent of my London national Sunday paper filed a story on renovations to the city's 1936 Olympic Stadium, and mentioned that it was in this arena that Jesse Owens won four gold medals. I put it through to the production department, they put it on the page, and the proof was duly read. All was well. Then some late-night copy editor, casting about for something to do, decided to 'improve' this item, so that it now read: '...Jesse Owens won *her* four ...'

Some of the most spectacular production errors involve photographs. In 2003, copies of the *Newbury Weekly News*, a local paper in the south of England, had to be recalled after a story about a priest facing child pornography charges carried the likeness of another, entirely blameless, churchman. Pictures of the unfamiliar can indeed be an accident waiting to happen, witness the apology once carried by the *Pasack Valley Community Life* in the US: 'In last week's issue, a picture caption listed some unusual gourmet dishes enjoyed at a Westwood Library party ... Mai Thai Finn was in the center of the photo. We incorrectly listed her name as one of the items on the menu ...'. The *Independent on Sunday*'s worst in this regard was when a photograph was ordered up of Gandhi, and captioned accordingly. Sad to say, the published picture was not that of the great man, but of actor Ben Kingsley playing him in a film. But for real 'heart-in-the-mouth, I'm-glad-that-wasn't-me' error, you must turn to a recent issue of the *Southern Reporter* in Scotland. This particular calamity arose from the ill-advised practice of the designer of the page writing some jocular words where the caption should be, safe in the assumption that a copy-editing colleague will replace them with something more suitable before the page goes to press. In this case, that did not happen. The paper carried a picture of people at a traditional Scottish ceremony, underneath which was written: 'Who are these pious *****ers? What on earth is going on in this picture – these people have got to get out more often for their peace of mind and sanity.' Exit one editor.

Then there are the idiocies of headline writers. Some are the result of not seeing all the implications of the words used: ('One-legged Escapee

Still On The Run' – *The Australian*, 'Man In River Thames Had Drink Problem' – *Reading Chronicle*, and 'Slimmer of the Year Vanishes' – *Daily Mail*); others betray an almost superhuman talent for stating the obvious ('Party Ends After Woman Is Murdered' – *Mooresville Tribune*, N. Carolina, and 'Some teens have an air of defiance' – *Washington Post)*.

But, in general, production errors are far less common than writer's slips, most of which are never seen by readers because copy-editors see them first. Sometimes they are impossible to spot, like the piece of bad reporting that once resulted in a sentence in the *New York Times* having no fewer than five mistakes. My favourite in this genre is the correction from a paper in Newcastle, northern England on a story about a woman's death from a rare disease. It read in part:

> We would like to point out that she did not go to her doctor complaining of a spot on her leg and she was not prescribed painkillers. She did not return to her GP for a second visit, nor was she taken into hospital on October 26. She was not rushed into emergency surgery and her death was not due to massive organ failure. Furthermore, her father is aged 45, not 52 a stated, her mother is 46, not 50, and her sister is 26, not 27.

Finally, for reporters who think the importance of accuracy is not quite all it's cracked up to be, a sobering story. It appeared in the *C-Ville Weekly*, a tabloid circulating in Charlottesville, Virginia. It told of the discovery by a female health club client of a two-way mirror that had been installed in the women's changing room. The paper also carried pictures and detailed graphics. The story went on to speculate freely (via quotes from a psychologist) about the motives of the person who had set up such a peephole. The story proved true in every detail, which was just as well because five days after it appeared, the owner of the health club was found dead in a local park. He had committed suicide. The repercussions for the reporter, had the story proved inaccurate in any way, hardly bear thinking about. The tale is a reminder that, since you never know the effects your stories can have, they had better be correct.

How should you respond to mistakes?

'Quickly and with candour' is the answer. This applies in spades if, as is often the case, you realise your mistake before anyone else does. Move speedily – there may be time to correct the mistake before the story is published, or, on larger papers, to correct between editions. Even if it is too late, a prompt confession (and, if the mistake is bad enough, contacting the source affected) will help to mitigate the consequences for the paper legally and for you personally. My experience is that, providing the error is not too crass, journalists who speedily hold their hands up and take responsibility emerge with reputations far less damaged than those who lurk in the shadows waiting to be unmasked. Those are the ones who are sacked.

With complaints from outside the paper, the first thing is to establish that the 'mistake' definitely is one. Sources often try it on, especially those whose openness with you may have caused them trouble within their own organisation. Many claims, especially of mis-quotation, prove to be nothing more than sources trying to cover their tracks.

Once an error has been established, a speedy correction should be published, preferably in a regular place. Some papers, such as the *Mobile Register* in Alabama, run all corrections on page one. At the Cleveland *Plain Dealer*, the correction goes as close as it can to where the original mistake was published and is indexed on page 2. The *Augusta Chronicle* does the same and, if the mistake occurs on page 1, then that's where the correction goes. Such policies are not an admission of weakness, but a simple matter of honesty and better informing the reader.

(Promptness is another virtue in corrections, but on a few occasions newspapers have not been deterred by the passage of time. In 1920 the *New York Times* publicly ridiculed Professor Robert Goddard, the father of space exploration, for his claim that rockets could operate in a vacuum. Some 49 years later, when Apollo 11 carried the first men to the moon, the *Times* published the following: 'It is now definitely established that a rocket can function in a vacuum. The *Times* regrets its error.' The record, however, is the 199 years that elapsed between the *Observer* of London reporting the death of Mozart as having happened on 5 December 1791 and it correcting this date to 3 December in early 1991.)

Honesty is not the only motive in correcting errors. Avoiding a law suit is also a pretty powerful reason for prompt correction. Some years ago, the following appeared in an Irish newspaper: 'In the edition of the *Sunday Press* dated March 18 1990 a photograph of Proinsias De Rossa TD was published with the caption "prospective monster". This should have read "prospective minister".' Similarly an English local paper ran this correction to a court report: '"Father head butts his son" should have read, "Father head butts his son's attacker".' And this, from the *Austin American-Statesman*: 'The band Raging Saint bases its music on born-again Christian principles. They are not "unrepentant headbangers" as reported in the Nightlife column last Friday.'

You can almost hear the rustle of potential legal proceedings in the distance as you read these corrections. No doubt the editors who ordered them into print were well aware that speedy correction can help stave off a defamation lawsuit, or at least form part of the subsequent defence.

Gilbert Cranberg, the former editorial page editor of the *Des Moines Register*, who surveyed 164 libel plaintiffs in 1987, found that most people who sued for libel did not originally want money. They wanted a correction. Only after they were brushed off by the paper did they then go to law.

However, unless corrections are being carried at the point of a lawyer's writ, they merely have to recall the mistake and amend it. There is no need to grovel, promise you won't do it again, apologise or launch into an explanation of how it was the regular editor's night off and his assistant was feeling under the weather. A few publications, like *American Lawyer,* actually name the reporter and editor who made the mistake. Others, like the *San Jose Mercury News,* go the other way and have eliminated any words of blame such as 'due to an editing error', etc. And there is, somewhere, a limit to what can be sensibly corrected. For instance, on the day after it carried a review of a new cartoon film, the *Boston Globe* carried the following: 'In our film review yesterday, statements made by Sylvester the Cat were erroneously attributed to Daffy Duck.'

Finally, factual errors are easy to correct; other types less so. Many complaints to newspapers centre on inappropriate or missing context, or a missing element which alters the overall story or the impression it gives. For these, papers can offer space in the letters page, or, more rarely, comment columns. To deal with such cases, the *New York Times* runs an Editors' Note to 'amplify articles or rectify what the editors consider significant lapses of fairness, balance or perspective.' It publishes about 25 of them annually. It is a useful device that deserves to be more widely copied.

Great newspaper hoaxes

In 1976 the following advertisement appeared in New York's *Village Voice*:

Cathouse for Dogs
Featuring a savoury selection of hot bitches. From pedigree (Fifi, the French poodle) to mutts (Lady the Tramp). Handler and Vet on duty. Stud and photo service available. No weirdos please. Dogs only. By appointment. Call 254 7878.

The same day a press release from the dogs' brothel was sent out, and, as stories appeared about the dog brothel, calls from pet owners (plus weirdos) flooded in. ABC began filming a documentary, requests for press visits came in and the story began to grow in other ways. The American Society for the Prevention of Cruelty to Animals called for the brothel's closure, as did the Bureau of Animal Affairs, vice squad, mayor's office and various religious and moral busybodies. The controversy was reported with relish. The US Attorney General even served a subpoena to the address of the service for illegally running a cathouse for dogs.

It was at this point that the man behind it all, one Joey Scaggs, stepped forward and revealed it was all a hoax.

Such attempts to hoodwink the press are by no means as uncommon as journalists think. Assorted hustlers, anarchists, gold-diggers and funsters have provided a rich history of spoof stories that found their way into print. Faked documents have been particularly successful. The Hitler Diaries took in *The Times*, *Sunday Times*, *Stern* magazine and others; the 'memoirs' of Howard Hughes (actually written by Clifford Irving) fooled *Life* magazine into paying $250,000; the Parnell Letters which expressed the Irish leader's approval of political murders humiliated *The Times* when it proved to have been written by a man called Pigott for cash; and the Zinoviev Letter showing the Labour Party as a 'front' for Moscow was eagerly swallowed by the *Daily Mail* and conveniently published on election day in 1924. It was a forgery. These are well-known cases, but other hoaxes deserve a wider audience.

The radiation-proof cockroach

United Press International was once approached by Dr. Joseph Gregor, a leading world entomologist, and persuaded that he had developed a strain of nuclear-proof cockroach. Their extracted hormones would cure arthritis, acne and anaemia and protect people from radiation. The resultant story, 'Roach hormone held as miracle drug' was sent round the world by UPI. Dr. Gregor was, of course, dog brothel inventor Joey Scaggs.

The topless string quartet

Large sections of the US press were duped in 1967 by stories about a forthcoming tour by these bare-breasted female musicians from France. The inspiration for this nonsense was one Alan Abel, who sent out press releases explaining that the musicians needed to play *sans* clothes in order to produce 'pure and unhampered tones'. He also hired four models to pose in white gowns for publicity shots. After the stories appeared, requests for recitals came in and Frank Sinatra's Reprise label even offered them a recording contract.

The earliest sayings of Jesus

In May 1991 the *Financial Times* published a long article about the discovery of what seemed to be the earliest surviving text of the sayings of Jesus. Only when the article was published did the paper realise the significance of the name of the supposed discoverer of the priceless find – Batson D. Sealing.

The Society for Indecency to Naked Animals

This was one of the more elaborate newspaper hoaxes, perpetrated by Alan Abel. The Society for Indecency to Naked Animals was invented by Alan Abel in 1959. Abel hired an jobless actor called Buck Henry to impersonate the fictional founder of the society, G. Clifford Prout Jr. He appeared on NBC's 'Today Show' to demand all animals over four inches high should be clothed for decency's sake, and Abel hired pickets to protest outside the White House and even set up a phone line and operator to take calls. Many newspapers published stories. The cover story was that SINA had been set up with money left to Prout by his father. This attracted the attention of the tax authorities and the IRS wrote to demand back tax. When no reply came, they visited SINA's offices, found a broom cupboard, and realised it was a hoax. Buck Henry went on to better things, getting a part in a soap opera and becoming a successful writer and actor in such TV series and movies as 'Get Smart', 'The Graduate', 'Catch-22' and 'To Die For'.

The Fat Squad

In 1983, John Corr of the *Philadelphia Inquirer* got a press release about a group of toughies called the Fat Squad, who were hired by the obese to physically restrain them from over-eating. Corr rang the man named as the organiser, Joe Bones, and wrote the story, which was then widely picked up. The affair climaxed with an appearance on ABC's 'Good Morning America' by Joe Bones and his strong arm squad. Joe Bones turned out to be persistent hoaxer Joey Skaggs. Some reporters, however, wise up before writing a story. One of Alan Abel's inventions was 'the Klu Klux Klan Symphony Orchestra', allegedly scraping away on their violins in an attempt to change the KKK's image. *Arizona Republic* reporter Julia Lobaco rumbled this straight away.

The great blonde extinction

In 2002, the BBC, NBC TV affiliates, British national tabloids and many other papers round the world reported that the gene responsible for blonde hair would die out by the year 2022. The forecast was attributed to the World Health Organisation, or 'experts in Germany'. The WHO disclaimed any role in the story (and pointed out the scientific idiocy of it), and, of course, the 'experts in Germany' were anonymous and so untraceable. A hoax, or irresponsible, small-time, news agency seem the most likely origin of the story.

Central to the success of all these hoaxes was the simple failure to check, and a taking at face value press releases or calls from plausible new 'sources'. Preventing such attempts being printed should be a straightforward matter of not letting the desire to get your byline on such stories overwhelm the simple precautions of asking questions and knocking on a few doors. Hoaxes are so much easier to perpetrate on reporters who never leave their offices.

The money paid for stories by some popular papers is so high (the *Sun* spends millions of pounds a year on payments to sources and freelances) that there have even been one or two people who earned a living as professional newspaper hoaxers. The best of them was probably a film stuntman called Rocky Ryan, alias Major Travis, Peter Bernstein, David Oppenheimer, Rocco Salvatore or one of the other false names he regularly used. He sold the *People* (a mass-market Sunday newspaper) a story about sex and drugs orgies among a Himalayan expedition, and to other media a tale that Gorbachev had resigned two years before he actually did (with the result that millions of dollars were lost on the foreign exchange markets), plus a story that top Nazi Martin Bormann was alive and well and living on a kibbutz in Israel. None of them was true.

He also made $18,000 by concocting transcripts of a phone conversation between Prince Charles and Princess Diana and then stung papers into paying for this. He got an actress friend to phone the *People* to say a friend in the security services wanted to talk about the royals. She gave a number in a smart part of London, and when the paper rang the telephone was answered by another friend who said he worked for British intelligence. He explained that they had been bugging Prince Charles's phone. He said he was prepared to sell the transcript of the phone conversation for $7,500. The *People* bought it, as did other papers. The reason they fell for it was that the hoaxers were giving them a story they wanted to believe was true – the art of the confidence trickster down the ages.

Journalism constructs momentarily arrested equilibriums and gives disorder an implied order. That is already two steps from reality.

Thomas Griffiths

12

Ethics

A gifted man who isn't interested in money is very hard to tame.
Alistair Cooke of the BBC

To the outsider, journalism and ethics are about as incongruous a mixture as you can get. Even to put the two words in the same sentence is to risk reducing the listener to helpless laughter.

To the insider on a mass-market tabloid, ethics are largely an irrelevance. Editors, pressured by intense competition for readers, demand that staff cut ethical corners; and competition among staff encourages some to respond. Lecturing these journalists about ethics is as pointless as advocating celibacy to sailors arriving in port after six months at sea.

To the insider working on a quality paper, where there is virtually unanimous agreeement about basic professional morality, ethics are a code of principles to which all journalists should adhere, or at least feel guilty about if they do not. They are rarely, if ever, required to step outside this code.

Ethics, more than any other aspect of the job, are where personal circumstance produces experiences so that the different ethics employed are barely recognisable as the same thing. The reason is that ethics, as actually practised, are conditioned less by morals than by what is rewarded or punished in any given newspaper. On a British mass market tabloid (or agency serving one) journalists may be regarded, paid and promoted according to how many dramatic, possibly invasive, stories they produce. Not too many questions are asked about how they obtained them or what degree of exaggeration is involved. Indeed the news desk, or higher executives, often tell reporters what line they want, regardless of any reservations reporters have. Not much scope for Mr. or Ms. Proper here. At the other extreme – on a US paper enjoying a monopoly and sharing the same city as its sources and readers – reporters are judged and rewarded differently, with ethics playing a far greater part in their lives.

Ultimately the main factor in deciding what ethics are actually practised is competition. In monopoly situations, papers know that there is no rival paper to scoop them, and readers have no alternative to turn to – save for giving up papers altogether. This lack of competition gives the journalists the moral luxury of generally being able to apply far more idealised standards of professional ethics. In a mass market, highly competitive and with a macho culture, almost the only sanction on what papers will do to get a story, or publish once they have got it, is the prospect of upsetting readers, especially to the point where they will not buy the paper. Only then will word go out to the staff, and the little news agencies that feed them, that it is time to call a halt (perhaps only temporarily) to stealing pictures from the bereaved, invading hospitals where sick celebrities are being treated, publishing pictures of royal children in private moments, condemning a community for violence without sufficient evidence, or whatever. On tabloids especially, the periodic little eruptions of ethics that are sometimes seen nearly always come from proprietors acutely aware that readers can always, and maybe are about to, buy another paper. Or that the government is about to legislate.

But journalists have a sanction, too. We do not have to be mere creatures of the papers we work for; we have a choice. Just as readers can stop buying, so journalists can change jobs. We can decide that there are some things we will not do and leave the paper – either discreetly after having found another post, or publicly, in a blaze of righteous indignation. If more of us did that, and made clear our reasons for doing so, journalism would be better for it.

This element of moral choice, the distinction between how papers acting under commercial pressures expect us to behave and how we can choose to behave, explains why ethics have a daily purpose – or rather, two purposes. The first is to provide some kind of moral compass, telling us how far we are diverging from a desired route. So far as I know, the magnetic north in our trade is found in the clauses of an unwritten contract which should exist between all newspapers and their readers:

- Every story in the paper is a result of decisions made free of political, commercial or non-commercial pressure.
- None are there because of any favours or money exchanged.
- All stories are written and edited in a spirit of free enquiry, and chosen for publication entirely on their own merits, be they real or imagined.

Second, ethics provides a practical guide to the production of safe and credible journalism. Honestly, with plain dealing and with the removal of conflicts of interest are the best ways to do this job because they are the safest ways to do it. At the most base level, they keep you out of the courts and help you to sleep at nights. And, at the risk of shocking some of the more raunchy reporters, ethics are the most decent way to do the job, too, giving us attitudes to readers (and sources) that are based on some sensitivity, rather than mere sly commercial calculation.

Viewed like this, ethics are not some optional extra but are integral to every aspect of the job. This book therefore deals with them as they occur – in handling sources, asking questions, writing, etc. – and not in some moral parking lot tucked away from the main action. There are, however, some general principles and these have been gathered together in this chapter.

General guidelines

There is a thought about ethics which I have found very useful throughout my career. It will sound exceedingly wet, as if this paragraph has been inserted into the book by the Society For Being Rather Nice To Each Other. But I am going to pass it on anyway, since it has proved so valuable to me. The thought is this: treat other people, especially sources and the subjects of stories, as you would like to be treated yourself. Written down, it does seem almost embarrassingly trite, but it will be a better guide to ethics than a hundred lectures on the subject. In fact, I would say that treating people as decently as you can will turn pretty much every ethical 'dilemma' into a clearer course of action. The alternative – treating people like temporary conveniences to be betrayed when it suits – is neither very attractive, nor a way to last long in this trade, at least not on newspapers worth working for.

If you doubt that, consider the behaviour of a US news editor many decades ago. Whilst it did not actually involve breaking the law, it is possibly the least ethical piece of journalism I have ever come across. It began when he received news that a young woman had just been found murdered. Her home state was a long way away, very little was known about her, and the news editor knew that if a reporter rang and told her parents of her death, they would not talk much. So he told a rewrite man to ring them, say that the girl had won a local beauty contest, and extract as much information as he could. He stood by the man's desk while he interviewed the parents, who were still oblivious of their daughter's death. Then, when he felt enough background, he hissed: 'OK, now tell 'em', and stood there while the reporter broke the news that their daughter was now a corpse. I had always assumed this was an urban legend, until I read a copy of an out-of-print book called *Reporters: Memoirs of a Young Newspaperman* by Will Fowler. In it, he reveals that the incident really did happen. The news editor was Jim Richardson of the *Los Angeles Examiner*, the date 1947, the rewrite man Wayne Sutton, the dead girl Elizabeth Short (whose killing, now known to history as The Black Dahlia case, is probably that city's most famous murder), and the poor parent was Mrs Phoebe May Short of Medford, Massachusetts. The story may seem amusing in a horrifying way at this distance in time, but I doubt Mrs Short ever saw it that way. (Will Fowler, by the way, was no angel himself. Once, he worked on the story of Mr Walter Overell, a wealthy property developer killed by his daughter and her boyfriend by means of a home-made bomb. No contemporary photograph of Mr Overell existed, and all that was left of him was a head and torso. What to do? Fowler and photographer George O'Day went to the undertakers, got them to prop the upper half of Mr Overell against a wall, took its picture, and then had an artist at the *Examiner* paint a coat, collar and striped tie onto the victim. No newspaper photograph has more deserved the phrase 'a head and shoulders').

If following the example of Jim Richardson does not appeal, here are some general guidelines on ethics:

Journalists should serve only their papers and their readers

If you want to be a propagandist, then go and work in public relations, or politics. Journalists should owe no loyalty to anyone or anything else; not a political party, source, commercial interest, non-commercial interest or particular cause, however worthy. Balanced journalism is difficult enough to achieve without such conflicts of interest. The *Washington Post* newspaper has a rule that its journalists cannot take part in any political activity. That includes marching on demonstrations. So when several *Post* reporters were spotted on an abortion rights demonstration, they were told they would not be allowed to cover anything touching on the abortion issue.

The dangers of allowing a missionary zeal for some cause to infect reporting are even more obvious. One of the more notorious examples is Walter Duranty, the *New York Times* correspondent in Moscow in the 1920s and 1930s. So taken was he by the ideology of the new Soviet Union that his reporting was often little more than propaganda. At the height of the famine in the Ukraine, for instance, largely engineered by Stalin to break local resistance to Soviet control, Duranty wrote of 'village markets overflowing with eggs, fruit, poultry, vegetables, milk and butter' at prices far lower than in Moscow. 'Anyone can see this is not famine, but abundance', he added; and a Pulitzer committee, knowing no better, gave him a prize. In fact, millions died, and Duranty knew this full well, telling colleagues in private that he thought the death toll was around ten million. Malcolm Muggeridge, the *Manchester Guardian's* reporter in Moscow at the time, called him 'the biggest liar of any journalist I have ever met.'

Every story should be an honest search for the truth

Each story should be an open-minded attempt to find out what really happened, accompanied by a willingness to print that truth, however uncomfortable it may be to our own, or the paper's, cherished beliefs.

Thus, journalists should not accept work which seeks to bolster a point of view in the face of evidence, or undertake reporting which aims to support a preconceived theory.

You would think this so self-evident that it would not need stating. But every day you can read reporting which stretches and strains the facts to fit a particular thesis. One of the worst examples in recent memory was committed by the *Sun*, Britain's biggest-selling daily. For reasons best known to himself, the then editor became convinced that Aids was a disease limited to drug addicts and homosexuals. On several occasions government statistics were wilfully manhandled to support this view. The most flagrant occasion was a story headlined 'Straight Sex Cannot Give You Aids – Official', which reported, among other absurdities, that the chances of getting Aids from heterosexual sex were 'statistically invisible. Anything else is homosexual propaganda.' Eventually, the volume of protests at this coverage produced an apology – which the paper ran at the bottom of page 28.

Here, and this is no isolated case, was reporting that deceived readers and possibly endangered them. Preconceived theories have no place in journalism. Newspapers should be at war with closed minds, not employing them.

No inducements to publish should be accepted

This means not only money and free gifts, but also the promise of advantage or preferment. It specifically means two things. The first is hidden advertising, where journalists or their papers take money for writing public relations pieces about firms or people which then appear in the editorial columns parading as normal stories. In recent years this has become a widespread practice in countries like Russia, and the temptation to write hidden advertising in places where pay is very poor is understandable. But that does not make it journalism. It is advertising, PR, puffs, whatever you call it, dressed up to look like journalism. It is a deception, and a damaging one. First, it breaks the basic contract with readers, with stories, purporting to be a normal editorial, in print only because money has changed hands. Second, such deceptions destroy any trust that should exist between readers and papers. Third, the practice makes editors suspect their staff have taken bribes to write about a company when their story may be perfectly honest. Fourth, editors and publishers will, like hotel owners paying waiters low salaries because of tips, use hidden advertising as an excuse not to pay journalists properly. Fifth, it establishes that the journalists who do it have their pens and minds available for hire. What will they accept money for next? Writing favourable stories about criminal groups? Keeping stories about wrong-doing out of the paper? That is but a short step away from collecting information with a view to selling its destruction or suppression. In other words, blackmail.

(Lest anyone think this a good original money-making scheme, an American publisher called Robert Harrison got there first in the 1950s with a magazine called *Confidential*. It specialised in Hollywood scandal and, by paying large sums for tips and information, he and his investigators obtained decidedly intimate details of the stars' private lives. Each story was well-researched and Harrison's staff were not fussy about their methods, hiring prostitutes to trap victims, secretly taping and filming encounters and confessions. Sales of *Confidential* soared and eventually hit four million. But soon the temptation to sell the negatives, tapes and other evidence to wealthy stars proved too strong. The inevitable court case happened, a staff member killed herself, the editor shot his wife and himself in a New York taxicab, Harrison sold the magazine and both he and it went into a richly-deserved oblivion.)

Hidden advertising (which should be correctly labelled 'advertising' and typographically treated accordingly), is very rare in developed countries. Far more common is the acceptance by journalists of what they call 'freebies', that is, free trips with vacation companies, free meals from restaurants or free tickets from theatres, all given so that journalists can review them. The danger here is that the writer will feel obliged to write a favourable piece. This need not be so, and the dangers can be minimised and faith kept with the reader if it is made plain somewhere in the piece or in a footnote that the ticket/trip/meal or whatever was given free to the newspaper.

The internet has thrown up another kind of opportunity for advertising masquerading as journalism (or rather quasi-journalism): commercial companies paying bloggers to write about their products. One of the distinctions between freelance online 'journalism' and the much-derided mainstream is that such a practice would instantly get you sacked on any Western newspaper or magazine. But on the Net, there are rarely any watching editors and no industry codes of ethics. So, at the time of writing (summer 2010), the going rate in the US for a paid blog about a product was from $25 to $200, with most earning at the low end of that range. There are now agencies that will match willing blogger to viral publicity-hungry company. Most insist the blog states plainly that the item is a paid one. You won't be surprised to learn this is a policy not always followed.

Don't make things up

In previous editions of this book, there was no specific statement that inventing quotes, sources, stories or facts is unethical. This was not an oversight, but because I was rather under the impression that such practices were self-evidently wrong. Until, that is, a student at a lecture I gave asked if I could give some guidance on what they called this 'difficult area'. I can. It's not difficult. Just don't do it – under any circumstances.

One of the most unsettling cases of story invention involved, ironically, a man who went on to be one of the best reporters of his generation. As a trainee, he worked for a paper in Australia that, one week, was particularly short of stories. In a mad attempt to save the day, the young reporter invented a crime story about a pervert he called 'The Hook' who lurked on trains and used a length of coast-hanger wire to lift women's skirts. The story even carried quotes from 'victims'. The editor was happy, the story published, and then the police came to visit him. So was he exposed as a liar? Not at all, the constabulary were calling to say that they'd caught 'The Hook'. To this day, the reporter does not know if he had, by some miraculous coincidence, invented a crime that really was happening; some sad individual had read his story and thought he'd copy the technique; or the police had arrested some entirely blameless person and framed them. The paper, of all things, was called *The Truth*, and the reporter was Phillip Knightley who went on to be one of the leading reporters for the London *Sunday Times* in its crusading heyday.

Journalists should not allow advertisers to influence, directly or indirectly, the paper's editorial content

It is not unusual, especially on smaller, less profitable or local papers, for advertisers to try to use their commercial weight to bully the paper. This pressure should be resisted at all times. It normally comes from the paper's advertising department who will say to the editor that it would be helpful if this important client could have some 'good coverage'. A few years ago the *Riverside Press-Enterprize*, a paper in California, published a total of eleven news pieces and 22 photographs of a new department store called Nordstrom's in the six days before, during and immediately after its opening in the town. These 400 column inches appeared in the same week as 20 full pages of ads for the store. A coincidence? Unlikely.

More rarely, groups of advertisers act in concert to try to force the paper to change its coverage. When I took over as editor of a British provincial paper, one of the things I did was to stop the *automatic* reporting of all shop-lifting court cases because they were so common as to be boring. Within a week, all the department stores in the city approached the publisher and told him that unless reporting of all shop-lifting cases was resumed they would withdraw their advertising, which was considerable. They said the coverage acted as a deterrent to would-be thieves. Luckily the publisher supported me. The advertisers' threat was not carried out.

The danger of giving in to advertisers' pressure, whether individual or collective, is that your content ceases to be freely chosen. You would also find that what is granted to one advertiser would soon be demanded by many. Give in once, and you would never be free of the pressure.

Do not use your position to threaten or gain advantage

A journalist has power. It should never be abused, either in the course of a story or in one's daily life. Prosecuting personal disputes with stores, neighbours, etc. by threatening exposure or reference to high-placed connections is bullying, and unsafe bullying at that. How could you ever write a future story about any person or organisation you have threatened in this way? How could you write about the connections you have used in your threat? You will be in their pocket for the favour you owe them. Neither should you use your newspaper's headed notepaper to write a letter demanding preferential treatment, compensation for some alleged negligence or faulty service. It implies to the recipient that your paper exists as a sort of private protection racket for its staff.

Do not promise to suppress stories for friendship or favours

It sometimes happens that you are asked by someone to 'forget' a story, or part of it, in return for some favour, or even cash. It is clearly wrong to accept such an offer, for the same reasons as it is wrong to put in a story for favours. When friends are involved, refusal might be more delicately phrased, but just as swift and sure. So should it be with colleagues, as these two stories illustrate.

The first case comes from Oregon in the United States where a few years ago a local television station reported that the long-time chief of staff of the state's Republican senator had served for 25 years as director of a bank that collapsed and was bailed out at a cost to taxpayers of $100 million. It was suggested that the man's involvement with the bank may have influenced the senator's position on bank deregulation and the subsequent bailout. The story was picked up by the Associated Press and was the talk of the state, but the main newspaper in the state, the *Oregonian*, chose to ignore it. It also ignored allegations a week later that the chief of staff's official travel, at taxpayer's expense, had included 52 trips to New York, where he published an annual guidebook to the city that had earned him more than $1 million.

The paper's reluctance to write this story may have had something to do with the fact that the chief of staff wrote a weekly column for the paper. It eventually published parts of the story only after the *Washington Post* gave the revelations national exposure.

Contrast this with a paper called the *Daily Item* in Sudbury, Pennsylvania. Among the daily stories from the police in one issue was an uncensored account of charges filed against a town resident for driving at an unsafe speed under the influence of alcohol. The item included the man's name, age, address and occupation – editor of the *Daily Item*. Which paper would you trust most, the *Item* or the *Oregonian*?

Do not invent or improve information

Inventing information is obviously wrong and dangerous. So, too, is even a light doctoring of the facts, embellishment of the truth or temporary amnesia about certain details that inconvenience the main thrust of the story. Your report will be a cheat. This applies with equal force to photographers and the dishonest 'set-up' picture, where an event or situation is staged to imitate some alleged reality.

Some news photographers in Western Europe also have been known to carry around in their cars certain 'props' to insert into pictures. A well-known ploy used to be to have a child's shoe, or teddy bear available, so that photographers covering disasters like train or air crashes, could set this prop among the wreckage for a 'poignant' picture. Such pictures have now become a cliché. Besides, there was always the danger that the passenger list, when finally issued, would reveal that there were no children aboard. Deliberate fakes, or at least the detected ones, are very rare. Perhaps the most famous recent example was Janet Cooke's Pulitzer-winning story in the *Washington Post*. It was called 'Jimmy's World' and told the story of an eight-year-old heroin addict. The story was published on the front page on 28 September 1980, and began: 'Jimmy is 8 years old and a third generation heroin addict ... He has been an addict since the age of 5 ... and every day Ron [his mother's lover] fires up Jimmy, plunging a needle into his bony arm, sending the fourth grader into a hypnotic nod.' Jimmy, however, did not exist. The story was an invention from beginning to end. When the fiction was revealed the *Post* saw that, with hindsight, there were many warning signs. Some staff, for instance, had harboured doubts about the story at the time, but had either thought it best to keep quiet, or thought the story 'too good to check'. This journalistically-lethal attitude was encouraged by Cooke's warnings that her (and Jimmy's) life would be endangered if checks were made. Nor did anyone think to check Cooke's own credentials. She said she was a graduate of Vassar, had a master's degree from Toledo, studied at the Sorbonne, was an accomplished pianist and spoke four languages. No editor thought this a tall order for someone aged just 25. Among these executives, ironically, was Watergate hero Bob Woodward.

You should not benefit personally from information you acquire

Using information you have acquired in order to make a commercial gain before the story is published is a temptation most likely to be faced by business reporters. A few years ago a reporter for the *Wall Street Journal* called R. Foster Whinans co-wrote a column based on information from sources that traded stocks. He decided to sell information to a stockbroker friend.

He was paid $31,000 to leak the contents of the column to several stockbrokers, enabling them to buy and sell shares in companies before this information became public and thus would affect the price of the stock. The brokers made about $690,000 from the leaked information. Whinans and the brokers were eventually caught and found guilty in court of violations of the Securities Exchange Act by misappropriating confidential information. Whinans was sentenced to 18 months in prison, five years' probation, 400 hours of community service and a $500 fine. Many Western papers now make their financial staff declare their investments and financial dealings.

Grey areas

The above issues are clear-cut. But a lot of issues in reporting are more complicated. Hard and fast rules are difficult to design and apply. Take phoney by-lines, for example. Plainly wrong if used routinely to give the impression a paper's staff is several times what it is, the practice is a good deal less harmful when sports editors use it to disguise the identity of, say, staff reporters from a daily moonlighting to cover events for a Sunday. Since the story purports to be written by someone who does not in fact exist, I would still contend phoney by-lines are a deceit. It is particularly unsafe where the story may be challenged, or even end in a law suit. Who do you produce in court? An actor taking the name of the fictitious reporter?

Privacy

There have been many attempts to be dogmatic about privacy, but none can be sustained beyond the most simplistic instances. We all agree that if a President fools around with a junior employee in his office, there is a legitimate story. If someone is asking for our votes (and our taxes to pay their wages), we have a right to know about them, their lives and how they impact on their duties. On the other hand, few would suggest writing a story about a second junior employee fooling around, in their own time, with a third. The sex lives of private citizens, however fascinating, are not regarded as a legitimate target for a story, unless the law is broken. But between these two extremes, in all the less clear-cut cases, is the gaping space where we argue about privacy.

The conventional, and largely sensible, guideline is that the person should be a public figure and the invasion of their privacy must have a legitimate justification based on the public interest, not merely tickling the public's curiosity. If a man standing for public office makes a great deal of public fuss about morality and the virtues of family life, but you can prove he has a string of mistresses, then it is right to publish a story. His double standards are clearly relevant to public life.

There are two problems with this conventional wisdom. First, if a paper thinks the story is sufficiently entertaining or salacious, almost any 'public interest' pretext can be dredged up. Second, justifications tend to be applied in a partisan way: papers defend the privacy of those they admire and invade the privacy of those they seek to destroy.

A fine example of what happens when sanctimonious motives operate was the case, in 2008, of the exposé by British Sunday tabloid, the *News of the World*, of Max Mosley, boss of Formula One motor racing. Mosley was a happily married man who had a taste for sado-masochism. He satisfied this by hiring specialist prostitutes who would arrange fantasy situations for him at private parties, during which roles would be played, and bottoms spanked. His wife knew nothing of these tastes, and no one was much harmed by these arrangements, especially not the women, who were handsomely paid. But one of the women, knowing that Mosley was a public name, decided to secretly film a session and sell the footage, and an account of proceedings, to the paper. The paper's justification was that, at this particular 'party', German was spoken, orders barked, and uniforms worn. They claimed this amounted to a 'Nazi death camp theme', and, because Mosley was the son of British fascist leader Oswald Mosley, the matter was of public interest. Mosley vigorously denied claims of a Nazi theme, and sued for breach of privacy.

The paper did not do well in court. The woman who filmed the party did not appear; the paper had, it turned out, failed to get translated the German dialogue spoken by the participants; and the fancy dress worn at the event, which the paper said were 'death camp uniforms', in fact bore more resemblance to hooped football shirts. Mosley won his case, and substantial damages, and many British journalists, to this, day, maintain that the verdict was defeat for press freedom.

But was it? It seems to me that the paper's motive was simply to bring its readers some entertaining revelations about the unusual sex life of a minor celebrity. As I wrote at the time in the Italian magazine *Internazionale*: 'As Mosley says, a perfectly legal private habit in which he had indulged for 45 years was made public because a paid informant had made a secret video. The resulting story came as devastating news to his wife and sons, robbed him of his dignity, and made his sex life – which had no bearing whatsoever on his public duties – common knowledge. It is hard not to sympathise. After all, imagine how your world would change if everyone you ever met not only knew your innermost sexual fantasies, but had also seen pictures of you acting them out.'

Part of the answer lies in that traditionally most unjournalistic of qualities: sensitivity. Journalists must have very good reasons for invading someone's privacy and should also be aware of the consequences of such reporting. A few years ago in Britain a policeman began an affair. His wife learnt about it and persuaded him to give up his mistress. The jealous lover then told a national paper and her account was printed under the headline, 'The Love Life of a Detective'. As a result, the couple's child was teased at school, the husband had to give up his job and the family had to move. Some may think that a fitting punishment for his original sin. I do not think so, and neither would I like to justify that reporting.

Restraint

For the average journalist, this is the ethical grey area most commonly encountered. And it's a curious one: you've found out, or been told, something, and now you're being asked to do something that goes against all your professional instincts and keep it quiet. These days (unlike times gone by when the press colluded to keep, for instance, President Roosevelt's confinement to a wheelchair – or Jack Kennedy's philandering – a secret) the request is made for what might be described as civic reasons. It might be a kidnap, where police ask for a news blackout until their operation is concluded; or some other investigation where premature publicity might endanger the lives of undercover officers. It may be that a political leader is visiting somewhere like Iraq, and the media is given advance notice in return for agreeing not to publicise the trip before it has finished. It might be something as routine as not publishing the addresses of children (to protect them from paedophiles); or an embargo, where the press is given sight of a report so that a journalist can fully absorb its contents and so write a full account at the time of its official release. These instances of restraint are everyday occurrences, and it is a pretty foolhardy editor who defies them.

So, too, is it fairly rash in, say, Russia or Africa, to publish an unflattering story about certain leaders, or prominent organised criminals. And so, many papers don't. We might from the comfort of our armchairs, call this self-censorship but the editors in question – unless they are among the very bravest – would call it self-preservation. Such restraint is understandable, but it is also undoubtedly rather shabby, as was the widespread decision by papers in 2005 not to publish cartoons satirising Muslims, their prophet, and Islamic terrorism. In this case, the restraint probably had as much to do with fear of a backlash among Muslim traders (quite large numbers of whom run shops which sell newspapers), as it did with not wanting to incite more civil unrest than was already occurring.

Paying for information or an interview

There are two basic kinds of paying for information. The first is when someone with some kind of extraordinary experience is paid for their exclusive story. Providing their experience is not a criminal one, there is nothing especially unethical about such a deal; and if they get the sum they are promised (and this is not always the case), it's a fair trade. Such payments have been going on a long time. As far back as 1912, the *New York Times* paid the *Titanic*'s wireless operator $1,000 for an exclusive interview. The second situation is where someone is paid in exchange for information, as opposed to their time and personal story. This is far more dodgy; for what has happened over the years is that a market has developed in which the sellers know that the juicier the information, the higher the price. It's no surprise that this produces exaggeration and outright lying, as the legal files of many papers (not all of them tabloids) testify. My view is that paying for information is a bad idea, not so much because it is ethically dubious (which it is), but because it is likely to prove journalistically unsafe.

Law-breaking

An issue which comes up less frequently is where journalists get involved in wrong-doing in order to investigate it. This is not a good idea. Breaking the law in pursuit of a story is both wrong and unsafe. It removes whatever moral legitimacy their reporting may otherwise have had.

Sometimes reporters investigating drug-dealing, crime or prostitution learn information that should be passed straight to the police. I think you should do that. Otherwise you are compromising your legitimacy, and may also be putting the lives of innocent citizens at risk. Only the police – not you – can judge that. (This condition about the safety of citizens also applies to the situation where journalists are accused of merely spectating in disaster or war situations and not doing anything to help those who are in danger. My rule would be that if you can have any influence on the outcome of a situation you should follow your normal instincts and act to help.) A classic case is that of Alan Dower of the *Melbourne Herald* during the Korean War. He and a colleague were told that some women were about to be shot because an informant had identified them to the authorities as communists. Dower, who was armed, pushed his way into a police station, in the yard of which he found the women lined up with their babies in front of an open pit. Two machine guns were trained on them. Dower demanded to see the man in charge, and said he would shoot him between the eyes if the women were shot. They were not. One shudders to think of a set of journalistic ethics that would condemn a reporter for 'interfering' in the story in this way.

Never accept a free ticket from a theatre manager, a free ride from the chamber of commerce, or a favour from a politician.

H. L. Mencken

13

Writing for Newspapers

The most essential gift for a writer is a built-in, shock-proof shit-detector.
Ernest Hemingway

Newspapers are not literature. But then nor is most literature. Writing for papers is different from writing a novel or short story, but not as different as some would like to think. All good writing has some things in common. It is clear, easy to read, uses fresh language, stimulates and entertains. Those things are as true of the well-written newspaper story as they are of the well-written novel. And they are true whatever language you are writing in.

Now for the bad news. Learning how to write is hard, lonely work. We all know people who say they want to write. What they often want is merely to walk around saying they are writers. What they do not want to do is to put their butts on a chair and stay there until they have covered some paper or a computer screen in words. That is what you have got to do. Many, many times. And the way you progress and develop whatever talent you have is to write hundreds and hundreds of stories and make mistakes. You leave vital things out and put irrelevancies in, write half the piece, then realise it is going wrong and have to start again, write clumsily, pompously or stiffly, turn in work that is confusing or trite, and commit to paper or screen whole paragraphs so silly that if you had to speak them, your voice would trail off in embarrassment mid-sentence.

Now for the good news. After a while, by hanging around a good newspaper and listening, by reading, studying the good and the bad and being your own sharpest critic, you begin to see a way. There will still be times when you take a long time to get a story to work, but by and large, the more you write, the more fluently you write. Writing is like a muscle, it will be a lot stronger if you exercise it every day; you will waste less time in false starts and chasing down the wrong route, less time in writing stories at the wrong pace for the length they should be and less energy trying to think of a fancy phrase when a simple one will be better.

And you find that essential thing without which no one can call themselves a writer – your voice. No more will you be experimenting with a style that is over-elaborate, too formal or too colloquial. Instead, you will have found a natural style that suits you, is consistent, has rhythms and expressions recognisably yours and – the crucial test – if read aloud would sound like an only slightly tidied up version of your speech. It will be your own. Not put on, not affected and not borrowed. Of course it will owe something to the writers you admire, your background, education, reading and so forth. But it will be yours – your words and idioms, your pattern of sentence lengths and your rhythm within sentences. It will be like a signature. Only more readable.

Planning

The most important part of writing is what happens inside your head between finishing your research and putting the first word down. You have got to think about your material and decide what it is about and what you want to do with it. Composition is not merely the business of arranging words, it is the business of organising thought. It does not matter how wonderful you are at conjuring up colourful phrases or witty remarks; if you do not have a clear idea of what you want to say it will show.

This is easy enough on some cataclysmic event or short, straightforward news stories, but most journalism is not like that. Stories can be complex, not as strong as you would like, or they can be long features covering many different aspects, or commissioned pieces where you are unsure if the subject is interesting to the reader. Then you have to think hard about what the story is actually about. And sometimes it is not immediately obvious. A feature, for example, about a man collecting and keeping exotic frogs in his apartment is superficially about amphibians, not a subject in which most people are automatically interested. But it is also a story about eccentricity and obsession, about how a hobby has taken over someone's life (and his home). That is a far more promising topic than frogs.

The most valuable phrase I have ever heard in relation to writing is one used by John Shirley of the London *Sunday Times, Observer* and *Guardian*: you have to *take command of the material*. By this he meant that before you can possibly hope to write a clear story, you have to have absorbed your research, made sense of it, ordered the main points of it in your head, and so be in a position to give a coherent verbal account of it. Consider, for example, something of significance to you that happened this year. If you wanted to tell someone of it, you could because you have experienced it, assimilated it, and rehearsed the telling of it, if only inside your head. You can do that because you are in command of the material, which is how you have to be with your news stories, especially complex ones.

And one other thing to remember when planning: news and features stories are not called stories for nothing. They should, if they have been researched and planned well, have the same coherence and development that the best short fiction has. This may strike you as odd, but it is well worth considering when you get past the novice stage.

The other thing you have to work out is the treatment for the story. Is it hard news? A soft news story or light human interest? Should it be told chronologically or by covering each aspect in turn? All these different ways of handling the story (and there are many more) affect the construction, the main framework of which you need to know before you start. In the case of simple news stories, planning what you want to say and the order in which you want to say it can be done quickly in your head. But with longer, or more complex, articles you need a written plan. Never be afraid to make a plan on paper. It is not the sign of an untutored novice, but someone who wants to get it right. It does not have to be very detailed – just the main building blocks of the story in order, with maybe a few notes of how to link them.

Construction gets its own chapter (Chapter 15), as does the intro (Chapter 14), that all-important first paragraph. Those sections discuss how you can grab the reader's attention immediately and sustain it through the piece – both essential features of good writing. There are, I think, six others: clarity, fresh language, honesty, precision, suitability and efficiency – and they are the subjects of this chapter.

Clarity

Each story must be clear in thought, organisation and language. If it isn't, it needs re-thinking or re-writing. You don't just have to take my word for that. The French novelist Stendhal wrote, 'I see only one rule: to be clear. If I am not clear then my entire world crumbles into nothing.' The British writer H.G. Wells put it less dramatically, 'I write as straight as I can, just as I walk as straight as I can, because that is the best way to get there.' Of no writing is this more true than that for newspapers. They are often read in distracting, noisy surroundings by people with other demands on their time and easier, albeit inferior, ways of getting news. There are specific points to watch for.

Achieve clarity before you have even put a single word down

To explain something to others, you must first fully understand it yourself. Until you do, don't write it down. A good tip for the confused is to tell the story to a colleague or friend. The obvious nub of the story (and its innate pattern) will probably come out of your mouth almost unconsciously.

Be careful to include each stage in a narrative, each event in a sequence and each step in an argument

Jumping from A to C leaves readers having to work out that B happened in between. That's annoying, confusing and sometimes misleading, especially in the cases when B actually happened out of place. And don't make leaps of logic. You may understand your thought processes but readers won't unless you explain them.

Don't assume readers have special or prior knowledge

When you spend a lot of time delving into a specialist or technical area, it is easy to forget that readers know only as much as you did before you began your research. Don't. And on stories that run for many days, weeks or months, don't assume that readers have a photographic memory of what has gone before or have dutifully made notes when they read your previous stories. They haven't. Instead, work on the assumption that until something has passed firmly into general knowledge, readers will need reminders and recaps.

Explain all jargon

The normal instruction on this subject is to avoid using all jargon, whether it is scientific, technical, bureaucratic or whatever. I think this is a mistake. Some jargon is useful. It takes readers inside a formerly closed world, adds to their knowledge of the language specialists use and, especially with bureaucratic jargon, shows the often-ludicrous phrases that officials dream up and thus their mentality. For these reasons, and for lovers of irony, it should never be banned from stories. What, however, should be censured is the failure to explain in everyday language what the jargon means.

This is not to say that jargon should be used often, even if it is explained. Journalists, especially specialist reporters, can easily slip into using jargon because they want to display their knowledge and sound like an insider. Well, by all means do so at a party if you think it will impress people, but not in your paper. Trying to come across as an insider or writing for insiders is elitist and obscurantist, neither of which characteristic is wanted on newspapers.

Then there is commercial and political jargon, which these days is perhaps the most damaging kind of all. It is widespread, sometimes difficult to detect, and journalists are especially prone to repeat it unthinkingly. Spokesmen for large companies say that their 'operation' (firm) is 'undergoing temporary cash-flow difficulties' (running out of money) due to 'market positioning problems' (people are not buying what they make) and so there will be a 'rationalisation of the work force' (people will be sacked). Government officials talk of 'correctional facilities' when they mean prisons and 'an imbalance between the supply and demand for domestic units' when they mean that there is a housing shortage.

These are euphemisms, a form of linguistic dishonesty which is particularly common where public relations people proliferate. They play on the natural tendency of politicians and business leaders to, if not lie, at least try to hide the truth when under pressure.

Ensure your sentences are totally clear

Don't write confusing sentences that oblige readers to go back to the beginning and read them again. Instead, you go back and re-write it. This is different, of course, from the deliberate device of writing sentences that lead readers to expect one thing and then deliver another. Surprise is important to keep the writing lively.

Avoid tricky writing and tricky language

Any writing that is self-consciously clever is almost certainly self-evidently bad. The idea is to communicate your meaning to others, not to keep it to yourself. So if you find yourself writing a showy phrase that you are particularly proud of, strike it out; if you verbally have to explain a passage to someone, change it; and if you feel tempted to use words to display your erudition, resist. And if you want a good guide to how intelligent, crisp, detailed, attributed news copy should be written, study those on the wires of the Associated Press and Reuters. If your paper doesn't subscribe, you can find plenty of fresh examples on Google News.

One final word on clarity – simplicity

This virtue is normally urged on journalists when they are writing, especially for mass-market newspapers. It is good advice, up to a point; and that point is where simplicity becomes simple-mindedness. Some papers, particularly in Britain and Australia, severely underestimate the literacy of their readers, with the result that they use a vocabulary and language which is restricted and stylised.

They defend this on the grounds that they know their readers – a questionable assertion. If they actually knew them, they would know that in speech and thought their customers' minds operate several levels above that of the paper. If anyone doubts that, they have only to compare it with the vastly more complicated language and vocabulary of television that their readers cope with every day. When simplicity means linguistic inbreeding, it is time to let in a little new blood.

Fresh language

The whole point of articles in newspapers is to give readers something they have not had before – information, insights, observations, thoughts. It is therefore a terrible waste to relate this novelty in language that is tired and worn-out through over-use. Do that and readers will feel even the newest material has an old, familiar ring to it. Points to watch out for are:

Regard each story as an individual, new thing

Don't fall into the trap of formula writing, where you say to yourself, 'Ah, here's "a he said – she said argument story"' and then trot it out to a well-worn pattern. Of course there must be a limit to the types of stories around, but that does not mean you must make all which bear a similarity to each other conform to a set formula. Professor John Carey, in his introduction to *The Faber Book of Reportage*, writes: 'Massive accumulations of standardised language and hackneyed story-lines lie in wait, ready to leap from the fingers to the typing page.' As he says, reporters have to see their story and tell it, as if for the first time. In this sense, beware especially a story which appears to write itself. If that starts to happen, stop, think and you write it instead.

Avoid all clichés

And here, for once, is something that is as easy to do as it is to say. Clichés are words and phrases that are familiar, too familiar, so recognising them should not pose any problems. A good rule is that anything you suspect of being a cliché undoubtedly is one and should be removed. Some are in general use, others seem to be purely confined to newspapers and are dealt with later in this chapter. But whatever they are, they are expressions so old and worn-out that they have ceased to have any impact.

Those that are similes pose an especial danger because their automatic use means they are often applied in the wrong place. For instance, describing a crash scene as 'like a battlefield' is both unoriginal and wrong, as those who have seen both accident scenes and battlefields will know. But whether they are similes, metaphors, catch phrases or single words, the cliché (a feature of which is that it is out of your head and into the story almost before you have realised it) should be deleted and something fresher put in its place. After all, clichéd words can so easily become clichéd thoughts.

Avoid all automatic words

These are normally adjectives which some reporters instinctively link with certain nouns. All deals have to be 'huge', all reports 'shock', all murders 'brutal', all concern 'widespread' and all wants 'long-felt'. The adjective has become like a parasite living on its host and has long since sucked the phrase of any impact it might have had. There are also phrases which seem to be used automatically in certain circumstances. Each country's newspapers have them. In English-language papers, for instance, disasters always have investigators 'grimly sifting through the wreckage' (as if they would be laughing) and civil disturbances overseas have 'baton-wielding police' and 'stone-throwing demonstrators'. Rain on parades always 'fails to dampen the spirits', disputes are settled after an agreement has been 'hammered out', rifles always 'high-powered' and loners in crime stories, you will be amazed to learn, 'always kept to themselves'. There are many, many others; or, as the knee-jerk writer would have it, 'too many to mention'. These are not just automatic, but are clichés, too – and used so frequently that they cannot even be accurate in a lot of cases.

Be very careful with puns

An outright ban would be a bit severe, because once in a while (say every three years) somewhere in the world a journalist comes up with a good fresh one. Meanwhile, many millions more that are anything but fresh get published. They normally take two forms: first where the writer on a certain subject thinks of every possible word associated with that subject and loses no opportunity to fill the story with them (as in 'Tennis Player Nets Fortune'); second where the story, normally a light one in a mass-market paper, seems to consist of nothing but word play. To those in the know, such puns are an infallible giveaway that the story is being written by someone with no imagination and also that the story is not worth the space it has been given.

There are no absolute rules in writing, but one that comes close is: never write the obvious. If you go to Las Vegas, don't write about the slot machines; if London, try to get to the end of the piece without reference to rain or Big Ben; if Paris, leave observations on the way women dress to someone else. So, too, with puns. They cannot put you in prison for writing a light story about cats which avoids all play on words like paws, nine lives or tail.

And contrary to the myth peddled by newspaper journalists whose stock in trade are puns, they are not at all difficult to write. If they were, there would be fewer of them in newspapers. A good general rule would be to allow someone else the glory of being the once-every-three-years hero who comes up with a pun worth repeating, and remove yourself from that competition by never writing with them. But if you really must use puns, try to attain the originality that Edwin Lahey of the *Chicago Daily News* did when he wrote a story about Richard Loeb, one of a pair of university graduates who killed a boy. Loeb, who had a passionate interest in literature, was murdered in jail after making advances to a fellow prisoner. Lahey's story began: 'Richard Loeb, the well-known student of English, yesterday ended his sentence with a proposition.'

Work hard at creating new similes, metaphors and phrases

Whenever you find yourself reaching in a semi-automatic fashion for a phrase, simile or metaphor, stop and think. Think hard about the real nature of what it is that you are trying to convey and try to find a phrase that fits the bill perfectly, not just the nearest off-the-shelf option. Experienced writers have all kinds of devices where they deliberately and cleverly invert or fool around with familiar phrases to give them new life. But they also put a lot of brain power into trying to describe something or communicate its nature exactly, and that means the hard work of inventing a phrase especially for it.

They also fight and argue with editors for the right to use colourful language. Sometimes this is necessary when you work on a paper which seeks to force a literary straitjacket on its staff. The editing staff at the *New York Times*, for instance, used to be notorious for the dead hand they would lay on the prose of its writers. Consider the experiences of Molly Ivens in the late 1970s. She once wrote that a man had 'a beer gut that belonged in the Smithsonian'. The copy-editor changed it to, 'a man with a protuberant stomach' – accurate, but dull. Then, another time, she wrote that a guy 'squawked like a two-dollar fiddle', and it appeared in the paper as 'an inexpensive musical instrument'. Editors who do things like that to fresh language should be working in a museum.

Beware the fashionable word or phrase

Language has its vogues, just like hem-lines and hair-styles. Each new fashionable word or phrase, however, rapidly becomes irritating to read. So do your writing a favour – be a trend-setter rather than a trend-follower. Use your own words, phrases and voice and let others mimic the passing fancy. As the style book of the London *Daily Telegraph* says: 'If you are tempted to use a word because all the smart writers are using it, change the word, your reading matter or your job.' Or, as Bernard Kilgore once wrote to his staff, 'If I read upcoming in the *Wall Street Journal* again, I shall be downcoming and somebody will be outgoing.'

Don't get too hung up on strict grammar

Don't adopt semi-literacy as a policy, but an over-obsessing with the more pernickity parts of grammar can get in the way of effective writing. For instance, when E.B. White was a reporter with the *Seattle Times*, he wrote a story about a man being asked to identify his wife's body in a mortuary. White wrote that, as her face was uncovered, the man exclaimed: 'My

God! It's her!'. An editor then changed that to: 'My God! It is she!'. Grammatically correct, but totally unrealistic. White decided to leave the paper soon afterwards.

Honesty

There are aspects of the process of journalism which often compromise truth. The lack of time to collate a totally comprehensive account, the lack of access to all the sources and information and the need to write the story to a finite, often quite short length – all these factors can prevent us presenting an account that is as complete (or as accurate) as we would like. That is fine as long as we are aware of these limitations and don't claim that we are presenting the definitive account in each story. And it is even better if we are doing all we can to overcome these limitations and difficulties.

But often when writing and editing news stories, journalists do things which actually put even more distance between their story and the truth. Writers know what editors prize as a strong news story and in writing the story as strongly as they dare, they often make omissions and use language which exaggerates or 'hypes' the story beyond its true value. And, on popular papers especially, if they do not do that, the chances are that an editor will. Avoiding this sometimes inadvertent, sometimes deliberate process is not easy, but here are a few points.

Write only what you know to be true

This is obvious and should not really need saying, but it does. Quite a lot of reporters when challenged on a part of a story will say, 'Well, it must be true.' Suppositions like this might be good enough for a chat in the kitchen with a friend, but not for newspapers.

All stories should be a conscious effort to be balanced and true to both the detail and spirit of the material

This is a tall order. It is not just a question of making sure you have included both sides (normally there are more than two) to the story and have quoted accurately. It is a question of making sure what you have put in the story accurately reflects what you know to be the whole picture. You may, for example, spend a great deal of time interviewing someone who is perfectly even–tempered, except for their response to one question. Of course you are entitled to report that touchiness, but even if you quote it with total accuracy, the whole piece would be dishonest unless you indicated that their general mood was benign. Anything else is slanted selection with a dishonest purpose.

Do not hype

This is the process whereby journalists use words that convey a stronger meaning than the material justifies. A lot of it is done automatically to conform to what the writer thinks are the required journalistic conventions, and thus is also a cliché. But whether his or her intention is conscious or not, the effect is to over-cook the story. Words like 'sensational', 'shock', 'dramatic' and 'disturbing' are used to describe things which are normally a good deal less than sensational, shocking, dramatic and disturbing. As one commentator once said: 'When you hear something described by a journalist as disturbing, you know you cannot take it seriously.'

When stories about the Sars virus were doing the rounds in 2004, the London *Daily Express* carried a story under this headline: 'PANIC AS KILLER FLU GRIPS BRITAIN'. There followed two pages of breathless reporting which somehow omitted to tell readers that, in a country of 58 million allegedly 'gripped' by the disease, there had so far been six cases, none of which had been fatal.

They were right about the panic, although not its location. The panic was plainly in the paper's newsroom, for there is no surer sign of a news publication in trouble than the ridiculous exaggeration of stories in a desperate bid to make an impact. It is the newspaper equivalent of using a padded bra, high heels, and whole heap of indiscriminately applied make-up to try and supply what nature so unfairly omitted to provide. Like that attempt at fraud, it is equally doomed to failure in anything but the shortest of terms and dimmest of lights. But while adding two and two and declaring in large headlines that the result is seven is unlikely to fool anyone for very long, the routine taking of stories to the very limits of their facts, and sometimes beyond, is an integral part of some newspapers' cultures. And it's a very damaging one.

The techniques of deceit are many and various: omitting facts and perspective that would detract from a crude black and white scenario, playing with statistics ('Suicides in jail soar ... up 30% in a year ... etc.' with the fact that they have merely gone up from six to eight only revealed in paragraph nine of the story), hyping language (words like 'dramatic', and 'sensational' dropped into stories like seeds in a vegetable garden, prosaic developments described as 'crucial', 'crime waves' hailed whenever two homes are robbed on the same night, the slightest setback called 'a disaster', and every disagreement portrayed as a 'row').

There are two other bad aspects of this habit. First, all these words involve a value judgement, which has no place in a straight news story. And hyping is the worst kind of comment – a sneaky comment posing as a legitimate description. It does not declare itself, but goes under an assumed identity. Second, let the facts speak for themselves. If the story is sensational, shocking, disturbing or whatever, tell the readers all about it and let them judge for themselves. Good journalism involves not only the readers trusting the paper, but the paper trusting the readers.

The final problem with this sort of breathless, exaggerated language is that it bears no relation to the language real people use. And in almost every country, many newspapers have evolved this 'journalese'. In Britain, for example, it is a world where two people disputing a point are 'confronting' each other, and where 'amid extraordinary scenes' (anything remotely out of the ordinary) 'soap-stars' (any actress who has had a walk-on part) have 'miracle' babies (used to describe infants born in anything but the most routine circumstances) which are 'dashed' or 'mercy dashed' to hospital to be operated on by 'heroic' doctors. Reporting in journalese is dishonest, at least several steps removed from reality and, because it is so over-used, ultimately has no impact on readers. It is a fossilised art form, performed to a set of rituals. It has no life. Replace it with fresh, honest language.

Beware of using simplistic, black and white headline language in stories

There is a great deal of difference between writing that brings an issue or subject to life and writing that gives the material a phoney life. A prime example of this is using words that have no shades of meaning, but are either very black or very white. This is best explained by relating briefly the roots of this in European mass-market newspapers. Over the last 50 or so years on such papers, headlines have become progressively larger in size. The unavoidable result of this is that the words used in headlines have got much shorter. And there is one great problem with short words: in almost every case they are far less good at conveying shades of meaning than longer words. They tend to deal in extremes of meaning, black and white and not grades of grey.

Thus if you and I hold different opinions on a subject and discuss it, we could be said to have a disagreement. If we are sufficiently interesting for a popular paper to want to report our debate, how will they describe it in their headline? Well 'disagreement' cannot fit, neither can 'debate', because all they have room for in type 4.5 cm high is a word of four letters. So our disagreement becomes a 'row' or a 'feud', something very different. Or we have a 'bust up', or I 'lash' you, or 'rap' you or 'blast' you, none of which happened. Typography and design has made a dishonest account of our meeting.

In many British papers, annoyance (meaning you are not pleased) is invariably now 'fury' (suggesting anger beyond control), an arrangement (meaning an informal agreement) is a 'deal' (meaning a far more formal agreement, with definite overtones of a financial, possibly even shady, side), bad luck is a 'curse', to criticise is 'to slam', failure to attend is a 'snub', internal dispute is 'civil war', possibility is 'threat', a proposal is a 'plan', to replace is to 'oust', a traffic jam is 'road chaos', etc. All of these examples (and there are many more to choose from) are shorter, more extreme and more brutal than the reality they describe. It is as if the story is being translated into another language by an angry man with a limited vocabulary.

This inaccuracy might be confined to the headline were it not for one thing: the language of today's headlines is the language of tomorrow's news stories. Editors and their senior executives control the culture of a paper partly through the language of headlines, which they approve. Reporters read the words used for headlines on their stories and, wanting to be thought in tune with the culture of the paper (and their editor) or a 'bright, lively' writer, they adopt it. And provincial reporters see such language in national papers and they imitate it, often badly. And then even some flagging quality paper, wanting to make its image more youthful, or its appearance more lively, will adopt larger headlines and thus imbibe some, if not the worst, of these excesses. Thus, in varying degrees, does the whole journalistic stream become polluted. If the language of your papers has not yet been invaded by the little black and white words, keep a wary eye out for them.

Precision

Journalism should be the enemy of imprecision. Stories should be written to answer questions in the readers' minds, not to raise them. And the questions a reporter should be trying to answer, and answer precisely, are:

- What? – What has happened?
- Who? – Who has it happened to? Who has done it? Age, appearance, position, credentials and any relevant background.
- Where? – Where did it happen?
- When? – When did it happen? What time, day, month?
- How? – How did it happen? Explanations.
- Why? – Why did it happen?

Other points to watch for are:

In all cases, abolish the abstract and use the particular

Writing which is not specific is not wanted. Reporting that talks of 'official organisations' without naming them is no good. Use specific words, name names, make lists and pin things down. You have to be careful where in the story you itemise these details, but they should be there. And don't just call a building 'tall'. How tall is it? In metres, please, plus some graphic idea of what that means.

Use known quantities rather than unknown ones

Writers often use words like 'really', 'considerably' and 'very' to express values or scale. But how much is 'very'? Be precise, use known values.

Be careful with 'up to' and 'more than'

A leading US copy–editor has rightly pointed out the infuriating habit of reporters of being mealy-mouthed with numbers, as in: 'An average caseworker might handle up to 100 cases a month or more.' As he says, this could be 'up to' (i.e., anything from 0 to 100) or 'more' (i.e., from 101 to infinity) – and it only 'might' be at that. Sentences like this say literally nothing. You can fiddle with this sentence a bit ('It's not unusual for a caseworker to handle 100 cases a month') but for all you know 100 cases a month might be extremely rare. The only real solution is that the reporter should go away and ask for specific data.

Don't use vague adjectives

There are some phrases in common use which communicate only vague ideas. 'Expensive tastes', for example, tells you that these tastes are not cheap, but that is all. What does expensive mean here? What the reader wants to know are concrete examples of what the money is being spent on, preferably with brand names and prices. Similarly 'fast car' – is it a Porsche, a second-hand police car or a Ferrari? And 'luxury' – what is that? The answer is, it is different things to different people. You should tell readers something that means the same to all of them. This applies also to descriptions of people. 'She is tall and attractive.' What does that mean? But if I write that she is blonde and stands six feet, then we both know what we mean. 'She is intelligent' is meaningless, except as a general indicator that she is not actually mentally handicapped. But if I write that she has a degree in politics, we begin to learn something.

Use specific quantities rather than vague ones

Writers often use words like 'very', 'considerable', 'big', and 'many' in stories. If challenged, they will say they are trying to express size or scale, but, in reality, what they are doing is two other things. First, annoying the reader with their imprecision. After all, how many is 'many'? How much is 'big'? The second thing they are doing is showing, by using such vague terms, their lack of research. News editors quickly learn that reporters whose stories are strewn with words like 'many' and 'large' are reporters who don't ask the proper questions when researching, or are trying to hype the story. Either way, their copy is bland and incomplete, and a sign of someone who is inept, dishonest or both. Give readers detail.

Don't proclaim it, show it

A lot of reporters fall into the trap of asserting, rather than reporting. Thus they will write that an incident is 'tragic' or 'disturbing', and think that this will add something to their story. It doesn't. Instead, show why the incident is tragic or disturbing – and if you can't, then it probably isn't.

Avoid euphemisms

This is the language of people hiding from reality. They speak, for instance, of someone 'passing on' when they mean dying, they refer to sex as 'being intimate with'. Victorian England was a rich source for the more absurd euphemisms: 'nether garments' for underwear, 'maleness' for penis, 'in a state of nature' for naked, 'smallest room in the house' for toilet, 'in an interesting condition' for pregnant. Even now, people invent words or phrases to describe the things they feel uncomfortable with, whether it is death, sex or their own emotions.

Journalists should not use euphemisms, unless with irony. But that does not mean that every last detail of sex cases, or killings, has to be spelt out. Most newspapers are produced for a general readership which embraces an enormous range of people with different sensitivities. You should neither write for the most shockable, prim and proper, nor for the most bloodthirsty.

When writing about violent deaths, be they the results of crime, war or accidents, use your judgement about how graphic you can be without making your readers feel sick. Precision does not have to mean gloating. It means describing things in sufficient *relevant* detail, without being insensitive. You should have a reason for giving the detail. In some situations, like plane crashes, readers will not be surprised to learn that the force of the crash or explosion has dismembered and mutilated the corpses. You need only spell out what is necessary.

In other situations, like war or terrorism, people need the horrors of what has been done brought home to them. You will do this all the more effectively if you use measured, cool language. Here is Robert Fisk, then of *The Times* of London, describing the scenes he found when he went to investigate reports of a massacre of Palestinians at a refugee camp at Chatila in September 1982:

> What we found inside the camps at ten o'clock next morning did not quite beggar description, although it would perhaps be easier to retell in a work of fiction or in the cold prose of a medical report.
>
> But the details should be told for – this being Lebanon – the facts will change over the coming weeks as militias and armies and governments

blame each other for the horrors committed upon the Palestinian civilians.

... Down a laneway to our right, not more than fifty yards from the entrance, there lay a pile of corpses.

There were more than a dozen of them, young men whose arms and legs had become entangled with each other in the agony of death. All had been shot at point-blank range through the right or left cheek, the bullet tearing away a line of flesh up to the ear and entering the brain. Some had vivid crimson scars down the left side of their throats. One had been castrated. Their eyes were open and the flies had only begun to gather. The youngest was perhaps only twelve or thirteen years old.

On the other side of the main road, up a track through the rubble, we found the bodies of five women and several children. The women were middle-aged, and their corpses lay draped over a pile of rubble. One lay on her back, her dress torn open, and the head of a little girl emerging from behind her. The girl had short, dark curly hair and her eyes were staring at us and there was a frown on her face. She was dead.

Fisk's report continues for another eleven paragraphs. Neither in these or the preceding thirteen is there is single word of comment, or emotionalism. You can be sure that is not because he feels no emotion, but knows that as soon as the reporter lets that infect the writing, then the impact – and veracity – of the story is lost.

Sex

For many years newspapers all round the world used the language of the nunnery to describe anything remotely sexual. Readers had to guess, rather than know, what was being described. Phrases like 'intimacy took place' and 'improper suggestion' were not only imprecise but also often left the reader with the impression that far worse had happened than actually did. One of the most abused terms was 'interfered with', which once led to the headline in a British paper: 'Girl Stabbed 65 Times But Not Interfered With'.

Yet the replacement of such bashful language with a clearer one is not a licence to write soft pornography. Detail should be given to explain and not to arouse. You will also find that being forced to describe events in a way that is acceptable to the broad band of your readers will frequently produce original and evocative writing. Here is Ben Hecht, an American reporter from the 1920s, writing the final line of a story for Chicago's *Daily News* about a priest who regularly made love to a girl in the basement of his church – until, one day, he accidentally kicked the gas jet open and died while having sex: 'Preoccupied by love, he had smelled no fumes than those of Paradise and given up the ghost while still glued to his parishioner.'

Suitability

Suitability is matching the style, tone and pace of the story to the subject. By no means all subjects require special handling, but some need more sensitive treatment than others. Most are obvious. Matters of life and death, for example, should always get serious treatment (unless you are writing a column and specialise in bad taste). Here are a few guidelines for the more straightforward situations.

Stories of action and movement should be written with real pace

The language and construction should be taut, the verbs active and direct, sentences economical and adjectives should be used sparingly. There are few better illustrations of this than Sergei Kurnakov's description of the frenzy in St. Petersburg, August 1914 in the hours after Germany declared war on Russia. It is a model of how to write something that reads at the same fast pace as the events it reports:

> When I got to the St Isaac Square it was swarming with people. It must have been about nine o'clock, for it was pretty light yet – the enervating, exciting twilight of the northern nights.
>
> The great greystone monstrosity of the German Embassy was facing the red granite of St Isaac's Cathedral. The crowds were pressing around waiting for something to happen. I was watching a young naval officer being pawed by an over-patriotic group when the steady hammering of axes on metal made me look up at the Embassy roof, which was decorated with colossal figures of overfed German warriors holding bloated cart horses. A flagstaff supported a bronze eagle with spread wings.
>
> Several men were busily hammering at the feet of the Teutons. The very first strokes pitched the mob to a frenzy; the heroic figures were hollow!
>
> 'They are empty! A good omen! Another German bluff! Hack them all down! No, leave the horses standing!'
>
> The axes were hammering faster and faster. At last one warrior swayed, pitched forward, and crashed onto the pavement one hundred feet below. A tremendous howl went up, scaring a flock of crows off the gilded dome of St Isaac's. The turn of the eagle came; the bird came hurtling down, and the battered remains were immediately drowned in the nearby Moika river. But obviously the destruction of the symbols was not enough. A quickly organised gang smashed a side door of the Embassy.
>
> I could see flashlights and torches moving inside, flitting to the upper storeys. A big window opened and spat a great portrait of the Kaiser at the crowd below. When it reached the cobblestones, there was just

about enough left to start a good bonfire. A rosewood grand piano followed, exploded like a bomb; the moan of the broken strings vibrated in the air for a second and was drowned; too many people were trying to out shout their own terror of the future.

There is not a spare word in this description. Each detail is fixed precisely with the minimum of adjectives. Like all the best writing, it defies editing.

If the events in the story are stark and horrific, resist the temptation to over-write

The lure to over-write is always greater when your material is extraordinary. Let the events themselves make the impact. And do not try to add drama by characterising the events in any way. Do not, for example, write that the story is 'sensational', 'disturbing', 'horrific'. Present the story without such comment and let the reader judge.

If the story deals with strong emotions, understate rather than overstate

This does not mean you should leave anything out, but that you should avoid language that strains for effect. A heart-rending story, for example, always works best if the language is low-keyed.

Beware of humour

In the movies, theatre and books, humour should have no taboos. Death, sex, cancer and hunger should all be fair game. But joking about these general subjects is a very different matter from trying to have a laugh about some specific person's misfortune in the following day's paper. Giving a light-hearted treatment to a story which involves injury, distress or upset is never a good idea. It is insensitive, and actually pointless. If there is a genuinely comic element to the story (of however questionable taste), people will find it and laugh anyway, especially if the tale is told straight.

Most journalists would agree that humour is very difficult to write. The trouble is, it does not stop them attempting it. Indeed so much writing in newspapers is humorous in intent, if not effect, that the failure of journalism textbooks to address this issue borders on the criminally negligent. Just the two words 'think twice' would be valuable. Of even greater worth would be for them to point out one of the basic truths of humour, because that at least might stop at the drafting stage a lot of the laborious, creaking efforts that get into print. And this truth is: being funny on paper is a God-given talent not granted to many of us.

Writing humour is like singing in tune. If you can do it, you don't need to be taught; if you can't do it, no amount of teaching will help.

And comedy out of tune, like singing, is excruciating to experience and embarrassing to do. Or should be. However, if you have got the talent, it comes relatively easily. Your ear instinctively recognises the rhythm that humour writing must have, and the words that are almost funny in themselves. You won't need to be told that jokes are funnier when delivered with a straight face rather than the literary equivalent of a whirring bow-tie. Your eye will see comic possibilities where everyone else sees what is merely on the surface, and your brain will be full of all the little cultural, social and historical references that make a joke.

If you have a good comic idea for a piece that is suitable, then work on it. It has to be tightly written, surprise the reader (which is why puns are not funny) and it has to have the punch line at the end of the sentence. Right at the end. Not in the penultimate phrase. Finally, if you are giving an article a particular humorous treatment or framework, it has to be strong enough to carry the whole piece right to the end. The soundest policy is always to let the humour flow naturally from the events and innate absurdities of your subject, rather than being a 'joke' that you impose on it from outside. Here, for example, is an intro written by *Wall Street Journal* reporter Tony Horwitz. Just after the end of the Gulf War, he filed a piece about Kuwait, the invasion of which by Iraq had started the conflict. Kuwait is an oil-rich, semi-feudal state presided over by a fabulously wealthy royal family. This is what Horwitz wrote: 'The emir of Kuwait, Jaber al Sabah, returned home yesterday, 15 days after the liberation of his land, and 10 days after his furniture.'

The moral of this section is that if you have any doubts about a joke or allegedly funny line, leave it out. If you have no doubts, then imagine standing on a stage delivering it to an audience of 500 readers. Only if you still think it will get a laugh should you go ahead with it. And remember that the addition of an exclamation mark at the end of a sentence does not render it funny! Just amateur!

Efficiency

In the last century and quite a way into this one, journalists in Britain and the United States were paid by the line. This system of payment gave birth to a generation of journalists who could write impressive amounts about nothing and almost endlessly about very little. And this in turn produced a bloated style of writing whose chief characteristic was its exponents' ability never to knowingly write one word where four or five could be deployed. As a result, their pompous and excessive language (a football, for instance, was known as 'the elusive leathern spheroid') made a lasting if inadvertent contribution to British humour. It was writing so spectacularly inefficient that, in its way, it was almost admirable.

Thankfully, journalistic style (and, in most cases, systems of payment) have moved on a little. Payment by the word has long since been recognised as a way of bribing people to write badly. Yet enough of the lineage men's spiritual descendants live on to make a few notes about writing efficiency worthwhile.

Make every phrase and sentence do a job of work

They must either convey fresh information or otherwise help move the piece forward. If any part of the story does not do this, cut it.

Avoid wasteful constructions

Every language has phrases that are used in speech to give the speaker time to form fully the thought that is coming. In English, examples would be: 'It is a well-known fact that ...'; 'Indeed, there is no doubting the fact that ...'; 'We can also observe that ...'. Avoid these and avoid also the leisurely constructions that slow a piece down. Journalism, especially news reporting, has to have pace. It can't if sentences like the previous one are constructed thus: 'It is an essential requirement of most journalism – features, sport, profiles and features, but particularly news reporting – that they should move forwards with that quality known as pace.'

Write without looking at your notes

You will write more quickly and more efficiently if you do so without looking at your notebook every five seconds. You should not even start to write unless the story is clear in your mind, and if you write without notes only the essential material will go in. The details, spellings and figures you can check with your notebook afterwards. There will almost certainly be one or two points you will add as a result, but the main draft will be written far more efficiently from your head than by copying out large chunks of notes.

Ruthlessly hunt down all obvious and silly remarks and remove them

Even the most experienced writers find themselves writing the most pitifully obvious things sometimes. These are often links between paragraphs that you have struggled over, and, in your desperation to try to weld one part of the story to another, you find yourself writing the purest nonsense. Only the other week I cut from a story the phrase, 'Of course, a ballet dancer's life is not all applause ...'. Well whoever thought it was? You often find that you do not need these links at all. Most readers can handle a small change of direction if it is accompanied with a change of paragraph.

Use the active, not passive voice

People and things do and say things, so it is always best to write this directly. Thus: 'Heathrow Airport will open another runway in 2003' and not 'It has been established that another runway will open at Heathrow International Airport in 2003.' Certain verbs, like come, leave and give, are frequently used for the passive voice as in: 'The demand came when Yeltsin asked ...' (better to say 'Yeltsin demands ...'), 'The earthquake left 3,000 people dead-...' ('The earthquake killed ...') and 'The move gave a boost to ...' ('The move boosted ...'). The active voice is not just more efficient, it is also, as the name suggests, more active.

Use bullets and lists to itemise points in a story

This can be overdone in a paper, but is very useful when you have a long catalogue of points to make. Instead of taking several long paragraphs to describe the effects of, say, government spending cuts on transport, itemise them like you would on a shopping list. But beware of doing this and then finding that you have to mention most of the points again in order to add detail to them. Put the detail with the list.

Avoid meaningless modifiers

Phrases like 'serious danger', 'unconfirmed rumours' and 'unduly alarmed' are, if you think for a second, complete nonsense. What, after all, is unserious danger? And if a rumour was confirmed it would no longer be a rumour, it would be a fact and an attributable one. Such automatic phrases can be cut down to the second word, along with other meaningless modifiers like 'rather unique'. It either is, or is not, the only one of its kind, and if it is not, then it is not unique, rather, slightly or otherwise.

Avoid tautology

This is the use of words that say the same thing twice. For instance, '*Some* of the remarks *included* ...' and 'it is an *essential condition*'. In both cases (and many others that could be given) only one of the italicised words is needed.

Do not use quotes to restate points already made in reported speech

This is a common and wasteful habit, as in: 'The ministry denied this. A spokesman said, "We do not accept this allegation."' Write one or the other, preferably the first.

Get to know the words that can be used instead of long phrases

'The subject to which I refer', for instance, amounts to the one little word: 'this'.

Finally, a useful exercise is to take a few of your recent published stories and, with a red pen, reduce the number of words used, without eliminating any essential fact. You will be surprised how wasteful you have been. That is why it is a very good experience for a writer to work for a period as a copy editor. There is nothing like the discipline of telling complex stories in 250 words to teach you efficient writing.

Revision

Writers have to be their own fiercest critics. It is essential that you read back what you have written, looking for any flaws, and revise it if you are not happy. Normally, by the time the story reaches another pair of eyes it will be too late – either for improvement or for your reputation. Some writers prefer to write a version of the whole story before subjecting it to, perhaps heavy, revision. Others, perhaps those who know more clearly what they want, revise as they go. The method does not matter, what is important is that the revision is comprehensive and not just a superficial search for spelling mistakes.

George Orwell, the author of *Animal Farm* and *1984* whose writing was noted for its clarity, thought there were four questions that any writer should ask of each sentence. This sounds laborious, and would be if this questioning did not become automatic and almost subconscious after a while. His questions were:

What am I trying to say?
What words express it?
What image or idiom will make it clearer?
Is the image fresh enough to have an effect?

Then, by way of important afterthoughts, he added two more:

Could I put it more simply?
Have I written anything avoidably ugly?

Those writing regularly will soon learn to ask those questions of their writing with no more conscious effort than they use to move their eyes from left to right as they read. I would, however, suggest that a couple of questions are knowingly asked of the drafted piece:

Are there any loose ends, is everything explained properly?
Does it read flowingly?

If it does, then leave it alone, resist the temptation to throw in a few more colourful phrases, as if you were a cook tossing a few more currants into a cake. And if it does read awkwardly, it may need more than a bit of light tinkering to put right. Punctuation, for instance, is not a quick way to give the kiss of life to dying sentences. Re-write and re-structure until you are happy.

And then cut it. Are there any words, phrases or sentences that slow the piece down? I rarely come across an article that could not be improved by cutting. It is like tightening the nuts and bolts on a piece of furniture. If left undone, the thing would be loose and unstable. Beware especially of anything that sounded good when you wrote it. As Samuel Johnson once said, 'Read over your compositions and, when you meet a passage which you think is particularly fine, strike it out.' Such parts often don't work as well as you first think.

The joys of writing

Inexperienced journalists can be almost overwhelmed at times by the problems of writing something clear and interesting that people will want to read. Older writers are not exactly immune from this sinking feeling, too, and to hear them speak of the pains of composition you would think that no sane person would write, unless at the point of a gun. The great American sports journalist, Red Smith, for instance, once said, 'There's nothing to writing. All you do is sit down at a typewriter and open a vein.' To which another American, Gore Vidal, probably gave the definitive reply when he wrote, 'When I hear about writer's block, this one and that one! Fuck off! Stop writing, for Christ's sake. Plenty more where you came from.'

Sure it is sometimes a real sweat. Of course, there are stories which seem a confusing and worthless jumble until you have spent many hours wrestling them into shape, and there are times of sheer panic as the deadline approaches with the thing only half done and ill thought out. But the pleasures of capturing something and pinning it down in words, your words, are immense. So too is the thrill of starting a piece with an assortment of disparate information and finding a pattern in it and new ideas about it as you write.

You will have to write and put away or burn a lot of material before you are comfortable in this medium. You might as well start now and get the necessary work done. For I believe that eventually quantity will make for quality.

Ray Bradbury

14

Intros

Always grab the reader by the throat in the first paragraph, sink your thumbs into his windpipe in the second, and hold him against the wall until the tag line.

Paul O'Neil, American writer

The intro is the most important paragraph in the story. It can make people want to read to the end, or it can turn them off and send them hurrying to another article. And they will not be slow to do this. Newspapers are often consumed quickly, by people with little time to read them, in places and conditions not designed for relaxation and contemplation – trains, cars at traffic lights, offices, the street, etc. There is a good chance that if the first paragraph does not grab their attention, they will never get to the second one.

That progress is not always determined by the quality of the intro. Other factors play a role: a good headline will sometimes inspire people to dig beyond the intro, and a strong interest in the subject matter may force them to plough on in case the story perks up. Readers are also influenced by the size of the paper (one of 96 pages obviously offering more alternative articles to sample than one of 12). As a journalist you cannot influence or have foreknowledge of these factors. (And don't say you know the size of the paper. Of course you do, but the reader may be buying several others.) The only way you can make a reader get beyond the intro is to make it a good one.

How to write sharp intros

Whatever kind of intro you are writing, on whatever kind of story, there are some general points to remember.

The intro should be direct, uncluttered and unambiguous

There should only be one question in readers' minds when they read an intro: 'Do I want to read this story?' The answer is liable to be 'no' if you give them extra questions raised by ambiguity and complication. It is also important to clear out any unwanted clutter, such as needless detail, precise titles, or attribution, that can wait until the second paragraph or later.

The intro should be self-contained

Except with certain types of features, it should not depend for its sense on what follows, only for its explanation and exposition. Neither should there be any unidentified facts, people, events, organisations or places unless strictly necessary.

Never start any story with a subsidiary clause

For instance, 'Despite the rising number of murders ...' or 'Although murders are increasing almost daily ...'. This approach is slow, delays the main point and puts questions in readers' minds. Subsidiary clause beginnings have this effect on any sentence and so should be used sparingly even in the body of the text.

Never start a story with numbers in digits

Spell out the number or, if it is a large one, find another way to begin the story. Do not just shove in the word 'about', as in 'About 47 people died yesterday when....'. This makes precise information sound like a wild guess.

Never start stories with official names of official bodies

Unless you have an exceptional reason or are being ironical, long bureaucratic titles are a bad way to start a story. If you begin: 'The Ministry of Agriculture and Fisheries Pollution Monitoring Unit yesterday announced ...', readers will turn away before they have a chance to read that all fish caught in a certain river are contaminated and should not be eaten. Begin instead with either a short form of the name, such as 'Government pollution experts', or, far better, tell people what has happened and attribute it later.

Only rarely begin with quotes

Beginning stories with quotes mystifies readers because until you tell them, they do not know who is talking. There are a few isolated occasions when a quote will be a good way to start, but, in these cases, the speaker should be identified immediately.

Avoid 'it' intros

The bad intro that I most commonly see is the one that begins 'It emerged last night that...'. This immediately begs the question: who or what is it? And 'emerged' is a silly word to decribe something being announced, revealed, said or published. The only story which would justify an 'It emerged last night' intro would be one revealing the Loch Ness monster's sudden appearance from the depths.

Do not get too obsessed with the length of intros

Some papers have rules about the maximum length of intros. If yours does, you have little choice but to conform. But otherwise, do not worry too much if an intro's length breaches some mythical 'limits'. I have never read a letter from a reader complaining about the length of an intro. So long as an intro is grabbing readers' attention, it is doing its job.

Normally when intros are written about in textbooks, the author will list various types of newspaper story (straight news, human interest, etc.) and set out the intros used in each case. This is unhelpful, stupid and wrong. It gives the impression that writing is a matter of acquiring techniques, that journalists can be provided with a bag of tricks or tools which they open and use according to the circumstances: 'Ah, here is a human interest story, so out comes the delayed intro approach ...'. And it produces the formula writing which is such a disease. Far better to set out the different approaches to intros and leave it to the writer to decide how to apply them.

For me, if there is a gold standard of hard news intro writing, it is set by two American reporters who worked forty years apart. Both feature in my *The Great Reporters* book. The first is Meyer 'Mike' Berger of the *New York Times*. On a major incident in 1944, he began:

> One hundred and thirty-nine dead and 174 badly burned persons were pulled from the charred ruins of the main Ringling Brothers and Barnum & Bailey circus tent in Hartford this afternoon after fire swept the enclosure end to end along its entire 520-foot length.

For today's mass-market tabloid that would be too long; but for any other purpose it is exemplary. It answers all the main questions (except, as you would expect in a report written just hours after the incident happened, the why), and even tells you the startling information that the fire swept from one end of such a large structure to the other. But Berger could also write an intro that, on a story far more prosaic (the falling of a blind man to his death on the New York metro), was more imaginative:

> The sixth sense that had preserved Oscar England from harm through the thirty-four dark years of his life betrayed him yesterday. One step too many in the BMT Union Square station and he was wedged, lifeless, between a north-bound express and the concrete platform.

That was written in 1936. More than four decades later, Edna Buchanan of the *Miami Herald* was writing very different kinds of intros on the stories that made her the world's leading crime reporter. These could be wise-cracking:

> They called it Operation Snow White because the drug was cocaine and the suspects included seven Miami police officers (1982)

> Angel Aguada saw a stranger across a crowded room. Their eyes met. The moment was spoiled when her husband shot Aguada three times.

Or ones that resembled the openings of short stories:

> There was a gold, diamond-studded Rolex watch on her wrist, and a bullet in her head.

Ones that imaginatively brought home the story's significance:

> Enough of a powerful hallucinogen to alter the minds of a million people was seized Friday ...

Others that collected all the 'sexy' facts and wove them into an intro:

> The double feature was 'Public Affairs' and 'American Desires'. It was the last picture show for a mystery man found dead in an aisle at the X-rated Pussy Cat Theater shortly before Fifi Royale's exotic dance act.

Punch-line intros where the most startling fact is delivered, like the pay-off of a gag, right at the end of the opening paragraph:

> He helped set up a major cocaine deal, using fluent English and Spanish. He spotted the undercover detectives outside and shouted a warning, setting off gunfire between suspects and police. He is 6 years old.

And intros that tantalise you so much that you could not fail to read on, like this, on the story of a woman whose husbands had a habit of dying prematurely:

> Bad things happen to the husbands of Widow Elkin.

Hard news approach

We are talking here about reporting news *in the first instance*. Stories written on a subject several days after the event may need a different approach and certainly would if they had in the meantime been reported on radio or television.

The aim of all intros is to grab readers and arouse their interest so strongly that they will want to read on. With hard news intros, this means that the most newsworthy aspect(s) of the story should be right up there at the top. This is particularly true if your paper's headline style is cryptic with little detailed information about the story underneath. All the more reason to come to the point as soon as you can. This is not normally difficult on strong or clear-cut stories. If 345 people have been killed in a plane crash, there is not much doubt about the hard news intro: 'At least 345 people were killed when a Global Airlines Boeing 747 crashed into an apartment block in the suburbs of Capital City last night.' But many stories are not as direct as that. They have several angles (aspects) and we cannot get them all into the intro without making it hopelessly cumbersome. You have to decide which is the most newsworthy.

That makes it sound simple, but it isn't. After all, a lot of highly experienced journalists spend many hours writing, rejecting and then re-writing intros. And the issue of what is the best angle for the intro is probably the part of the job that causes more arguments in more newsrooms around the world than anything else. There is invariably no simple right and wrong, just conflicting opinions.

So if you are in two (or three) minds about how to write the intro for the story, is there any help available? Thankfully there is. It was some advice given to me many years ago by Peter Corrigan and I think it is the single most useful tip anyone has ever given me. It is called the *Parable of The Friend On The Hill* and it goes like this:

> Imagine you have all the story's information in your head and you are walking in the country. Suddenly, on top of a hill, you see a friend who you know will be keen to learn about your story. You run towards him, up and up, and when you get within reach of him you only have enough breath for one sentence before collapsing. What is it that you blurt out? That is your intro.

There are variations on this theme, such as to imagine you are sending a telegram about the story, the charge is £10 a word and you are paying. Set yourself a very severe target for the number of words in the telegram: six, or even four. What that will do is force you to think of the key word or words in the story. You can then build the story around that. Geoffrey Murray, an experienced Reuters correspondent, tells an anecdote which perfectly illustrates this. It involves the Reuters correspondent in India covering Mahatma Gandhi at an engagement in 1947. The yarn conflicts with the version in the official history of the news agency, but that does not detract from its therapeutic value to the confused writer of intros.

The Reuters man was at a prayer meeting attended by the Indian leader when an assailant suddenly leapt forward and shot him. Gandhi was badly wounded, but not immediately dead. The reporter ran down the road to the nearest post office to send a cable to London, but found he only had enough money to transmit four words. What should they be? 'Mahatma Gandhi shot here'? – well, you can probably assume your office will know the leader's full name and be aware of his, and your, whereabouts, so 'Mahatma' and 'here' are wasteful. What he filed was: 'Gandhi shot worst feared' – thus conveying an assassination attempt, the victim, method and likely outcome, all in four words. He had also alerted the office to prepare the obituary to run – a vital thing for the agency and all its clients.

(But beware: brevity can breed ambiguity. A message from New York was received at Reuters' London office in September 1901 which read 'McKinley shot Buffalo' and was spiked by a young sub-editor with the words, 'These Yanks. They seem to think we're interested in their President's shooting excursion.' The story was rescued by the editor in charge who realised that Buffalo referred not to the animals but to the city in New York State. Thus did the agency first flash the news of the assassination around the world.)

Other approaches

In most cases where you are reporting on news of general interest, and doing so in the first instance, the hard news intro is the best choice. Yet there are, of course, many other ways to begin a story and some of them can be applied to news stories in the right situation. Feature openings are generally a lot more free-form and, for these especially, the only criteria are what works, and that they are fresh and inventive. This point is equally true of intros to analysis, colour, comment and personality pieces.

Every writer should make intros a lifetime's study, taking every available paper or magazine as a potential text. Once you begin to study intros you soon realise that what you thought were about four or five main types soon multiply into scores. The following are some of the main sorts found on news stories and features. Some of them raise the issue, dealt with more fully in the chapter on construction, that intros are often conceived not as one paragraph but as several.

Narrative

This is an intro which deals with the story in a chronological way. Used commonly on features, it is sometimes used on news stories where how it happened is more interesting or important than what happened. Use, and subsequent abuse, of the chronological start in news features by the *Sunday Times* of London gave birth to a now much-derided school of intro writing. For example:

> At 12.47 p.m. two men in identical blue suits, each carrying a Samsonite attaché case, left the Ruritanian Embassy by the rear entrance.
> They hailed a taxi, asked the driver to take them to Victoria Station and sat back in its black leather upholstery. In the 25 minutes it took the driver to negotiate the capital's heavy lunch-time traffic, neither let go of his innocent-looking case for one second.
> At Victoria Station the taller man took out a brand-new £5 note and paid off the driver, 47-year-old father of three Harry Wingfield. Little could he have known their final destination ...

And so it might go on for another few paragraphs. This novel-style approach has its uses, but one warning: tantalising the reader like this means that when you finally get to the point, it had better be a strong one. If, in the example above, they were smuggling secrets or were off to blow up a rival embassy, all well and good. Not so, however, if they had been given a half-day off and were merely on their way home to spend an evening with their stamp collections.

Anecdote

This is an intro which relates a self-contained anecdote to illustrate an aspect of the story's subject, and is often used on lengthy news features either to introduce main players, show their relationships, or relate an unknown vignette from the story's otherwise well-known sequence of events. It is vital to ensure the anecdote is good and makes a point. One thing to watch is the habit of applying this kind of start to hard news stories. Page one stories that begin with sometimes seven or eight paragraphs of colour about a person, place or intro can seriously aggravate readers who find they are wading through line after line of apparently inconsequential description and anecdote while wondering all the while why they're being told all this. If you must write stories with lengthy delayed drops, here's a thought: why not, early on, let the readers in on the secret of why they're having to read all this. And if there really is no secret, if your delayed drop is merely a delay before you get to the point, then maybe it's a sign you should be rethinking the piece.

Delayed drop

This is an intro of several, sometimes many, paragraphs where the story's point is saved up, like the punch line of a joke. It is often used on soft news stories and light-hearted articles where ordinary everyday events are described for a few paragraphs, followed by the introduction of the nub of the story in a paragraph that inevitably begins, 'Now ...' or, 'And then ...'.

Somewhat stylised and hackneyed, it often produces banalities of the 'Little did they know ...' variety, as in: 'It was a perfect flight. The weather clear, the wine good and the meal excellent. But little did they know as they fastened their seat belts for the landing that two minutes later the plane would catch fire, fall to the ground in seconds and that only two of them would survive.' Perhaps its worst manifestation is the 'he, she, they or it' intro which states a series of things well known about the subject, but gives them a spurious mystery by using a pronoun rather than subject's name. Thus:

'He was the greatest pop star of the 1950s, had a string of number one hits and his home is now a shrine to his fans. He died decades ago and yet sightings of him in petrol stations and shopping malls are regularly reported.' The fact that the headline and picture will almost certainly identify the subject as Elvis Presley does not stop this witless style of intro. The writer then follows these statements of the obvious with a new paragraph beginning: 'But now ...' which will reveal fresh information that ought, in intelligent hands, to be the substance of the intro. A variation is the intro: 'For years this and that has been happening, and such and such are the consequences. Blah, blah, blah. But now ...'. Constructions like this have long since become a cliché. If you use them, you are saying more about your writing skills (or lack of them) than you are about the subject.

Single statement intro

This is the opposite of the story above. Here the whole story is encapsulated in one telling sentence. Economical, evocative and powerful when it works but disastrous when it doesn't; it needs experience, real talent and good judgement. The most appropriate use is on a story which is important, not entirely unexpected and which will be run by virtually all news media. One of the best was on the death of Hitler in May 1945. Imagine that was your story. What could you write on this (already reported on the radio) that would not read as if it were too obvious and unexciting? It is a tall order. But the British *News Chronicle* began its story with the stark sentence: 'The most hated man in the world is dead.' Running it a close second was an intro written by Jack London, author of *White Fang*, for *Collier's Weekly* in April 1906. His assignment was the earthquake and subsequent fire which destroyed most of the buildings in San Francisco and made 225,000 people homeless. London began his report with a paragraph of just four words: 'San Francisco is gone.'

Summary intro

This surveys the territory into which the reader will be taken by the writer and is used to its best advantage to distil the main elements of a complex chain of events. For instance, a story about a very complicated betting fraud involving horse racing could have begun: 'A betting syndicate yesterday tried to swindle £400,000 from bookmakers across Britain.' But a better alternative might be: 'Joe Martin was a gambler who was so keen to win on the horses that he invented a racecourse, held a "meeting" there, got his friends to bet on its fictitious results and nearly, very nearly got away with it all.'

This type of intro is used also when the story's interest lies not in one main point but in a number of developments. Although very useful, the danger with the summary intro is that if it is insufficiently comprehensive it only delays the problem of deciding the most important aspect until the second paragraph. Perhaps the best way to avoid this is to think of it as akin to a film trailer, giving highlights of what is to come. Then it is especially valuable on stories surveying a broad range of subjects or people, or on profiles of individuals. For example: 'Farouk is not just the King of Egypt. He is also a road hog, racketeer, womaniser, glutton, pickpocket and, now, an overweight playboy in exile. He is, in fact, the king who never grew up.'

Singular statement intro

This is an opening where the writer throws a bizarre or amazing statement at readers in the hope of tantalising them into reading on. A war reporter once began a piece with the line, 'This morning I shaved in vintage red wine ...', before going on to write that the unit he was with had just taken one of the more important vineyards from the Germans.

Jolt intro

This is where you take two pieces of information in the story, most probably the origin and the outcome, and put them together so that they provide a jolt. Deliberate understatement is often essential. For instance, this by an American writer on what might have been a fairly routine accident story: 'Billy Ray Smith lit a cigarette while soaking his feet in petrol. He may survive.'

But make sure you give enough information to make the reader appreciate the shock value in what you have to say. The *Cincinnati Inquirer* did this correctly in the intro on a 2008 story about a man known as 'Clermont County's version of Hannibal Lecter': 'David Allen Chapin, who ate the brain of his roommate after he shot him 30 years ago in an argument over whose religion was better, is up for parole in June.' Sales of security locks in the city no doubt perked up.

Scene-setter intro

This is an intro where the writer paints a word picture of a scene that is unusual or else vital to understanding the subject. Used most commonly on long soft features or on colour pieces, it has to be both well-written and have its significance explained soon afterwards. It is at its best when there is some 'the clock struck thirteen' peculiarity to it. As in:

> Imagine the scene. It is winter and inside an unheated apartment sits an old man wearing nothing but a thin gown. He is bent over a table, examining something through a microscope. A small candle burns by his elbow. All of a sudden, he leans back, smiles, takes a $5 note from his pocket, puts it in the candle's flame and uses it to light a small cigar.

You are compelled to read on to discover what it is that he is looking at, why he has no need of heat or warm clothes and what he is doing using dollars to light cigars. He is, the story goes on to explain, a banknote forger fallen on hard times. The trick is to write something where the reader yearns to know what happens next, as in Anthony Burgess's intro to his novel, *Earthly Powers*:

> It was the afternoon of my eighty-first birthday, and I was in bed with my catamite when Ali announced that the archbishop had come to see me.

Question intro

This is a dangerous opening, since readers are apt to give an immediate answer and pass on. So best not ask them direct, easily solved questions. Nor ones to which there is a surprising reply, since this is an infallible indicator that the information given in the answer would be better deployed in the intro. It is often used (ill-advisedly) on soft lifestyle features, as in, 'How many times did you wash your hands today?' but is best used on features where the question has a complex solution(s), could not possibly be answered by any reader and you delay answering it completely until the end of the piece. Even then, it should be used very sparingly. Its application to news stories (which are supposed to provide answers, not questions) would be absurd.

Joke intro

This is one of the most common of all intros, but, as indicated in the previous chapter, humour is attempted more often than it is achieved.

Despite this, it is a very effective opening when successful because readers feel they are in the company of an amusing writer and will always read on in anticipation of more humour.

The opening can be a one-liner, like this from P.J. O'Rourke of the American magazine *Rolling Stone*: 'There are probably more fact-finding tours of Nicaragua right now than there are facts.'

Or it can be a number of sentences that build up to a punch-line, as in this, also by O'Rourke:

> My friend Dorothy and I spent a weekend at Heritage USA, the born-again Christian resort and amusement park created by television evangelists Jim and Tammy Bakker. Dorothy and I came to scoff – but went away converted. Unfortunately, we were converted to Satanism.

Philosophical intro

This consists of making some broad and sweeping, epigrammatical statement that is supposed to sound profound and yet rarely is. Be aware that the thought you conceived about the condition of humanity, which came to you just as the clock ticked towards your deadline, is unlikely to look so rich in meaning the following day.

A variant of this is that old college essay trick of putting up a statement in the intro solely for the purpose of demolishing it in the rest of the piece. The problem with this approach is that it often comes across as a writer's trick rather than an inventive start springing naturally from the material.

Historical intro

This is when a story begins with a statement about the subject's history, as such: 'In 1948, the Ruritanian government decided that henceforward their borders would be effectively sealed, thus ending their long tradition of automatic hospitality to foreigners.' With this type, either the historical fact itself must be fascinating enough to grab the reader, or the twist (usually provided in a second paragraph that begins: 'But-...') must be strong. Otherwise it can appear very flat. It is nearly always better re-worked with the information from the second paragraph in the intro.

False intros

Finally there is one species of intro which is not a type at all but a widely made mistake. Called a 'false intro' it is an opening which the writer thinks is selling the story to readers but which is entirely disposable. Commonly used on features or light news stories, it has two usual forms. First is the failed joke, as in this on a story about a new sports car: 'Move over girls, here comes a curvy desirable object that's going to replace you in your man's dreams.' Second is the narrative opening which starts one phase too early, as in this on the story of a couple's disastrous holiday: 'Olive and Ian Meredith were really looking forward to two weeks of fun on the sun-soaked beaches of Thailand.' The fact that they arrived to find the hotel only half built and the beach covered in untreated sewage is only revealed in the second paragraph. It should be in the first. After all, most people *do* look forward to their holidays.

Do you always write the intro first?

In both the above cases, the piece would be far better without the annoying, inane intro. Practice intros are like a dancer's warm-up routine – perhaps essential to the performance, but certainly not part of it. They are a private thing and should not reach the public. They are also a reminder that we often need to get something down on paper or screen just to get ourselves going. There is nothing wrong with that; any behind-the-scenes routine that delivers the goods in the paper is worth following. Just don't let anyone else see it.

Some feature writers, if they have the time, prefer to write in longhand and then type the result, polishing as they go. They claim to choose words more carefully and write more economically if they have to do so manually, rather than on a computer. They maintain that fast, sensitive electronic keyboards encourage verbosity and loose sentence construction, and make writers compose 'off the top of the head' rather than forming and reforming sentences before they write them down, as they would do with a pen and paper.

There are as many writing habits as there are writers (Nabokov, for instance, often wrote standing up; Victor Hugo naked). But there is one habit which is decidedly dangerous – writing the piece without a proper intro and then going back to compose the first paragraph last. The great problem with this is that the process of writing the intro is often what gives you a clear idea of the piece, its construction and the tone you should adopt. If you draft a piece and then go back to write the intro, you may find that the article should have a totally different tone and structure, which means a re-write.

The only time when this habit may be useful is if the story has a clear, probably chronological, structure and you can start at the beginning of the narrative and then go back and put a summary, declaratory, or some other kind of intro on it. The most obvious instance of this is with major incident stories when you have to start writing before the final outcome, cause or death toll is known. This is called a running story because it is still running when you have to begin writing. With these, it is always best to start at the chronological beginning of the incident and then, just before deadline, add the intro and, possibly, a final few paragraphs.

A word about feature intros

A lot of inexperienced reporters produce feature intros that are obscure, opaque or obtuse – or even contain some little homily on the subject which has all the originality and profundity of the words inside a greeting card. Good feature reporters are content to let the facts speak for themselves – and there is a reason for this, quite apart from their skill as writers. Consider these three intros by Gay Talese, then of the *New York Times*, one of the best newspaper and magazine writers of the twentieth century. The first is on a 2,662-word feature about the dummies in Manhattan shop windows:

> At 4 am, Fifth Avenue is deserted by all but a few strolling insomniacs, some cruising cab drivers, and a group of sophisticated females who stand in store windows all night (and day), wearing cold, perfect smiles – smiles formed by lips of clay, eyes of glass, and cheeks that will glow until the paint wears off.

Then this, on a man's odd occupation:

> Every time Bernie Fein listens to the jokes of nightclub, television or Broadway comedians, he chuckles, roars, slaps his thighs and doubles up in convulsive laughter. Mr. Fein is a professional laugher. He will laugh at anything for a fee.

And a third on the short (452 words) news feature on a meeting of an unusual organisation:

> Kinderhook, N.Y., Feb. 2 – The big farmer rapped his raw knuckles against the wooden table a few times yesterday, and soon 80 men stopped talking and began to lumber toward their seats. The 141st annual meeting of the local Society for the Detection of Horse Thieves was about to begin.

In each case, Talese is upfront about the subject. Why? Because the material he has gathered on it is fascinating in its own right. And that's the reason he writes directly and lesser reporters fanny around at the start, are obscure, or use lengthy delayed drop intros. What I'm sure they are doing, whether they realise it or not, is trying to hide the fact that they haven't got much of a story to tell. But to the trained eye, they haven't disguised anything. What they've done is reveal very plainly the thinness of their material. And therein lies one of the biggest truths about journalism – if you haven't got much of a story to tell you'll always struggle with the writing.

Bad writers are those who write with reference to an inner context which the reader cannot know.

Albert Camus

15

Construction and Description

Anything that is written to please the author is worthless.
Blaise Pascal

Good story construction is a matter of clarity, organisation and efficiency. It ought to be a simple matter and generally it is, especially on hard news stories of up to about twelve paragraphs. Once you have the most interesting information in the intro, arranging the rest of it is not the most challenging of tasks. The oft-quoted model for this is the inverted pyramid, a pseudo-technical phrase for the rudimentary matter of placing the material in descending order of interest and importance. Do that, and you will be at the end of the story before you know it. And it should have the same effect on readers.

Problems of construction come with articles that are more lengthy, complex or both. This is especially true of news stories that do not have a chronological sequence of events. Feature-style reports are also more difficult to construct because they often involve a lot of different themes and strands. Parts of the story seem to fit in several different places and others seem to fit nowhere.

The construction difficulties mostly centre on this: how do you present often diverse aspects clearly and logically in a way that presents a coherent picture at the end? What goes where and how does it hang together? These problems at their worst are like trying to solve a jigsaw puzzle where the pieces can be an almost infinite number of sizes and shapes and the picture on the box is missing. Fortunately you are in *command*, a word which is at the heart of this process. Good construction is about taking command of the material. That means you have to survey the information you have, decide on its essence, envisage the overall picture and effect you want to achieve, decide which pieces you need and which you don't, what size and shape they should be and how they should fit together.

If there is a secret of good construction it is in thinking of the story as being made up of building blocks. These are sections of information that make up units with which you will construct the story. When you first spread out your information and survey it, you are looking for what is essential and what is not. Then you start to see these essentials falling into several different building blocks or aspects of the story. You then start allocating the more minor information to these blocks and also begin to think of what order the sections will go in. Links between them then occur to you. In anything but the most elementary cases, some of this planning will be done on paper, even if it is only a few scribbled headings.

A lot of this process becomes unconscious after a while and setting it out as above may give the impression that it has more in common with filing than composition. What cannot be reflected here is that, with experience, story planning becomes a more intuitive business.

Construction guidelines

Deal with each aspect of the story in one place

Don't jump about from one part of the story to another and then back to the first part. This is confusing for you and the reader. Deal with each aspect separately and clearly.

Make the links between building blocks as natural as you can

You can always tell a badly planned story by the proliferation of 'meanwhiles', 'buts' and 'howevers'. You should be able to move logically from one block to another without using a lot of these. Such words are used to introduce something which conflicts or contrasts with what has gone before and are a great construction trip-wire. Unless you are careful, you can easily find yourself wanting to use them every third or fourth sentence. Minimising them is a matter of putting together all the material that argues in one direction, and then following it with the contradictory information, where possible. If you do need a linking thought or sentence, make it a smooth one.

On longer stories, think of the intro as a building block in itself

It is often helpful to think of the intro as being not just one paragraph but a block of maybe three or four. This would contain not only the opening paragraph but also the highlights or summary of the story that follows. Typical second or third paragraphs on news stories (where the main angle is in the first paragraph) are the amplification of that angle, a quote to support it, or a summary or taster paragraph. This is a sentence or two of the story's highlights, telling the reader what is in store. A highlights paragraph is useful when, for some reason, these good points will be dealt with well down the story.

Beware of blind alleys

When making your plan, be on the look-out for any building block that does not lead naturally to another. Typically these are peripheral side-issues or side-effects of the main thrust of the story. Such blind alleys should be left to the end of the story, otherwise, as with the real thing, you will find yourself having to reverse out of if you want to go anywhere else.

Watch the second paragraph

Let's get three things clear: in all but a few cases, the second paragraph of a hard news story is not for: a change of subject, a chunk of background, or a quote that merely says the same thing the intro has already done in reported speech. The paragraph after the intro should, as Dennis Jackson and John Sweeney's excellent book *The Journalist's Craft* says, drive the story forward with information that adds to that provided by your intro, together – perhaps – 'with some foreshadowing (of juicy detail or developments to come) or tantalising detail.'

If the events in the story have a chronological structure, use that

A chronological narrative is simple, easy to follow and is often the best option. After your intro paragraph(s), don't be afraid to say 'It all began when ...' and then proceed from there to the end.

Make denials follow accusations as closely as possible

If there are two conflicting sides to a story, ensure where possible that the denials or challenges closely follow the accusation. Separating these by several paragraphs is one of the easiest ways to confuse the reader. It is also wasteful because distance between these two parts means you may have to recap the original claim.

Never be afraid to spell things out

Some stories are highly complicated and there is a danger of readers getting lost, however good the construction. In these situations don't be shy of setting things out textbook style and telling readers what they are going to get, as in: 'There are four aspects to this complex issue: 1...', etc.

Don't put background in large, indigestible chunks

Some stories need to contain a lot of background or recapping of previous stories either to make sense or to be at maximum strength. In most cases, this kind of material is best woven into the main narrative and given succinctly in passing. In rare, highly complicated cases, you can however resort to the 'The story so far ...' device.

Beware the consequences construction

This is a way of writing light human interest stories that has become depressingly over-used. To paraphrase Keith Waterhouse's parody of this technique in his superb book *Waterhouse on Newspaper Style*, an example would be:

A little Bolton schoolboy will never forget the day he got his head stuck in the school railings. *(A short jokey characterisation of what happened, which does not give the final game away.)*
First ... this happened. *(Names, time and place are introduced,)*
Then ... that happened. *(The chronological narrative continues.)*
And ... something else happened. *(And continues...)*
But ... *(Feeble news point goes in here).*
And now ... everything is all right *(Otherwise it would be written another way, see?)*
So ... *(The final consequence and quotes from all the main parties.)*

Use quotes to change the pace in a long section of reported speech

Just as a long section of quotes would be tedious, and also inefficient in terms of length, so prolonged reported speech can get monotonous. Insert some variety, and a human voice with a quote or two, however brief.

Reported speech statements in the intro should be supported by quotes later in the story

This should always be done, but applies particularly when the reported speech statement is controversial.

On follow-up stories remember to recapitulate

When constructing a follow-up story, you should take care to recap enough of the original to make your new story intelligible. This can either be done as a glancing sentence, or as a longer background section. It is vital when recapping that, if an accusation has been denied in earlier stories, any follow-up story which repeats the accusation also repeats the denial.

Don't forget the context paragraph

For some reason a lot of reporters, when writing a follow-up or a story that is part of a long-running sequence or issue, forget to remind readers

of the topicality of their story. In such circumstances, you need a sentence
or two that fixes your story in context and normally begins with 'the news
comes as ...' or 'Just three days ago ...' or something like that.

Analysing story structures

Most of us spent endless hours of our youth sitting in schoolrooms and
university halls, studying and deconstructing poems, short stories and
novels. But suggest to journalists, young or old, that their own writing
would benefit from giving newspaper articles the same analytical
treatment and they will look at you as if you had just advocated the
neutering of all males over 25.

Yet there is a lot to be gained from a little time devoted to such analysis.
It does not have to take long, and the objects of your attentions can be
good or bad; you can learn from both. All you have to do is make some
notes of the job each part of the story does. Here, by way of illustration,
is an example:

Speech stories.
Intro stating most important news point, with or without supporting
quotes.
Any further major points, with or without quotes.
Elaboration of intro with direct quotes.
Development of speech and quotes.
Summary of other main points.
(Note: audience reaction, demeanour and appearance of speaker,
essential background, etc. given as passing clauses unless significant.)

Payoffs

American writer Ernest Hemingway once claimed he re-wrote the ending
of *Farewell To Arms* 39 times before he was satisfied. Not many newspaper
stories would get published if this practice was imitated (although more
than a few intros could benefit from such attention), but it is a reminder
that endings are important as well as openings. Not as important, but
still worth thinking about.

Longer articles, especially, are better when rounded off. They do not
have to resolve themselves in the same way as a piece of nineteenth-
century symphonic music does. And they should certainly not come to
one of those dreadful phoney, forced conclusions where the writer feels
he has to give a verdict or give the reader a kind of farewell wave in words.
But neither should they end abruptly, as if the writer just got bored, nor
just meekly fade away.

Anecdotes, preferably without the writer's quasi-philosophical wrap-up remark, are a good way to close. So are short descriptions of a final scene, a telling quote, ironic fact or statistic, some twist to the main thrust of the story that you have held back; maybe even an echo from the intro or something else earlier in the story. Anything, in fact, that gives completeness and prevents the reader concluding that the author got so far and then suddenly remembered a pressing engagement.

Here is one of the finest closing sentences in the history of the printed word. It was written by the American-born correspondent of the London *Daily News*, J.A. MacGahan, at the conclusion of one of his dispatches that revealed the Turkish atrocities against the Bulgarians in 1876. After a controlled account of the slaughter in Batak (the one extensively quoted in Chapter 1), he concludes by surveying the scene where thousands of bodies lay, and then adds: 'The harvests are rotting in the fields, and the reapers are rotting here in the churchyard.'

Attribution

If there is one thing that American journalists can teach the world, it is how to be disciplined in sourcing stories. For some reason, attribution is an area where a lot of reporters have an attitude problem. They feel that anything other than the bare minimum of information-sourcing involves a certain loss of journalistic virility. This, of course, is nonsense. In properly sourcing a story, all you are doing is giving readers what they need to help them judge your story, or the separate pieces of information within it. The reader should never have to ask, 'How does the paper know this?'

The degree of sourcing depends on the nature of the story and the type of publication. Controversial stories and specialised publications generally need attribution that is more detailed and prominent. Here are some other points on when, where and how to source.

Where sourcing is not needed

Attribution is obviously not needed on what you might call general knowledge, information that is in the public domain, and which can be verified immediately by a host of other sources. No one should feel the need to write something like this: 'Budapest is the capital of Hungary, a foreign ministry official said today.' Nor, if a major fire occurs, is there a need to have a source for it, unless someone in authority is doubting its existence. Generally, however, the contents of most news stories will need sourcing in print. And that means every statement should have a clear derivation.

Source everything that is, or might become, contentious

In the example of the fire above, you would need a source for casualty figures, damage and cause – all of which might be challenged by another source. Any information that is contentious, or might be, should be sourced, as should anything judgemental or which you feel might not be immediate public knowledge (for example, if the fire was a bomb and you felt the authorities would contest that a bomb had gone off).

Never use passive attribution

Do not write, 'It was said', 'It was announced', or 'It was understood'. They all beg the question, by whom? Somewhere in the world there is the person or organisation that said it, announced it or believes it. Tell us who they are. Apart from anything else, passive attribution uses the impersonal voice of the bureaucracy claiming omnipotence – and we all know how reliable that is.

Make clear how information was obtained

If it is relevant, and it usually is, make clear how your information was obtained. This need not take much explanation, just a simple phrase will do, such as 'said in a prepared press statement' or 'told reporters in answer to questions'.

Be as specific as you can

Sources carry so much more weight when they have a name, title and anything else that establishes their credibility or helps readers judge the information's quality. 'Army spokesman Ronald Elwill' is far better than 'army spokesman'. Add any extra information that may be useful. If your source was at a meeting or on the scene of an incident, then say so. Sources carry more conviction if they are on the spot, as opposed to sitting in headquarters, miles, or even continents, away.

Unnamed sources

When you cannot name a source (negotiating and dealing with this situation is dealt with in Chapter 6) you should give as much information about the kind of person they are, and their credentials, as possible. Don't just write 'sources', 'analysts', 'experts' or, God forbid, 'this newspaper's sources'. Be as specific as you can, and use the plural only when justified. If it is a single source then say so. Finally, if your information comes from a variety of anonymous sources, do not attribute each item. Write,

'Interviews with senior bankers revealed differing reactions to the news. Some said ...'.

Develop ranks of unnamed sources

Readers will be helped considerably if you grade unnamed sources. Reuters uses the following categories:

- Authoritative sources exercise real authority on the issue in question. A defence minister is an authoritative source on defence matters but not on finance.
- Official sources have access to information in their official capacity, but their competence as a source is limited to this field.
- Designated sources are, for instance, diplomatic sources, intelligence sources or sources in the mining industry. As with an official source, they must have access to reliable information on the subject.

One of the great troubles with no-name sources is that, unless you give such guidance, the reader does not have the first idea whether you are quoting the President or the man who cleans his shoes.

Placing of attribution

Sourcing should come high in every story and be in the intro if the story is contentious. Intro sourcing need not be inelegant and is always better than those ugly constructions which start a story with a bald, unsourced statement and then follow with a second paragraph which opens, 'That is the opinion/view/finding, etc. of ...'. This applies particularly if the story is about something being said rather than done. Intro sourcing should, however, be minimised as much as possible to avoid clutter. Full and official titles, for example, can be given lower down.

Elsewhere in the story, attribution can be given discreetly at the end of sentences. Where one source covers most of the story, it does not need to be repeated more than is strictly necessary. However, every statement in the story, unless it is covered in the exceptions above, will need sourcing. This does not mean every sentence, for it is usually possible to write the story to make it clear that clumps of information have the same source.

Starting with the source

There are two situations where a news story is better understood by readers if it starts with the source. They are both 'say stories' (ones about someone saying something). The first is where the statement/ accusation/ claim has been made by a figure of such prominence and significance that his or her identity should be known before what is said is revealed.

The second is where a highly contentious accusation or claim has been made, often of a personal nature. It would, for instance, be absurd to read a story that began, 'President Bogdorov of Ruritania has killed off many of his country's old people with his new health policies, says opposition leader Mr Yuri Snickerov.' Far better to write, 'Ruritanian opposition leader Yuri Snickerov has accused President Bogdorov of killing off ...'. The first is an apparent statement of fact, followed by a source; the second makes it clear that this is an accusation, and, given who it comes from, a politically motivated one.

Description

Description, or colour as it is sometimes called, should be part of most stories. It is easy to be so consumed with relating the bare facts of the story that you forget to describe people or places at the centre of it. Even if the description is only a few phrases giving readers a basic idea of what a building or person looks like, it is worthwhile. Descriptions, whether they are passing remarks or whole passages, add extra information and help readers to imagine better what has happened, to whom and where.

You are the reader's ears, eyes and nose. Almost every day you meet people and see things that readers will never experience. If you don't tell them what these things are like, they will never know. If, for example, you are interviewing a well-known politician, readers will want to know what his or her office is like. Is it grand, or surprisingly modest? How is it decorated? Are there any interesting personal possessions about? Is the person nervous or calm? How do they appear to treat those who work for them?

You cannot rely on a photograph in the paper doing these things for you. Instead, you have to paint a word picture, however brief. And your words can convey things that pictures cannot. Description brings the story alive, takes readers to where you have been and evokes atmosphere. It can put flavour in the most arid and dry news story and make the difference between a report that satisfies and one that does not. So long as you remember that description goes into a story to aid readers' understanding and not provide you with an opportunity to display your latest vocabulary, it will be an aid to clarity and not an obstacle to it.

Description in news stories, or any kind of writing for that matter, is not a matter of adding the occasional adjective but of giving detail and conjuring up pictures in the readers' minds. Easier said than done, but a good idea of what this means in practice is often found in the articles of two of the best descriptive writers ever to apply words to newsprint: the *New Yorker's* A.J. Liebling and Hugh McIlvanney of the *Observer* and *Sunday Times*. Here's a few examples, starting with the way Liebling described the men who hang around Izzy Yereshevsky's less than reputable I&Y Cigar Store on Broadway:

> Most of Izzy's evening guests – their purchases are so infrequent it would be misleading to call them customers – wear white felt hats and overcoats of a style known to them as English Drape. Short men peer up from between the wide-flung shoulders of these coats as if they had been lowered into the garments on a rope and were now trying to climb out.

And here's Liebling using his subject's dialogue to others to describe him. It comes from a profile of Clifford C. Fischer, a show producer famous for his ranting in rehearsals, which begins with the statement that 'A rehearsal by Clifford C. Fischer ... is one of the finest shows imaginable', and went on:

> 'Get out of here on the boat and go back to Paris!' Fischer will yell at a show girl, a vision of ecstatic beauty, who has failed to switch her hips. 'The next boat – out!' Then, with a sweep of his hand toward any three or four acrobats or stagehands present, he will shout, 'And take them jackasses with you! Im-med-jutly!' His voice sinks, and as he slumps into his chair, he gurgles, 'Quick. Before somebody kills you, already.' Odette Puig, a calm, blonde Frenchwoman who is his secretary, provides him with a glass of water. Then an electrician misses a cue, and Fischer is up again. 'Rudy,' he screams, 'Rudy, did you forgot again? I want here ma-Gen-ta! Not PINK! Ma-Gen-ta! Oh, my God!'

McIlvanney worked at a shorter length than Liebling, typically in the 1,200–2,500 word range, and was a wittier man. Hence the crispness of his descriptions:

On a championship fight between the ill-matched Mike Tyson and Leon Spinks:

> ... an event whose violence could scarcely have been briefer or more one-sided if the electric chair had been involved.

On a famously thin snooker player:

> Never has a wearer of dinner suits been so urgently in need of dinners.

On the scene at a press conference given by Diego Maradona after his expulsion for drugs from the 1994 World Cup Finals:

As a mass of hands holding microphones closed around him like a carniverous plant, the drawn, slightly hunted look on his Spanish-Indian face said more about the nature and origins of his predicament than the predictable words of denial and complaint that came from his mouth.

There is not a single adjective or adverb in these extracts – proof that the best description does not need them. And finally, just to ram home the point, here is another one of the greats, James Cameron, describing the aftermath of the Six Day War in the Middle East:

... Yesterday I went on the first survey of the whole peninsula, perhaps one of the biggest single battlefields ever known, the place where the Egyptian Army died. In a lifetime not too unfamiliar with such things I have never seen anything like this ... An Egyptian force of five infantry and two armoured divisions abruptly eliminated; an army of some ninety thousand or more men disintegrated, with some tens of thousands killed or captured, or left, ignored, to wander and struggle somehow or other in the general direction of anywhere. Several million pounds worth of extremely expensive and sophisticated military ironmongery now reduced to booty or to crushed and blackened scrap. The tanks and vehicles litter the desert like the nursery floor of an angry child.

Here are a few points on description:

What is familiar to you may not be to the reader

Too often journalists take for granted that readers have seen the people, places and events they are writing about. Even the reporter's most familiar surroundings may be strange and unknown to readers. How many readers, for instance, ever go inside a parliament building? They may have seen it fleetingly on television, but do they know whether it is overheated or cold? If the seats are comfortable? What pictures are hung there? What the atmosphere is like? Such information helps to take readers there.

Avoid big chunks of description

Unless the main purpose of a piece is to be descriptive, colour is best doled out in small helpings here and there rather than in long, unbroken passages. You can tell readers a lot in a series of asides. The thing you have to watch is where you place these. The fact that the person you are quoting is red-haired and collects stamps is worth recording somewhere, but probably not in the intro or immediately after you quote them calling on the government to resign.

Relevance is the key. Introduce description where it helps, not where it is incongruous. More detailed descriptions of a certain person or place are, however, best given in one part of the story and not sprinkled through it. It is irritating to read a piece where, every time someone is mentioned, you are thrown another little crumb of description about them. Just how irritating is shown by this example, from Kingsley Amis of what is called in the US, the 'gorged snake' construction:

> Briton Chris Mankiewitz, 26, has been named to lead England's soccer squad against Ruritania next month.
> The Warsaw-born father-of-two said at his recently rebuilt £150,000 Deptford home, 'My attractive wife Samantha, 24, and I are just over the moon with the news.'
> Success has come just in time for the whiskered former schoolboy hurdler champion star of Clapton Occident's injury-stricken midfielders. The much-photographed hat-trick specialist and avid sports-car driver, a familiar local figure in his blood-red Halberstadt D-VII...

Bring people alive to readers

Even the smallest piece of information about people helps readers. After all, a name does not tell you very much about someone, apart from their sex. Age adds something, as do details of appearance, demeanour and so on. Try to stick to facts rather than judgements and be sensitive about the source's feelings.

Be precise

Precision applies especially to description. Avoid vague, judgemental adjectives and descriptions. To say that an office is 'imposing' tells you something, but not very much. Far better to say that it is so big that you could park two cars in there, that it has plush red carpet, a new black desk with brass fittings and that the windows command a view of the capital. That gives a far better idea. Apply this thinking to people, too. Avoid words like attractive, handsome, good-looking, pretty, impressive. Instead describe their hair colour, how they are dressed, their height.

Precision is also the best motive for using adjectives – to qualify nouns in a way that adds information. Using them to try to add emphasis will degrade the impact and lead to wordiness. Descriptive writing is about finding ways of bringing something to life, not the random sprinkling of adjectives through a piece.

Take care with similes

Writing that something is 'like ...' is only effective if you choose a simile that matches and is fresh. Phrases that exaggerate, unless you are writing humour, are immediately spotted for what they are and anything tired and clichéd will have no impact. A near-perfect example of a fresh simile is at the end of this short extract from Floyd Gibbons of the *Chicago Tribune*. He was the first reporter to cover the effects of the Great Famine in the Soviet Union of 1921:

> A boy of 12 with a face of sixty was carrying a six-month-old infant wrapped in a filthy bundle of furs. He deposited the baby under a freight car, crawled after him and drew from his pocket some dried fish-heads, which he chewed ravenously and then, bringing the baby's lips to his, transferred the sticky white paste of half-masticated fish-scales and bones to the infant's mouth as a mother bird feeds her young.

Develop an eye for detail

The small things are often the most telling – little details or moments in a scene that can be described and used to make a point about the whole story or event. Develop an eye for detail, learn to focus on such things and paint a word picture of them for readers. This is especially effective when you have been sent to write a colour or atmosphere piece about a big scene or event. But detail can also be used to great effect in all reporting, when you observe a little thing that seems significant. You do not have to cast a great spotlight on it, or give the detail immense symbolic significance. Such lines are often most powerful when delivered simply and starkly without further elaboration.

Curzio Malaparte covered the battle of Leningrad for the Italian paper *Corriere della Sera*. One of the eventual saviours of the city, after much suffering, was the 'Lagoda Life-Line', the convoys of food taken across the lake by boat in the summer and over the ice in winter. In researching his piece, Malaparte took a walk over the frozen lake:

> Under my shoes, imprinted in the ice as in transparent crystal, was a line of beautiful human faces, a line of glass masks like a Byzantine icon. They were looking at me, staring at me. The lips were narrow and worn, the hair long, the noses sharp, the eyes large and very clear. They were the images of Soviet soldiers who had fallen in the attempt to cross the lake. Their poor bodies, imprisoned all winter by the ice, had been swept away by the first spring currents. But their faces remained printed in the pure, green-blue crystal.

That image of the faces is imprinted on the mind of the reader just as surely as those soldiers' features were marked in the ice. (Malaparte's real name, incidentally, was Kurt Suckert, and his father was German. Nevertheless, he fought for the French and Italians in the First World War, was decorated by both countries, and, in 1933, was arrested for anti-fascist reporting and imprisoned for three years on the Lipari islands, off the coast of Sicily.)

However, if you are going to use detail, make sure you get it right. A reporter covering an earthquake in Central America and wanting to make plain its effects on ordinary people, wrote about how he had even seen starving families eating rats. In fact, they were eating small guinea pigs, which are a standard local delicacy. The reporter thus earned the nickname Rat Man for ever more.

Use familiar references

Always think how to tell readers information in a way that they can immediately grasp. That often means using imagery and comparisons familiar in their own lives. If a building is 50,000 square feet, you should say so, but then add that this area is equivalent to five tennis courts or whatever. If someone has been on some travels covering 8,000 miles, say that this is the distance from London to Tokyo, or the same as going from London to Aberdeen ten times. Use comparisons that people can relate to. Say, for example, you have the job of capturing in a memorable way, just how small the European state of Liechtenstein is. How to do it? By stating the miles from one side to another (five)? By giving the population (33,717 in 2006)? Or by giving the country's GDP ($825m)? Gay Talese of the *New York Times* had to do this in a short feature he wrote about the place in 1961. Here is what he wrote: 'Liechtenstein, an Alpine principality of 15,000 citizens and 5,000 cows, is so small that its telephone directory has only three pages.'

Look for descriptive stories

Far too many journalists content themselves with writing stories which have the conventional minimalist detail and description. The people who inhabit most reporter's articles appear to have only names, ages, occupations, and, possibly, hair colouring. What they don't have is a life beyond the immediate confines of the subject in hand. It was reflecting on this two-dimensional approach that gave rise, in the 1960s, to what was called the New Journalism; pieces whose storytelling owed more to the conventions and pace of fiction than the wham-bam, just-the-facts-ma'am attitude of news reporting. The result was stories with rich detail, dialogue, description, and a sense of being there, all written at decent length and peopled with characters who are more than a name and age. Stories, even, that have been found far from the newspaper's offices, rather than merely being the metropolitan topic of the moment. Of course this requires space, but any intelligent editor will give this if he or she is presented with quality writing. So why not look for stories that will bear this approach and invest some of your own time in researching and writing them. This, after all, is how many of the top journalists broke out of routine reporting and into a better-paid life of writing longer, high-profile pieces.

The wastepaper basket is still the writer's best friend.
                                        Isaac Singer

16

Handling Quotes

Journalism largely consists of saying 'Lord Jones Dead' to people who never knew Lord Jones was alive.

G.K. Chesterton 1914

And now, let me reveal a little-known secret of the journalistic trade: you cannot be arrested for writing a story without quotes. I know this runs contrary to what many young journalists are told, but it is true. Most stories benefit from quotes, but it is not illegal to write without them.

I pass this on because quotes have become something of a fetish with many editors. They have come to believe that every story must have quotes dropped into it at regular intervals, like buoys marking the entrance to a port. In mass-market sport reporting, this belief has been taken to extremes, and story after story is little more than a series of quotations laid end to end with odd, linking interjections from the reporter. Spurred, perhaps, by the belief that television has robbed them of the need to relate what happened, they confine themselves instead to reporting reactions to what happened. For their work, the post-event interview has become more important than the event itself. As Hugh McIlvanney of the *Sunday Times*, in my view the best writer ever to apply words to newsprint, has said: '... there is so much more concern with what is said off the field than what is done on it that reporting by ear rather than eye has become their norm. Sprinkled among their number are reporters whose efficiency would scarcely be diminished if they went blind.'

Quoting excess is a sure sign of either reporters who are trying to pad the story to a length way beyond its real worth, or ones who are not confident about their own writing or observations. They thus become like a novice swimmer who, afraid of being out of her depth, constantly seeks the security of the shallows – in this case, the shallowness of the average quote. It was striking, when I was surveying the best journalism of the last 150 years for my *Great Reporters* book, that the outstanding reporters used quotes very sparingly. This was generally because they could express ideas and information better – or more succinctly – than most interview subjects. That may sound arrogant, but it is so. The great reporters save quotation for when someone says something in an original way, with an authentic voice, or when they want to capture some characteristic of the interviewee, be it authority, cheekiness, pomposity, sharpness, etc. Here's three examples, two of which are from the reporting of A.J. Liebling, the legendary *New Yorker* writer who, for all his capacity for neat phrasing, was renowned as a great listener. The first was in a piece about a man called Rubin Fisher who had read 146,444 New York gas meters without making a mistake, and had now been invited by his company to give a seminar to other meter readers. Liebling establishes that Mr Fisher is almost excruciatingly tedious not by assertion, but by judicious quote. Having established just how obsessed he is with meter reading to the exclusion of all else ('... A meter reader sees a lot of things, but it is none of his business.'), Liebling wrote: 'He is not a playboy. "When I get home," he said, "I just like to sit quiet."'

Liebling also once interviewed the last elephant leaper with Ringling Bros circus, which had abandoned this kind of act in 1908 due to the number of broken necks. The quotes Liebling used in this piece are an almost perfect example of capturing an authentic voice: 'Charlie Bell sat on a trunk by one of the entries to the circus ring, watching the elephants. "Ain't nobody leaped over 'em for twenty-four years now," he said pityingly. "I don't see how they handle 'em. Nothing keeps an elephant in place like being leaped over. Makes 'em feel they ain't so big."' Finally, there is the quote that expresses an idea in a way a reporter would perhaps never think of. Interviewing a Titanic survivor, *Boston Post* reporter (and later novelist) John P. Marquand asked her: 'So you came to America on the Titanic? "Well," she replied, "Part way".'

Finally, what good reporters don't do is wallpaper their stories with yards of quotes in the mistaken belief that not only is this the approved way of filling the space, but it is also the means of bringing enlightenment to the reader. As A.J.Wiggins, editor-publisher of the *Ellsworth (Maine) American* has said: 'A newspaper cannot really congratulate itself on having got at the facts impartially when it has quoted at length from two uninformed idiots on opposing sides of an issue.'

That is not the only problem with quotes. Some journalists, and a lot of journalism trainers, find the issue of tidying up quotes a terrible ethical dilemma. Others are hugely exercised by how to attribute quotes, or how to use them partially. Time, then, for a few guidelines.

When do you use quotes?

Generally you should always use reported speech to convey information and quotes to add personality, immediacy, authenticity and a change of voice and pace to a story. Quotes can also be used to report verbatim an exchange between interviewee and questioner, especially if you wish to show what built up to some sudden confession, particularly dramatic statement or to show evasiveness. Normally, however, quotes should be reserved for allowing people to comment, or to give an impression of themselves, their opinions or feelings. They are not to be used as mere padding, and, least of all, as substitutes for reporting. And never forget that you can write a lot more efficiently than most people can speak. For example, instead of 'A United Nations spokesman said, "We utterly deny this claim is or ever was true"', just write, 'A United Nations spokesman denied the claim.'

Accuracy

At opposite ends of a collection of words are two little marks. These indicate that what is inside them is a verbatim record of what was said. Not an edited version of their words, or a tidied up or summarised account. Nor what someone meant to say, or would have said if they had only been sufficiently well educated to speak in such grammatical sentences. But a word for word, syllable by syllable, accurate report of their actual words. If not, what on earth is the point of those little marks at either end?

And if you do not have a verbatim note or tape, or the person you would like to quote does not speak in a way that, when written down, makes sense, then you use reported speech. Unless, of course, their incoherence is part of the story. In which case you quote them, accurately, with every unfinished sentence, every ungrammatical statement, and every misuse of words faithfully preserved. This is the best protection against complaints of being misquoted. But then, with some people, you can't win. Pedro Guerrero of the St Louis Cardinals once complained: 'Sometimes they write what I say and not what I mean.'

Ums and ers

A proper reverence for the sanctity of what you place within quotation marks does not normally extend to solemnly reporting every um, er and strangulated throat-clearing. In most situation, reporters naturally filter out the ums and ers – either when taking notes or writing the story. But sometimes, when writing colour pieces, profiles or news stories, giving warts and all quotes is called for. A story, for instance, where the quoted person's hesitancy or uncertainty is a relevant element would be a case in point. Knowing the difference between such relevance and gratuitous unfairness is, however, a judgement for the experienced.

Lack of grammar

Some papers, such as the *Philadelphia Inquirer* will allow minor grammatical errors in quotes to be changed, both to avoid confusion and to prevent the speaker looking foolish. I would not even go this far. My aim would be not to save the blushes of the source, but to achieve accuracy and clarity. This means using reported speech to give a clear picture of what is going on or is meant, but using, if it is relevant, quotes to convey the authentic voice of those involved in the story.

After all, if someone's speech is ungrammatical, that's how it is. And if accurate reporting of it makes them look stupid, too bad. Many journalists working in the political field regularly tidy up the language of politicians. They think it is part of their job to take the inarticulate ramblings of politicians and turn them into neat, rounded sentences. It is not. First, cleaning up their quotes gives a false impression. Second, if the politician in question cannot speak his own language properly, it is your job to let readers know. They can then decide if they want to vote for him.

The real problem with allowing reporters to clean up speakers' grammar is that they tend to apply it unevenly; unconsciously tidying the speech of the educated and the official, but leaving other, more hum-drum voices with their quotes unimproved. Be aware of this class bias and resist it. Smooth out no one's quotes.

Incoherence and dissembling

Far beyond poor grammar comes incoherence. There are two issues here and the first is clarity. Your job is to find out what is going on, and if the person your are talking to cannot give a straight or comprehensible answer, then find someone who can. If their words are convoluted and rambling, but their meaning discernible, then use reported speech.

Sometimes, if the source is someone in authority, and their incoherent or dissembling words are a legitimate part of the story, they deserve to be quoted. Consider this, from a White House press conference given by American President Richard Nixon's press secretary Ron Ziegler in 1974. He was asked if certain tapes which may have recorded the President discussing illegal actions were still intact. The question seemed to demand a straight 'yes' or 'no'. Instead, Ziegler gave the following 99-word reply:

> I would feel that most of the conversations that took place in those areas of the White House that did have the recording system would in almost their entirety be in existence, but the special prosecutor, the court, and, I think, the American people are sufficiently familiar with the recording system to know where the recording devices existed and to know the situation in terms of the recording process, but I feel, although the process has not been undertaken yet in preparation of

the material to abide by the court decision, really, what the answer to that question is.

If the incoherence is habitual, it can become a story in its own right. After all, repeated incoherence is a pretty good indicator of a failure to think straight, having something to hide, substance abuse, or all three.

Dialect

This can be very delicate territory. All social groups, whether they are a self-conscious sub-culture, a band of enthusiasts for some activity, an ethnic group or people who merely share the same work, have a language and dialect that is their own. Some use this dialect only when speaking to each other, others use it whatever their audience. In many cases, quoting people's actual words poses no great problems. If the footballer says, 'We was robbed blind' on the late night television news, that is authentic and everyone understands it. To render this in next day's paper as 'We were robbed of a deserved victory' is wrong and fools no one.

The problems begin when dialect is not immediately understandable. Do you translate so the meaning is clear, or keep the authentic voice and confuse a lot of readers? It is perhaps the most difficult of the authenticity versus clarity issues, especially where ethnic groups are involved. In recent years Eskimo Indians have objected to an Alaskan paper tidying up their quotes into standard English and so depriving them of their own, stripped-down form of speech. And in Florida, the *St Petersburg Times* came under fire for verbatim quotes of a black athlete's own argot. The athlete was happy, but black readers thought the paper was holding his speech up to ridicule.

My policy would be to be wary, and where a dialect is not clear to all readers then generally to use reported speech on news pages, but feel more free to use authentic quotes on specialist or feature pages, especially in pieces of greater length. I see nothing patronising about that. And if you are going to quote extensively in dialect, do so only if your ear (and your notes or tapes) are good. This is not an area for the tone deaf.

Efficiency

Shorten quotes only by visible deletion

There is only one honest, safe way to shorten quotes and that is by omitting phrases and sentences, but making plain by dots that you have done so. For instance, 'I think it is outrageous that we should be asked to do this ... We have no intention of giving in. We are going to fight this all the way.' Never just remove the surplus words and join the parts together as if they were said in continuous speech. If you still cannot achieve the brevity you require, use reported speech.

Quoting in fragments

This is the habit of quoting not sentences, but phrases or even single words. In his *Troublesome Words*, Bill Bryson cites these two examples:

He said the profits in the second half would be 'good'.

...loneliness was a 'feature' of Hinckley's life...

The problem here is putting quote marks around a word which is perfectly ordinary and predictable. It suggests either the reporter's note-taking was so poor he only managed to get down one word per sentence or that the writer is trying to signal scepticism about the quoted word. The impression given by the first example above is that there will be something not quite kosher or distinctly qualified about the goodness of the results. The second example conveys irony or even mistrust of the source. The moral is use quotes around single words or phrases only when the words used are particularly emphatic, as in:

He said the profits in the second half would be 'sensational'.

or

He said the profits in the second half 'did not bear thinking about'.

Attributing quotes

Said, claimed or commented?

When it comes to the verb that goes between the name of the quoted and their words, many reporters think that the word 'said' can be regularly replaced by synonyms like commented, claimed, asserted, etc. This is fine so long as the words quoted really are a claim, comment or assertion. To write:

'My dog then hurled himself at the thief,' commented Mr Black.

is idiotic, since Mr Black is not commenting, but stating what he knows to be a fact. Claimed in such a circumstance would be even worse, since it suggests that Mr Black's words should be treated as a statement which may be challenged or subsequently regarded as a delusion. Unless you have the evidence for this, it is misleading to use 'claimed' when you mean 'said'. Even more unsafe are words which carry a pejorative meaning, like 'admitted', or 'confessed'. Admissions generally involve fresh information which is negative, something the speaker would have preferred to keep to themselves and which has been conceded by them in the face of persistent questioning or under some other duress.

Similarly sloppy is the substitution of words that have a particular meaning and therefore cannot be used as direct synonyms for 'said'. Declared is a frequent delinquent here, as in:

'I am 24,' she declared.

She may have said 'I am 24', but if she declared it, then it suggests she raised her voice several decibels and declaimed the words, as if from a rooftop. This, implying that she is either proud of her age to the point of eccentricity, or that it has recently been in question and she wishes to clear the matter up very publicly, gives an entirely different meaning to merely saying the words.

Said versus says

These words are not interchangeable, as many think, but have different functions. 'Said' is for the specific:

'We were astonished when Christmas came twice this year,' said Ms Brown.

But 'says' is for the general, recurring sentiment, as in:

'Christmas comes but once a year,' says Ms White.

Inverted sentences

Some reporters think they can introduce hitherto absent variety into their writing by inverting sentences at will. This is strangely common when approaching a quote, as in:

Said Mr Smith, 'I am the happiest man in London.'

As Keith Waterhouse points out in *Waterhouse On Newspaper Style*, this became such a disease on *Time* magazine that the *New Yorker* magazine commented, 'Backward ran sentences until reeled the mind.'

Inventing quotes

Growing quotes from one-word answers

There is one other unsafe practice with quotes and that is the habit some reporters have of putting statements to people, getting a 'yes' or 'no' answer (or even a nod or shake of the head) and then putting that statement in direct quotes as if it was said by the source. For instance, 'Have you ever leaked Cabinet papers to the press?' And when the subject says no, the reporter writes in his story, 'He then said, "I have never leaked Cabinet papers to the press."' Or, even worse, '"Have I ever leaked Cabinet papers to the press? No."' Any such exchanges should be mainly, or all, in reported speech, making clear what the question was and the extent of the reply.

Playing fast and loose with the results of a snatched conversation is regarded on a lot of papers as standard practice. For instance, in his book, *Dog Eat Dog: Confessions of a Tabloid Journalist*, Wensley Clarkson, once of the *Mirror* in London, reports the following exchange between himself and Paul McCartney when rumours were rife about a split in the former Beatle's first marriage. Clarkson waited for hours outside the star's home in East Sussex before a red Mercedes containing McCartney and wife appeared. It stopped and the window was wound down. This was the conversation:

McCartney: 'Yes, what can I do for you?'
Clarkson: 'I'm Wensley Clarkson from the *Sunday Mirror*. I can see from both of you that these marriage rift stories aren't true.'
McCartney: 'Yep. Load of nonsense.'
Clarkson: 'I suppose you wish these gossips would stop.'
McCartney: 'Yep. Sure do.'
Clarkson: 'Would you call them muck-spreaders?'
McCartney: 'Yep.'
Clarkson: 'These rumours first surfaced a year ago. They're obviously no more truthful now than then.'
McCartney: 'Yep. Now why don't you go off home?'
Clarkson: 'Yep.'

Two days later, on page three of the *Sunday Mirror*, appeared a story headlined: 'Paul's Fury at Love Rift Lies'. The opening paragraphs read:

Superstar Paul McCartney has hit back at the rumours that his marriage is on the rocks.
   'I want the world to know that Linda and I are as happy as ever,' he insisted.
   'I just wish these gossips would go away and stop talking rubbish.'
   Paul, 40, was speaking on the eve of a West German court case in which a 20-year-old girl who says she is his illegitimate daughter is claiming millions of pounds maintenance from him. He was tight-lipped

about the court case – but with Linda at his side he angrily denied show business rumours of a rift in their 14-year marriage.

'We're targets once again for these malicious muck-spreaders,' he said.

'Last time these rumours started about a year ago and, as you can see, they're no more truthful than they were then.'

Paul spoke exclusively to the *Sunday Mirror* at his cottage in the East Sussex countryside, near Rye.

There is no doubt Clarkson put words into McCartney's mouth. On the other hand, the resulting story, although a travesty of an accurate report of the exchange, is true to the spirit of McCartney's feelings. But there are obvious dangers in such an approach; and it is a slippery path, not all that far down which, I suspect, begins total invention. Start putting words into people's mouths and you might lose interest in what they do actually say for themselves.

Don't invent quotes to protect a source

A silly habit adopted by the inexperienced is to try to disguise the identity of the story's source by writing inaccurately that they refused to speak to the paper. Or, even worse, by quoting them as saying, 'No comment'. First, it is not true. Second, if the identity of the source ever comes out, it can be proved that at least part of the story was deceptive.

'Experts say ...'

Of all the witless phrases over-used by reporters, this one takes a lot of beating. It crops up all the time and is used in two circumstances. First, where the reporter remembers (or mis-remembers) a claim by scientists, doctors, climatologists, or some other specialists, and can't be bothered to research the matter back to the original source. The danger here is that it's quite possible that the original claim is not as the reporter recalls it. Second, reporters use 'experts say' because they've been told to include something in the story (so it will then fit with their editor's prejudices) but can't actually find a specialist to say it – often because the claim bears little relationship to any known science. To an experienced news editor (and more readers than you imagine), 'experts say' is a dead giveaway that you have not done the research, are being deceitful, or both.

Overheard in the street

Making up quotes ought to be as patently ill-advised as sticking a wet hand in a light socket. But some reporters seem to feel that the obvious wrongs of this are somehow suspended when they are doing a story which involves, or would be enlivened by, a few words from the man or woman in the street. Dishonesty is almost the least of reasons for not doing this. First, no words a reporter can invent will be as original or revealing as the public's real ones. Second, the kind of reporters who go in for this, and specialise in filling their pieces with quotes 'overheard on the train', invariably have no more idea of how people actually speak than someone who has been deaf from birth. The normal retort to such 'inventive' reporters is that they should be writing fiction. But, actually, they shouldn't. Ideally they should not be writing anything.

All successful newspapers are ceaselessly querulous and bellicose. They never defend anyone or anything if they can help it; if the job is forced upon them, they tackle it by denouncing someone or something else.

H.L. Mencken 1919

17

Different Ways To Tell A Story

A journalist is a person who works harder than any other lazy person in the world.

Anon

Medieval Christians believed that those condemned to hell had to endure the eternal torture of alternating extremes of intense heat and terrible cold. This bothered theologians greatly. If that was so, they puzzled, would the wicked and the damned have one exquisite moment as cold turned to heat? Would their thawing souls have a fleeting moment of ecstasy? And where, they wanted to know, was the punishment in that?

Similar hair-splitting debates go on every time someone tries to define the difference between a news story and a feature. A lot of journalists think that news reporting is always arid, dry and impersonal, whereas features are rather jolly free-form things. They see the reporter as an earnest collector of 'facts' and the feature *writer* as someone who wanders around thinking of fine phrases which save them the trouble of doing much research.

At the extremes – say a report of 68 people dying in a fire on one hand and a gardening advice column on the other – there is not much danger of confusing the two. One is a news report, the other plainly a feature. But in between these two extremes are the vast majority of stories and at what point does a news story become a feature? When it reaches a certain length? When it lacks a certain amount of facts? When it deals with certain subjects like lifestyle and relationships that really interest people? When it ceases to deliver fresh information in stories with news pyramid structures?

The truth is that trying to make distinctions between news and features does not get us very far. In fact, it is positively dangerous. It produces narrow thinking which can restrict coverage of news to conventional subjects and puts writing it into the unimaginative straitjacket of a formula. With features, it encourages the insidious idea that normal standards of precision and thorough research don't apply and that they can be a kind of low-fact product, instantly recognisable from their lack of capital letters. The opposite, of course, is the case. Most news pages could benefit from a greater sense of adventure and a more flexible approach to stories. Similarly, most features sections cry out for sharper research and less indulgent writing. There is no great divide between news and features. Best to think of it all as reporting.

Different approaches

Having jettisoned this rigid thinking, you can then appreciate that there are an almost infinite number of ways to write, supplement or follow-up a story (whether it appears on news or feature pages). Some of these approaches are relatively common, some are not. Some make sidebars or panels, some separate pieces paired with the main report, others can appear on comment, feature or analysis pages. All of them, if used judiciously, can bring variety and life to pages.

Colour piece

An article describing a scene or event which throws light on some of the themes or people involved in the main story. Often regarded by writers as convenient camouflage for their own opinions, colour pieces are at their best when precisely descriptive. The most telling often alight on some detail and use that to symbolise the wider situation. The effect of this, however, can be destroyed by making heavy-handed analogies. The best approach is usually to provide the detail and trust the reader to see its significance.

Fly on the wall

The journalist as observer, pure and simple, asking no questions; merely watching, recording and noting the behaviour, speech and interactions of the subject(s). The published report will probably use a lot of quotes and verbatim exchanges between people. This type of piece is commonly written on some place or institution which is exotic to your readership.

Behind the scenes

This has similarities to the above but differs in being an explanatory, rather than observational, piece. It should describe how something works. This approach is often best on subjects that readers take for granted, but in reality know very little about. How, for instance, does a national railway timetable get planned? How does a credit-rating agency work?

In disguise

The journalist assumes the role of the subject to see how people react. This can be done for two reasons. First, for fun, such as dressing up as a priest to see how this affects people's behaviour (a London journalist recently did this, and in addition to just wandering around in his disguise, also went into bars and nightclubs). Second, it can be done for a serious purpose, such as taking the role of a homeless person to see what treatment is available. Several years ago a reporter roamed America posing as an HIV sufferer to write about people's reactions when he slipped this 'fact' into conversations.

Profile

Normally a study of a personality at the centre of a story, but it can also be the portrait of a place, organisation, religion, etc. It can be a report of one encounter with the subject, or gather many views and give a rounded portrait.

Interview

Can be either written as a story, with context, background and comments, or given as a verbatim, but edited, account of the interview. If the latter, the questions should not be too long, should be more carefully phrased than usual and any editing of the answers should be made clear with ellipses (...). The subject needs to speak well and interestingly, as there is no scope for making good this deficiency with entertaining commentary from the interviewer.

Factboxes

Simple lists of facts associated with the story, or previous instances of the event at the centre of your story. These are usually blobbed or given by date, rather than written through as a single piece.

Chronology

Relates 'the story so far' in short items, with each usually starting with the date in bold, followed by the development at that time. Often best written in punchy, abbreviated language shorn of definite articles, etc.

A history of ...

This is most appropriate when the subject has been around for a long time and is suddenly thrown into prominence by events. This will also work well on familiar subjects whose history is not broadly known. Works best when it is a true history and not merely a summary of the last few years' developments.

Full texts

When you have a story which deals with an important speech, statement or document, it is worth thinking about running the complete text.

My testimony

Personal experience written by a journalist after interviewing the subject, or written by the subject him or herself. The latter method always has the edge, as it provides the unmistakably untidy and honest tones of a real person speaking, compared to the smoothed-out sentences of the paper's journalists.

Backgrounder

A piece explaining the recent past of the issues or themes at the centre of a story. This gives a sense of such developments being part of a continuing process, rather than unprovoked eruptions of fate. Writing such pieces is often an object lesson in the kind of material you should be routinely including, albeit in a shorter form, in everyday reporting.

Analysis

A piece examining the reasons why something has happened, or not happened. Even if you are an experienced reporter, this is best done after consulting experts rather than off the top of your head.

Vox pops

Short verbatim quotes from people you have telephoned or stopped in the street for their reaction to the story. Often fails because the questions are so predictable (e.g., variations on 'Do you think murder is wrong?'), too facile to get anything more than a knee-jerk response, or the responses are too prosaic. Ask questions that elicit replies that give personal experiences or highly individual reactions. And don't go back to the office until you have a good variety of responses.

Experts' round-up

The same as the above, but with specialists rather than members of the public. The same precautions apply.

Opinion poll

A poll of people's views carried out by an accredited research organisation. Having your own staff carry out the poll is not a good idea. The results will be unscientific and therefore meaningless.

Review

Just as you review films, plays or new cars, so you can review other things, such as a new health service, museum, newly opened historic house, park or any other public service. A refinement is to go with someone at whom the service is aimed (such as taking a claimant along to test a new welfare service), and writing a review based on their experiences.

Extended reporting

There is one type of journalism where the boundaries between news and features is truly blurred, and that is reporting in depth and at length – in articles of 5,000 words and upwards. Such articles are more likely to be found in magazines, but some American newspapers will carry reporting of great length, normally in a series spread over several issues. More papers should follow their example, for the impact of such journalism can be considerable. A year after the dropping of an atom bomb on Hiroshima, for example, the *New Yorker* magazine carried a 31,000 word report on the experiences of six residents of the city, written by John Hersey. The magazine was a sell-out, copies were soon changing hands at up to $20, requests for reprints came in from all over the world (Albert Einstein asked for 1,000 copies), the Book of the Month Club reprinted the article and sent it to every member, Hersey's report was read out over radio, and, three months later, it appeared as a book and has been in print ever since.

These days, unless you have the good fortune to work for the *New Yorker*, the most likely outlet for such in-depth reporting is as a series in a paper, or online. Such was the case with the work of *Philadelphia Inquirer* reporter Mark Bowden. His subject was the battle of Mogadishu in Somalia, when US special forces trapped in that city had to fight their way out. More than five hundred Somalis died, as did 18 US servicemen. Having extensively interviewed US military and Somalis, Bowden was able to reconstruct the battle in the smallest detail, and this was published as a 29-part series in the *Inquirer*. You may have heard of it; the title was 'Black Hawk Down'. It became a book which topped the US best-seller list, a television documentary, an audio book, website, and, most famously, a Hollywood movie. Such journalism is expensive, and fewer and fewer editors are prepared to underwrite the costs involved. But, with the option of the journalist doing the work in their own time and themselves putting it online at virtually no cost, the wonder – given the personal and public rewards – is that more of us do not attempt to emulate the Herseys and Bowdens.

> *I never open a newspaper without finding something I should have deemed it a loss not to have seen; never without deriving from it instruction and amusement.*
>
> Samuel Johnson

18

Comment, Intentional and Otherwise

No story is fair if reporters hide their biases or emotions behind such subtly pejorative words as 'refused', 'despite' 'admit' and 'massive'.

Ben Bradlee

Journalism is by nature a subjective process. It can no more help producing and projecting views of the world than a cow can help making milk. Be it intentional or unintentional, overt or covert, comment comes with the territory. To deny this is to deny that ink makes a mark on paper.

As far as intentional comment is concerned (columnists, leading articles) no one would want to deny it. After all, a newspaper without such opinion would be like someone who has had a personality by-pass operation. The problem comes with comment that goes in disguise, dressed up as straight reporting, speaking in its voice and aping its mannerisms. The problem, too, is with comment that creeps in under cover of a paragraph in a news story and has infiltrated before either the reader, and sometimes the writer, realises.

Comment, then, is only a problem when it does not advertise itself. We can never eliminate this, but we can hope to minimise it by searching for it, studying it, thinking about it and trying to recognise it for what it is. This, plus the more up-front types of comment, is what this chapter is about.

Comment in news stories

There are three types of comment in news stories: overt, covert and inadvertent. Overt comment is where the reporter passes judgement or states an opinion in a direct and open way. This type of comment is simply banned on news pages in many papers around the world. Indeed in Britain and the United States, it is thought to be so obviously wrong that many journalism textbooks do not even give it more than a passing mention. The authors take it for granted that none of their readers would contest the view that news pages are for information given as straight as it can be, and comment is for columnists and opinion pages.

In most circumstances (the exceptions are dealt with later) this is right. Readers will know where they are and can read stories assuming that what they are getting is an attempt to present facts, even if it is not always successful. As noted in the chapter on news value, everyone has a comment, relatively few have fresh information. The one is commonplace, the other scarce. That is why news is invariably more interesting than comment and it is certainly why there is a real risk of devaluation when the two are mixed. For when they are, hard information becomes tainted and so loses its worth.

But there are exceptions. The highly experienced reporter writing a background piece on a subject which he has followed for a long time should be allowed to let his judgements inform a story, and hence the readers. The same latitude should also be given to specialists or foreign correspondents who have been resident in their posts for a long time. Their comment should not appear in the form of drum-banging opinions of the 'Well he may say that, but here's what I think ...' variety, but appear as asides, little nudging remarks which give the story, or aspects of it, context. They work best as little notes of scepticism, forecasts of the likeliest scenarios, views about which policy might be adopted, etc., preferrably displayed in a different way from hard news reports. And an opinion that springs naturally from the facts, or a reporter's observation of them, is more potent than a viewpoint (or prejudice, as they are known when we don't share them) merely asserted. One of the best such passages is from a report from the frontline of the Greek-Turkish War written by American journalist Richard Harding Davis for *The Times*.

There was no selection of the unfittest; it seemed to be ruled by unreasoning luck. A certain number of shells and bullets passed through a certain area of space, and men of different bulks blocked that space in different places. If a man happened to be standing in the line of a bullet he was killed and passed into eternity, leaving a wife and children, perhaps, to mourn him.

'Father died,' these children will say, 'doing his duty.' As a matter of fact, father died because he happened to stand up at the wrong moment, or because he turned to ask the man on his right for a match, instead of leaning toward the left, and he projected his bulk of two hundred pounds where a bullet, fired by a man who did not know him and who had not aimed at him, happened to want the right of way. One of the two had to give it, and as the bullet would not, the soldier had his heart torn out.

These two paragraphs say more about the real nature of war than ten thousand leading articles. It was also, lest anyone be under the impression that news stories from more than ten years ago couldn't possibly teach them anything, written as long ago as 1897.

Such comment should be used sparingly but perhaps deployed more often than it is. Conventional facts-only reporting must be the mainstay of the paper's news coverage but other, broader forms should be used more often, especially in longer, overview-type pieces. As television news channels and websites proliferate, such comment is an important part of newspaper content. And it is plainly hypocritical for newspapers to spurn any idea of overt comment when other forms are unavoidably part of news stories. The only stipulation is that overt comment should be honest and immediately apparent for what it is and not try to hide itself or masquerade as something else.

Surreptitiousness is what is wrong with covert and inadvertent comment. The difference between the two is that covert is intentional, inadvertent is not. But they both deliver the same thing and by the same routes: in the language, material and sources they use, or omit. In news writing the chief vehicle for covert and inadvertent comment is loaded words. These are words with pejorative meaning and there are many examples in every language. Here are two situations which produce many examples in almost every language.

Attribution of speech

The words 'said' and 'told' are neutral verbs. They merely inform us that the words quoted were spoken. Reporters often look for alternatives, but the problem is that many of those alternatives are not neutral. The words 'confessed' and 'admitted' do not merely tell us that words have been spoken, they communicate more than that. They mean that someone has either been pressured into revealing some hitherto unknown, perhaps shameful, act; or that they have decided, after wrestling with their conscience, to tell all. Both cases are rather different from 'said'.

'Concede' also implies an admission (or concession) of guilt, while 'alleged', 'claimed' and 'maintained' can also carry the implication that you do not believe what is being said. Meanwhile, 'emphasised', 'stressed' and 'pointed out' all imply that you support the speaker. Similarly, if someone is explaining some of their actions or decisions, do not write without reasons that they 'tried to justify' their actions or 'defended' them. That would only be appropriate if they had been criticised or were under some other pressure to explain.

Another rich source of unintentional comment is the story that begins, 'Fears that ...' or 'Hopes that ...' and omits to mention who it is that is doing the fearing and hoping. There is no harm when the fears or hopes are ones that every person would share, as in: 'Fears are growing for the safety of three children who failed to arrive home yesterday after attending an after-school party.' But when the story is: 'Hopes rose yesterday that a lower price for gold is coming ...', you really have to say whose hopes. Gold producers, and those whose economies benefit from higher gold prices, will presumably be fearing rather than hoping.

Politics

Describing briefly someone's views and political position throws up all kinds of problems. Terms like 'reformer', 'radical', 'hard-liner', 'reactionary', 'moderate' and 'extremist' are used all the time as if they were fixed reference points in the same way that party labels are. But they are not. They are frequently on the move, and most depend on the position from which you are describing them. And they are all used pejoratively. Someone who disagrees with you, or the mainstream, is an 'extremist', which carries all the implications of 'excess' that are so obviously in the word's antecedents. Never lose sight of that old adage that one person's 'freedom fighter' is another person's 'terrorist'.

There are many more loaded words where these came from. Their use often depends on your prejudice, conscious or otherwise. Action by the authorities against a particular group of people is, depending on your point of view, a 'crusade' or a 'witch hunt'. People you approve of make 'mistakes' or 'errors', people you don't care for 'bungle' or 'blunder'. Demonstrators you disapprove of are a 'mob', others constitute a 'crowd'. And people can be 'refuseniks' or 'rebels' and so on.

The moral is that you should choose words with great care and always be aware of their connotations. The most innocent choice of phrase can convey the wrong impression. In the United States and elsewhere, for example, abortion rights have been a highly contentious issue for many years. Call what is growing inside a woman an 'unborn baby', however early in its gestation, and you are unwittingly lining up with those who would restrict abortions. Call their protagonists 'pro-abortion campaigners' and you double the offence. 'Aborted foetus' and 'pro-choice campaigners' are the more neutral descriptions.

The big I

The personal pronoun is one of the most contentious words in any language. Some journalists will go to great lengths to avoid ever typing it, writing such variants as 'this reporter', 'your correspondent', or 'this paper's representative'. Others will use it at the slightest excuse, making almost every story they write an exercise in informative vanity. There has to be a middle way and preferably one that is a lot closer to the modesty option.

Yet achieving this is not always easy. When President John F. Kennedy was composing his inaugural address, one of the most memorable speeches of this century, he told his advisers that the personal pronoun would be banned. Some of the best brains in America worked on successive drafts, but 'I' still crept in four times.

Reporters covering 'big stories' are particularly vulnerable to the temptations of the first person, perhaps feeling that some of the importance of the story has rubbed off on them. Then there are those journalists who believe that their reactions to a story, their emotions, their doings, are so fascinating that they should be frequently included. As a character in British dramatist Tom Stoppard's play, *Night and Day*, says, 'A foreign correspondent is someone who flies around from hotel to hotel and thinks that the most interesting thing about any story is the fact that he has arrived to cover it.'

Of course, as a reporter, you are seeing things, meeting people, having experiences that are, by definition, interesting – after all, you would not be there if they were not news. But what the reader wants to know is *what* you saw and *what* you discovered, and not *how* you saw it or found it, and certainly not what you ate, drank, or felt while finding it. In as much as anything in reporting is a rule, this is one, unless you are a big name journalist whose stock-in-trade is personal reporting.

On the assumption that you are not, you should save highly personalised writing for when you have a personal experience to relate which is utterly fascinating (to the readers, not to you and your family). In any normal career, such occasions will be few and far between. As an example, here is a piece George Orwell wrote while covering the Spanish Civil War. The personal approach is justified here because Orwell had an experience considerably out of the ordinary and one that many people wonder about – being shot. It is a model of understatement:

I had been about ten days at the front when it happened. The whole experience of being hit by a bullet is very interesting and I think it is worth describing in detail.

... Roughly speaking it was the sensation of being at the centre of an explosion. There seemed to be a loud bang and a blinding flash of light all round me, and I felt a tremendous shock – no pain, only a violent shock, such as you get from an electric terminal; with it a sense of utter weakness, a feeling of being stricken and shrivelled up to nothing. The sandbags in front of me receded into immense distance. I fancy you would feel much the same if you were struck by lightning. I knew immediately that I was hit, but because of the seeming bang and flash I thought it was a rifle nearby that had gone off accidentally and shot me. All this happened in a space of time much less than a second. The next moment my knees crumpled up and I was falling, my head hitting the ground with a violent bang which, to my relief, did not hurt. I had a numb, dazed feeling, a consciousness of being very badly hurt, but no pain in the ordinary sense.

Political correctness

In the last decade or so there has been radical, and overdue, change in the way newspapers write and think about different groups in society: women, blacks, the disabled, homosexuals. All of these have been – and often still are – patronised and discriminated against. One of the main targets of those trying to correct this has been the language applied to these groups. Although the more extreme advocates of political correctness have provided endless amusement to the mainstream with their excesses, very few of us would want to go back to the days when, for instance, women were called 'ladies' and always with a brief note attached telling the reader whether they were 'pretty', 'vivacious' or 'attractive' and what colour dress they wore.

Political correctness is now an intense preoccupation to journalism schools in many parts of the world. One recent textbook gave more space to how to write about the disabled than it did to news values. This is silly, because the matter can be resolved into three broad principles, all of which involve applying the sensitivity any educated person would use in normal life:

- Do not refer to someone's race, or disability unless it has a direct bearing on the story.
- Do not apply different standards to writing about one group in society from those you would apply to another. Don't, for instance, describe a woman politician's dress and hairstyle unless it has a bearing on the story or possesses news value in itself. The test is: would you describe a male politician's appearance in the same situation?
- Be precise and do not use euphemisms. The fashion in some countries is now to refer to a blind person as 'visually impaired'. They are not, they are blind. A visually impaired person is one who can partially see, and is thus better called 'partially-sighted'. Best of all, do not use any vague phrases; be precise. Instead of 'disabled', which many object to, say what the disability actually is – providing it is relevant to the story.

Analysis

Any news story or feature of substance should have some measure of analysis in it, whether it is woven in with the main fabric or written as a separate section. But often a story is of such a size or sudden importance that a piece which is nothing but analysis is called for. This will dissect events, themes, issues and developments in an attempt to explain what is happening now or will happen in the future. It should also try to explain the significance of these events and their context.

Such pieces should not merely be a series of assertions. Neither should they be old news stories reheated and served up with a few opinions. They must bring fresh evidence and fresh insights to bear on the story. These can either be yours, or, preferably, those of named authorities and experts. The accent should be on interpretation and explanation. This approach can be applied to other types of stories. Profiles of prominent public figures, for instance, can often be a fairly superficial recycling of well-worn material. But they can also be a serious attempt to set their lives into a context, with some detailed research into their backgrounds and work. The views of those who have encountered them can be collected and added to present a rounded portrait.

Interpretive pieces are needed by readers even more now that they often receive the first reports of events from television, radio and the internet. As well as reporting in depth as the broadcast media cannot, newspapers should also explain what the events and developments mean. This need not be some quiet backwater of the paper, where commentators suck their thumbs, ruminate and, as American journalist A.J. Liebling said, 'write what they construe to be the meaning of what they have not seen.' It should be to report new understandings and insights – a new sense of what things mean.

Obituaries

To most journalists, obituaries are an ignored backwater, the kind of thing you write when you get too old for news or feature reporting. Yet, on leading American papers and British national quality dailies, here is where some of the best writing in all journalism is found. Two examples, the first from the *Daily Telegraph*: 'The 3rd Lord Moynihan, who has died in Manila aged 55, provided, through his character and career, ample ammunition for critics of the hereditary principle. His chief occupations were bongo-drummer, confidence trickster, brothel-keeper, drug-smuggler, and police informer.' And then there is this, by Douglas Martin of the *New York Times*: 'Selma Koch, a Manhattan store owner who earned a national reputation by helping women find the right bra size, mostly through a discerning glance and never with a tape measure, died Thursday at Mount Sinai Medical Center. She was 95 and a 34B.' A perfect instance of the punch-line intro.

But most papers, especially provincial ones, still persist in not writing or publishing proper obituaries. They might report the death of a local citizen, but a news story, laden as it often is with hollow tributes from colleagues and family, is not an obituary. It is a get-well card that arrived too late. What we readers want is the telling of someone's life story – and they don't have to be well known. Some of the best obituaries are those of non-celebrities who just happened to have been fascinating people. In recent years I have written about: Enric Fontlladosa, Spanish confectioner who, when he launched the famous Chupa Chups lollipops, got Salvadore Dali to design the logo; Dorothy E. Tate, an American foster mother who, in 23 years, cared for no fewer than 680 troubled and otherwise unwanted children; Rosa Maria Cardini, whose tenacity popularised the salad dressing invented by her father, Caesar; Gerald Watts, an English golf club official who was so obsessed with smart dress that he even polished the soles of his shoes; and Alberta Martin, the last American Civil War widow, who, in 1927 as a 19-year-old, married 81-year-old William Martin, veteran of the 4th Alabama Infantry. When he died, she wed his grandson.

The scope in a life story for comment is temptingly wide, ranging from the weighty judgement on a career to the discreet aside couched in what you might call 'obituary language'. Even today, when British newspapers are more open about the faults of the departed, understatement is still generally preferred. Thus, 'not suffered fools gladly' translates as foul-tempered psychotic; 'something of a perfectionist' normally means the dearly departed was a deranged obsessive, and 'not a book lover' is often code for the subject being little short of an idiot. And, when it comes to a subject's sexuality, much innocent fun can be had deciphering euphemism, for example, a woman described as 'highly sociable and popular with men' can be taken to have been a nymphomaniac, and a man discreetly gay invariably goes to his maker with the words 'although handsome, he was rarely seen in female company'. In US papers, especially small-town ones (where obits are often written by relatives and treated as advertisements, with charges to match) euphemism even extends to the fact of death. The following have all been recorded: 'ushered to the angels', 'received his final marching orders', and, for two sportsmen 'teed up for Golf in the Kingdom,' and 'went fishing with Christ'.

Leaders or editorial opinion pieces

Serious comment pieces that read interestingly, and have some pace and authority, are very difficult to write. Too often seriousness comes out as solemnity, authority as pomposity, and the subject is as predictable as tomorrow's date. Such pieces have all the freshness of last week's bread.

It is a near-universal convention that each issue of a paper should have a column that gives the paper's view on some topical issue(s). In countries where basic freedoms are under threat, editorials can be a ringing voice in the defence of people's rights. They send public word to regimes that they are being watched and opposed. They bolster and inspire those who are fighting for freedom and justice.

Elsewhere, in more comfortable circumstances, the value of these daily editorials is more debatable. I have sat in many editorial conferences where for some considerable time the assembled minds rummaged hopefully through recent stories for a subject – any subject – that the paper could sound off about. The clock would tick steadily onwards, until at last some issue was agreed on (invariably one of the ones suggested at the beginning of the meeting). With the problem solved for another day, everyone then heaved a collective sigh of relief. Except the poor devil commissioned to write the thing. A lot of us find it very testing to write a good comment piece unless we have a genuine conviction about an issue. Fabricating one will often produce a piece that is hollow and insincere; trying to write the piece without one leads to inconclusive waffle or, worse, a succession of comments saying it is too early to pass judgement on this matter – a dead give-away that the paper has chosen the wrong subject, or the wrong writer.

Some larger papers have specialists employed to write nothing but editorials. This gave rise, on the *Daily News* of Chicago, to a practical joke from one of the better-class journalists. Groups of readers used to be regularly shown round the paper, which was known for the high moral tone of its editorials. Knowing that such a party was due, a reporter called Eugene Field, later a poet, got together with a member of staff who was the readers' guide and hatched a plan. As the prim matrons of the town reached the door marked 'Editorial Writers', the guide opened it to reveal a figure seated at a desk, composing one of the paper's pious editorials. It was Field, unshaven, snarling, and dressed in the arrowed uniform of a convict, complete with ball and chain. 'He's a trusty from the state pen, up for murder, you know', explained the guide, 'Our editor Mr Stone is very economy minded, always thinking of the paper's expenses. He used his influence to get this fellow in twice a week. A free editorial writer, get it? Doesn't cost us a dime.'

However, if you are a more conventional member of the paper's staff and have been commissioned to write an editorial on something about which you have no burning convictions, you have two choices. You can either speak to experts inside and outside your paper and collect strong views, or retire to a dark corner and rapidly acquire some. This is not as cynical as it sounds. It is surprising how often a few moments' contemplation suddenly focused by the approaching deadline will give birth to original opinions.

Originality, however, has its limits. Joseph Medill, the ultra-conservative owner of the *Chicago Tribune* wrote an editorial in 1884 on the problem of the city's large mobile population of homeless, jobless men. Not for him any plea for work to be found for these unfortunates. Instead, an editorial written in vindictive seriousness and which read in part:

The simplest plan, probably where one is not a member of the Humane Society, is to put a little strychnine or arsenic in the meat and other supplies furnished to the tramp. This produces death within a comparatively short time, is a warning to other tramps to keep out of the neighborhood ... and saves one's chickens and other portable property from constant depredation.

Passion, too, has its limits which were certainly reached and appreciably exceeded by the *Messenger*, an English-language paper in Cameroon in July 1995. A front-page piece was headed 'Kill This Man', and read in part: 'Such a man is not fit to live and should be wiped out of existence. Such a treatment, however harsh, befits Oben Peter Ashu, Governor of the South West Province.'

Editorials, like all opinion pieces, should not be a series of wilful assertions laid upon each other. As well as a fresh point of view, they should contain sufficient elements of background and analysis to make them understandable to those who have not read the story(ies) they are based upon. They should be arguments constructed as tightly as a well-wound spring.

And if you wish them to have impact, concentrate your creativity on a few memorable phrases. The list of newspaper editorials that have lived beyond the paper's next issue is not long. In fact it is very short. But those that have achieved any kind of immortality owe it not to a brilliantly argued case, but to a memorable phrase. That indeed is all they are remembered for: C.P. Scott's 'Comment is free, facts are sacred' (*Manchester Guardian*, 1921), 'Communism with a human face' (*Rude Pravo*, Prague 1968), 'The smack of firm government' (*Daily Telegraph*, London 1956), 'One picture is worth a thousand words' (*Printers' Ink*, US 1927).

But there is a thin line between presence and pretentiousness. Just as politicians are only politicians, papers are only papers, not players on the world stage. There is nothing more preposterous than a squeaky voice from a newspaper, especially a small provincial one, 'calling on the United Nations to act now'. Witness the *Skibereen Eagle*, a four-page sheet published once a week in the city of Cork, Ireland in late Victorian times. Once, when the Tsar of Russia had done something to displease the *Eagle*'s proprietor, one Frederick Peel Eldon Potter, a vehement leading article informed its 4,000 readers: 'The *Skibereen Eagle* has its eye on Russia.'

Individual classified advertisements have done more to change the world than all the billions of words of blustering newspaper editorials in history. The battle of Gettysburg, one of the bloodiest in the American Civil War, for instance, was caused by an ad for footwear. It appeared in the *Gettysburg Compiler* and had been placed by a shoe store announcing fine new boots for sale. It was seen by Confederate General James Pettigrew who at the time was marching his bedraggled army through Pennsylvania.

They were in a sorry state, having worn out their boots and many were marching barefoot. Pettigrew ordered his men to change direction and head for Gettysburg. On the way they were spotted by Union forces and so began the bloody, three-day battle of Gettysburg. At the end of it, 5,662 men lay dead and 27,203 wounded.

Indeed, it is very hard to find a single case of a newspaper comment actually changing the world. The one usually cited, Émile Zola's famous 'J'accuse' about the Dreyfus case published in the French paper *L'Aurore* in January 1898, was actually an open letter to the government and not an editorial (and had only a limited direct effect). The other case was where the comment was actually made in error.

In April 1888, Ludwig Nobel died. He was the elder brother of the moody yet idealistic inventor of dynamite, Alfred Nobel. A leading French newspaper misread the report and ran an obituary of Alfred, calling him 'a merchant of death'. Reading that obituary and being stung by the idea that he would be remembered as a 'merchant of death', was one of the main reasons why Nobel changed his will and left his fortune to establish the Nobel Prize awards for peace, literature and the sciences.

Columnists

Anyone who has reached the stage of a column either has no need for advice; or has (or will soon acquire) an ego which precludes them from taking any. Indeed, of all the bizarre and disturbing creatures that inhabit newspapers and magazines, none are quite so preposterous as columnists. Reporters are often obsessive, copy-editors pernickity to the point where you want to head butt them, and editors, however scholarly, tend to have much in common, psychologically, with the leaders of military juntas. But columnists, quite definitely, are the strangest of the lot. To be fair (as commentators invariably write in the final paragraph when they have spent all the previous ones being outrageously unfair), columnists are not one species, but a vast family of them, plus assorted subspecies and mutants. Some are mildly annoying, like the self-obsessed me-columnists, who write under the impression that the minutiae of their lives are as fascinating to us as they obviously are to them. These are usually either a thirtysomething woman wittering on about how hopeless she is at everything and doing her best to set back the cause of feminism thirty years; or a slightly older male anxious to prove how far he has progressed down the road to New Manhood. Neither are convincing.

Better by far are the satirists, not all of whose work is immediately obvious. For some years, America marvelled at the outrageous right-wing opinions of Ed Anger, who fulminated in the *Weekly World News* against 'commies, pinkoes, and vegetable eaters', and wrote such lines as 'God gave women knees to pray on and scrub floors with'. How delicious it was to later learn that Mr Anger was in fact the alter ego of Rafe Klinger, a small, slightly balding Jewish liberal with two degrees. Mr Klinger has long since moved on, but Ed continues to rant, courtesy of other mischievous pens. But the star names of the comment world are the current affairs columnists with their instant, stir-fry solutions to global dilemmas. Or, as American writer Westbrook Pegler described them fully fifty years ago: 'Of all the fantastic fog-shapes that have risen off the fog of human confusion since the big war, the most futile and at the same time the most pretentious is the deep-thinking, hair-trigger columnist or commentator who knows all the answers just off-hand and can settle great affairs with absolute finality three or even six days a week.' They come at us daily, opinions flourished like banners at a demonstration: the political pontificator, ever wise after the event; the why-oh-why merchant, deploring some incident as symptomatic of how the country is going to the dogs; the hired celebrity cashing in with a few clichéd thoughts; the resident minority group spokesperson, ever ready to tell us all how prejudiced we all are; and the 'murder is wrong' columnist, bravely condemning terrorists, paedophiles and people traffickers.

Yet what such columnists lack in humility (and originality) they can normally make up for in 24-carat vanity. Whether it is, like Arthur Krock in the 1940s, returning home each evening to demand his family fall silent so he could read them his *New York Times* column, or the crazed insistence that none of the column's words or facts, however wrong, can be altered, columnists are the prima donnas of print. Nothing shows this more than their fussiness about the personal photographs that often accompany their words. I have known these to be of such extreme vintage that a columnist who wrote from home managed to pass completely unnoticed when she did finally show up in the office. No one recognised her, and, when she introduced herself, they took her, from her lack of resemblance to the column's ancient picture, to be an imposter. But if their faces don't age on the page, their words certainly do. I own dozens of books that are collections of columns by the great names of the trade, and most of these articles are rendered, by the passage of even the shortest time, either utterly irrelevant or bafflingly obscure. Good news reporting, of whatever age, tells a story; columns of the past are barely even ephemera. Newspapers, I fancy, would be a great deal better if more journalists followed the example of American Bob Considine, who, in 1973, wrote the shortest column on record. It read simply: 'I have nothing to say today'.

Reviews

There are three schools of reviewing and two of them should be closed down. First, there are those professional journalists who are perfectly good reporters when given a story, but when presented with a book, play, film or concert to review are stricken with a sudden desire to prove they are 'writers'.

Then there are those amateurs, often a rival (or, worse, a friend) of those whose work is under review, who grind in-crowd axes in public, to the bewilderment or deceit of readers. In both cases what we often get is a piece where the writer fails to describe the content of the work, so anxious is he or she to discharge opinions, fanciful divinations of meaning, wild guesses at the artist's intent and, of course, what he or she hopes will be the resonating verdict.

Readers should beware these schools of reviewing. So, too, should writers. As Vladimir Nabokov observed of book reviewers: 'Criticism can be instructive in the sense that it gives readers, including the author of the book, some information about the critic's intelligence, or honesty, or both.' The school of reviewing that deserves preservation is that whose prime aim is to give information about the work in question; to describe it as precisely and fully as possible, to scrutinise its style, content and thinking. And remember, it is permissible to write a review that contains no glib opinion. If you feel tempted to ignore this advice, just remember the *Odessa Courier*'s anonymous book reviewer who in 1887 wrote of a novel: 'Sentimental rubbish. Show me one page that contains an idea.' The book reviewed was *Anna Karenina*.

Of all the fantastic fog-shapes that have risen off the fog of human confusion since the big war, the most futile and at the same time the most pretentious is the deep-thinking, hair-trigger columnist or commentator who knows all the answers just off-hand and can settle great affairs with absolute finality three or even six days a week.

Westbrook Pegler

19

How To Be A Great Reporter

Trying to be a first-rate reporter on the average newspaper is like trying to play Bach's St Matthew Passion on a ukulele. The instrument is too crude for the work, for the audience and for the performer.

Ben Bagdikian

Reporters, like most people in an occupation that requires a little bit more than mere attendance, have a choice. They can do enough to get by – content to be a run-of-the-mill journalist – and seek real satisfaction elsewhere in their life. Or, if they're the kind of psychological misfit many of us are, they can strive to be a very good, even great, reporter. If the latter path sounds like more fun (and I can promise you it is), then this chapter is for you. It tells you how, having become a good reporter, what you need to progress to the next level.

To hand out advice on achieving that elevated state may seem a little presumptive. After all, I am not a great reporter. But I do have a pretty good idea of what it takes to be one. First, because, at the *Observer, Independent* and *Independent on Sunday*, I've had the fortune to work with a few; second, because I spent two years researching great reporters for my book of that name; and third, because for many years I have read all the outstanding reporting I could get my hands on. The fruits of that obsession follow – the qualities I think you need to be a great reporter.

Hard work

A lot of reporters will interview musicians, athletes, actors or dancers and write pieces about how the star has intensively studied their discipline, is always trying new techniques, and practises five hours a day. The piece will invariably conclude, or at least imply, a direct connection between the subject's dedication and their success. As lessons in life go, it's hardly a shocking one. Yet it never seems to occur to a high proportion of these reporters that their own careers might benefit from a little of the same application. I often give seminars about various aspects of reporting, and I see the look of horror on many of the faces ranged before me when I suggest that they ought to dedicate an hour or so a week to exploring potential stories online; to reading books of, or about, journalism; and, from time to time, to acquiring new techniques, perhaps by taking themselves through an online tutorial. It is as if I've suggested that they volunteer to have a limb amputated without anaesthetic.

Well, if you're content to be an average reporter on an average paper, fine. But if you're not – and have realised life's a lot more fun if you're good at what you do – then you need to know that becoming an outstanding journalist requires commitment to your own development. Training does not stop when you get some trifling certificate and start your first job. That is when the task of training yourself begins – and it is a constant one. The class acts in journalism work at their own skills incessantly. They keep up to date with new technologies, and read, study and work at whatever it needs to make them better at the kind of reporting they do. If they are a general reporter, they will use their own time to become better at searching on the Net, mastering database management and other techniques of computer assisted reporting, to searching the Net for stories and keeping up to date with new online sources of them, to asking themselves why that story last week did not read as well as they initially hoped – in short, doing the equivalent of what Tiger Woods has done to make himself the world's best golfer. If they are a specialist, they will give their own time to keeping up with what's being published, to knowing the new online sources, to cultivating contacts, and to showing up at meetings and lectures in their field.

All I know of great reporters tells me that they regard such tasks as essential parts of their working lives. And, like Tiger Woods, what makes this easy for them is that they don't think of such activity as work at all. And there's a reason for that: if you're a true journalist, it isn't.

The application of intelligence

I have never met a very good or great reporter who was not also highly intelligent, reflective and thoughtful. To be really good at this job, that is essential. Decent journalism, never mind great journalism, is not a matter of technique, it is a matter of intelligence. And the best reporters are relentless in applying their intelligence not just to the collection of material, but to the material once they have got it. They think, and worry away intellectually at it, asking themselves: What have I got here? What does it amount to? What has caused this? They know the limits of what they have discovered when researching a story, realise they have not found out everything and that the situation, issue or character they are writing about is almost certainly more complex than given credit for.

And they have the honesty, and intellectual humility to recognise this in their story. Above all, they see subtleties where other reporters see only stereotypes to be allocated a pigeon hole. All the outstanding reporters I have worked with are conspicuous for their intelligence. They have technical skills, but it is the brainpower that accompanies these which makes them so good.

Intellectual courage

Some of the best reporting challenges a current orthodoxy, a widespread belief, or an assumption generally subscribed to. That is what William Russell of *The Times* did when he outraged the London establishment by reporting the callous shortcomings of the British Army in the Crimea (and kept on doing so, alone, in the face of official denials); what J.A. MacGahan did when he proved rumours of Turkish atrocities in the Balkans to be true; what Ida Tarbell did when she exposed the inner workings of the trusts in early twentieth-century America; what Bob Woodward and Carl Bernstein did when they reported the corruption that was Watergate; and what Randy Shilts did when he revealed the beginnings of Aids in the US gay community. To report at that level requires many qualities, but perhaps the most important of them – and the reason why reporting of that standard and impact is so rare – is intellectual courage. When the powers that be rubbish your stories (and that was true in an intimidating way in all the above cases), and when the rest of the press is conspicuously not following up your stories, it takes considerable mental fortitude to stick to your guns, your stories, and the trail. Most of us would be deflected, compromise, or lose our nerve. Great reporters don't, and one of the reasons is not just that they have intellectual balls, but because they are generally more meticulous in their reporting than most journalists.

Meticulousness

I still encounter reporters who, when you point out factual errors in their copy (or, more likely, omissions of important context), will shrug their shoulders as if such mistakes were acts of God entirely beyond their control. Well, they seem to be saying (and sometimes do actually say), accidents will happen. It is a characteristic trait of the kind of person who will forever be a poor reporter and a liability not just to themselves, but to their papers.

Outstanding reporters do it differently. They go well beyond a mere passion for accuracy that any journalist worth the name would have. Instead, they exhibit a neurosis about getting things right that is often not easy to live with – either for themselves or anyone around them. They will double, treble and multiple check contentious points, ring editors at all hours of the day and night to make minor changes for even greater accuracy, and will be psychotically protective of every nuance in their stories. The reasons (beyond the obvious one of getting the story as real and right as possible) are twofold. First, because they are operating at the spotlighted end of the trade where they are not just trying to describe something or someone, but also to make sense of it. And, if you're doing that, and sometimes going out on a limb in print, you have to be utterly sure of the facts upon which your story is based. Second, the thought of getting something wrong, even an incorrect initial in someone's name, disturbs them in ways mere ordinary mortals cannot imagine and drives them into despairs that can last days. And it is this – and the fear of having even a triviality wrong under their by-line (and to them, there is no such thing as a triviality when it comes to accuracy) – that drives them to be precisely correct more often than lesser reporters. If that sounds to you like a serious case of losing perspective, it is unlikely you will be a great reporter.

Consuming appetite for books

I have never met a great reporter who was not also a voracious reader, especially of non-fiction. This reading is both a cause and an effect of their brilliance at reporting. The compulsive curiosity that makes them outstanding journalists also makes them constantly seek knowledge and the experiences of others – found at their most lucid, comprehensive and considered in books, rather than online. And this volume of reading, in two crucial respects, makes them better reporters. First, and most obviously, those who read a lot of good writing tend to absorb (both consciously and unconsciously) new words, expressions, and constructions. If nothing else, you will recognise what, in a writer, constitutes a 'voice', as opposed to the faltering, uneven sentences of someone who is not at ease with communicating on paper or screen. Second – and this is the vital legacy of all that reading – the knowledge and mental horizons of reporters who read a lot of books are constantly expanded. Their ability to make connections, and to be aware of how what they are reporting slots into the schemes of things, is hugely enhanced. If, for instance, you are unaware of great swathes of history (or at least the parts of it that relate to what you write about) how can you possibly hope to report with context and intelligence?

Behind this lies what I think is almost a law of journalism: that the well-read reporter is always a good one, while the ill-read reporter is always a poor or shallow one. In 35 years in the business, I have never met an exception to this rule, nor come across anyone else who claims to have done.

A good knowledge of journalism's past

By this I don't mean knowing when the *Huddersfield Examiner* was started, when the *Minneapolis Bugle* folded, or the impact of Rural Free Delivery on early twentieth-century advertising revenues. What I mean is a knowledge of the best reporters of the past and their work. For an experienced reporter to be ignorant of this is like a musician trying to compose symphonies without ever having heard a single work of Mozart, Beethoven, Tchaikovsky, Brahms, Mahler and so on. This may seem like the tritest of truisms, but I come across so many journalists for whom the best of reporters of the past might as well be fourteenth-century stonemasons for all they know of them. If you're one of these, you need to ask yourself: How good would Norman Mailer be if he knew nothing of the great novelists of the past? What kind of movies would Stephen Spielberg make if he had never seen a film made before 1970?

If you talk to the outstanding people in any field, from golf to moral philosophy, you find that they have a deep awareness of the great practitioners of their craft. And the best reporters are no different: they have read Russell of the Crimea, Liebling, Harding Davis, Marguerite Higgins, James Cameron, Gay Talese, Robert Fisk, Red Smith, David Halberstam, Hugh McIlvanney and Ann Leslie or a host of other great reporters. And they have learned a lot from them: not just different ways of writing, but how to think about the job, interview techniques, the level of detail that a great reporter collects and deploys, the way to quote people (or not), the range of knowledge that should be brought to bear on even the most apparently straightforward story, and much else. To not do this, to ignore what this trade's finest reporters have produced, is to declare that all the best journalists of the past two centuries have nothing to teach you; that you instinctively know it all. It is, when you think about, not very likely.

Obsessive nature

If you haven't already guessed it, the truth is that being a really outstanding reporter requires a single-mindedness that is not always compatible with being a well-adjusted human being, let alone an acceptable husband, wife, or partner. There are exceptions – Ann Leslie of the *Daily Mail* is one, Geoffrey Lean, the great environment editor of the *Independent on Sunday* is another. But the qualities needed to be a high-quality reporter and an easy-going, tactful and considerate person do not always coincide. A perfect illustration of this is a story told by the war reporter, editor and commentator Max Hastings. A famous correspondent returns home, after a lengthy assignment, to the wife he has not seen for weeks. That night, they naturally begin to make love. The phone rings. It is a foreign radio station asking if he will do a down-the-line phone interview. He agrees, and for the next 15 minutes, proceeds to answer questions about the complexities of the Middle East – while lying on top of his wife in the position he was in before the phone rang. 'It was then,' the wife later said, 'that I realised that something of the romance had gone out of our marriage.'

But then, in a curious way, I don't think this guy's nature gave him much choice in the matter. The impulses that drove him to treat his wife so casually were also those that powered his journalism: a compulsive curiosity, a constant itch to tell people what he'd discovered (and what he thought about what he'd discovered), and no little ego. He couldn't – although this is unlikely to be her point of view – help himself. As someone once said, to be called a reporter isn't so much a job description as a diagnosis. But then, to some of us, it's the best diagnosis in the world.

It is part of the social mission of every great newspaper to provide a refuge and a home for the largest possible number of salaried eccentrics
Lord Thomson, one-time owner of *The Times*
and *Sunday Times* of London

Reading for Journalists

There are very few books on journalism worth reading. Official histories of newspapers tend to be public relations exercises, not literature; editors' memoirs often seem to be written to settle old scores, drop names or justify expenses; press critiques are invariably a thoughtless recitation of the predictable outrages of the tabloids; and 'how to' volumes are compiled mostly by those whose unfitness to be employed at the top level has given them the time to write the book. However, there are honourable exceptions:

Collections of reporting

The *Bedside Guardian* series is a treasure trove of good, sharp work, as are the compilations of the year's best offerings from *Observer* writers, now, alas, no longer published. Disappointingly little good reporting ever makes it into hard covers, which is why *The Faber Book of Reportage*, edited by John Gross, is so valuable. Some of the best passages, as opposed to whole articles, ever captured are to be found in *The First Casualty* (Andre Deutsch, 1975), Phillip Knightley's survey of war reporting. More likely to be collected are the more polemical or humorous writers, and the best examples of each approach are found in *Distant Voices* by John Pilger (Vintage, 1992) and anything by P.J. O'Rourke. If you want to see what an intelligent and entertaining long feature or magazine piece looks like, turn to Ian Jack's *Before the Oil Ran Out* (Vintage, 1977) and Blake Morrison's *Too True* (Granta, 1999) or any book of pieces by Hugh McIlvanney or A.J. Liebling. For shorter newspaper features, two collections of Meyer Berger's articles are worth tracking down: *The Eight Million*, and *Meyer Berger's New York*. My own book *The Great Reporters* (Pluto Press, 2005) has many excerpts from the work of those I profile. And a good collection of work by reporters who witnessed some of the last century-and-a-half's defining moments is *The Mammoth Book of Journalism* edited by Jon E. Lewis (Carroll & Graf, 2003).

Reporters' memoirs

Foreign correspondents tend to hog the limelight here, since references to Ho Chi Minh city and Dushanbe obviously make for more glamorous reading than tales from the Manchester magistrates courts. Among the best are *Anyone Here Been Raped and Speaks English ...* by Edward Behr (New English Library, 1978), and *Point of Departure* by James Cameron (Granada, 1969). The life and techniques of a top tabloid reporter are described in helpful detail in *Exposed!* by Gerry Brown (Virgin, 1995) and Wensley Clarkson's *Dog Eat Dog. Confessions of a Tabloid Journalist* (Fourth Estate, 1990). Bill Deedes's *Dear Bill* is the autobiography of a reporter who became an MP, minister and editor, but always remained a reporter and finally reverted back to the job. The book is a striking illustration of how a lifelong curiosity about anything and everything is a reporter's best asset. For those in search of how it used to be on Fleet Street, the authentic sounds of scuffling shoe leather and old invoices being pulled from pockets can be heard on every page of Alfred Draper's *Scoops and Swindles* (Buchan and Enright, 1988) and anything by Derek Lambert. If you want to hear from one of the best and most versatile reporters, then read Ann Leslie's *Killing My Own Snakes* (Macmillan, 2008). And even experienced journalists could not fail to get a lot of practical working tips from the autobiography of the great modern crime reporter, Edna Buchanan, *The Corpse Had a Familiar Face* (Pocket Books, 2004).

Press critiques

Almost all of these are written about the popular press by academics or quality newspaper editors and writers, both of which groups seem solely preoccupied with sniffily disapproving of what they find. You search in vain for anyone with a more complicated diagnosis of the accumulated lies and distortion than rampant commercialism combined with immorality. A partial exception is *Shock, Horror!* by S.J. Taylor (Corgi, 1991). Americans do this kind of thing better. *Media Circus* by Howard Kurtz (Times Books, 1994) is a sharp survey of the values and foibles of modern US journalism, and *Who Stole the News?* by Mort Rosenblum (Wiley, 1995) is an ex-Associated Press correspondent's thoughtful reflections on news. A more general diagnosis, with a lot of valuable historical context, is Andrew Marr's *My Trade* (Macmillan, 2004). And no one operating in the post-internet, cuts-bedevilled newsrooms of today should fail to read Nick Davies's *Flat Earth News* (Vintage, 2009). It is polemical, a bit swift to condemn, and argumentative, but it is thought-provoking and a good corrective to the phoney romanticism still fed to trainees.

'How to' books

All The President's Men (Quartet, 1974), Bob Woodward and Carl Bernstein's account of their Watergate reporting, is easily the best description of the attitudes and some of the techniques essential to the high-quality reporter. As for books on writing, these are invariably written by those who have a tin ear when it comes to a rhythmic sentence or original phrase. Turn instead to reading examples of good writing and absorbing its virtues that way. If you must have a manual by your side, choose *Waterhouse on Newspaper Style* by Keith Waterhouse (Penguin, 1993). For copy and picture editing, the best books are still *Handling Newspaper Text* and *Pictures on a Page* both by Harold Evans (Heinemann). *Secrets of the Press* (Allen Lane, 1999) is Stephen Glover's collection of essays by contemporary national newspaper journalists. Worth getting for two practical pieces alone – Ann Leslie on being a foreign correspondent and Lyn Barber's guide to interviewing. Americans do helpful reporting manuals better, and the Associated Press *Reporting Handbook* (McGraw Hill, 2002) is well worth reading, as are these excellent volumes: *The Journalist's Craft: A Guide to Writing Better Stories* by Dennis Jackson and John Sweeney (Allworth Press, 2002), and John Brady's *The Interviewer's Handbook* (Kalmbach Publishing, 2004). The best guide to the online world is *The Net For Journalists* by Martin Huckerby (UNESCO, 2005). Finally, although it is a collection of biographical essays on the people I think were the best ever performers in print, my own *The Great Reporters* (Pluto Press, 2005) is full of detailed descriptions of how the best of our trade worked and operated.

Statistics and Numbers

There are many dry and learned tomes on the subject, but Darrell Huff's little Penguin *How To Lie With Statistics* wears its learning very lightly. It is a classic and should be read and re-read by any journalist.

Finally, a book which fits into no category, but which is the most thoughtful I have ever read on newspapers – John Allen Paulos's *A Mathematician Reads The Newspaper* (Penguin, 1996). A man with the unusual combination of a lifelong love of both newspapers and mathematics, Paulos goes hunting for logical and statistical illiteracy in newspapers and finds many examples. The book will tell you how chaos theory relates to news values, and permanently change the way you look at stories.

Index